Arthur Stein and Andrew Vidich ... *Let* ... *Light* ... ...
have most certainly offered us yet m... ... *Light* ... ... !
global ethos. This is such an importa ... *book, an* ... ... :
Their work is skillful, written with wonderful simplicity* ... ... e
with scriptural references, personal epiphanies, and tales from the world's wisdom
traditions. Theirs is an outstanding contribution to the interfaith/interspiritual
literature, and I am most grateful to be able to refer our students and faculty, along
with other colleagues, to this amazing resource.

—Rev. Joyce Liechenstein, Ph.D., Associate Director of One Spirit Interfaith
Seminary and One Spirit Learning Alliance, Order of Universal Interfaith (OUnI)

Let There Be Light *is a comprehensive guide, tradition by tradition, to the*
globe's unfolding Interspiritual Age. Drs. Stein and Vidich provide the rich detail
needed to understand the unfolding tapestry of an emerging Universal Spirituality.

—Kurt Johnson, co-author of *The Coming Interspiritual Age*

Let There Be Light, *beyond serving as an important and informative intro-*
duction to some of the most fascinating of the world's mystical traditions, fosters
the crucial recognition of the unity of all these paths in search of the Mystery of
all mysteries. Vidich and Stein have a gift for crafting a text that is both engaging
and enjoyable, and which serves as an excellent reference and guide for readers
interested in exploring the mystical insights and paths to achieving the direct inner
experience of inner Light.

—Yuval Ron, Emmy Award winner composer, recording artist, oud master, educator and author of *Divine Attunement: Music as a Path to Wisdom*

The amazing experiences of the Luminous and Cosmic Song had by mystics
and saints of authentic spiritual traditions from ancient times to the present are
thoughtfully researched and beautifully portrayed in this valuable tome. These
experiences are actually within everyone's possibility. In 1961, at the age of sev-
enteen, I had my first unsought, puzzling, but transformative experiences of inner
Light, which eventually assumed the form of a radiant guide. I encourage the reader
to make the experiences of the past saints and mystics your very own. Humans were
created to serve and love the creation and also to return consciously to the Creator.
This book will inspire and gently inform our own journey to the Inner Light.

—Arran Stephens, CEO/founder of Nature's Path Foods, author of *Journey to the*
Luminous, Moth and the Flame, and *Compassionate Diet*

A marvelous, complex, carefully rendered exploration of exemplary experienc-
es and understandings of this key dimension of transformation shared by each of

the world's religious traditions. "Enlightenment" will never seem the same again, as the reader comes to grips with these revealing spiritual facets of our common humanity.

—Prof. James W. Morris, Department of Theology, Boston College

This ambitious work shows that the experience of divine light is a common and continuous thread in all the world's religions. Demonstrating a compendious knowledge of disparate faiths, the authors use traditional teaching stories and scriptural references to illuminate the many linkages between them. A chapter on quantum physics and near-death experiences connect ancient spiritual traditions with contemporary scientific endeavor, and the authors conclude by weaving all these threads into the grand tapestry of eternal mystical experience. This book appeals to students of contemporary spirituality, as well as followers of the Great Tradition from which all religions arise.

—Dawson Church, author of The Genie in Your Genes and Soul Medicine, CEO of Elite Books, and international speaker on Emotional Freedom Technique

This wonderful book by Arthur Stein and Andrew Vidich is a must read for all seekers of Truth and Light. It offers an interspiritual lens into the history, experience and mystery of the One Light, both as metaphor and literal experience. Intentionally and uniquely, Let There Be Light confirms the truth that lies at the heart of all the world's religious and spiritual traditions—God, the Divine, the One—call it what you will—is the pure Light that, like a prism, gives color and texture not only to the world's religious and spiritual traditions, but is in truth the singular Source that gives life and sustenance to everything that is. Read this book, not only because it sheds light on a profound truth, but also points to and reminds us of the One Light that shines in every living being.

—Rev. Robert V. Thompson, author of A Voluptuous God: A Christian Heretic Speaks; past Chair of the Parliament of the World's Religions

Let There Be Light is destined to become a classic for the 21st century and beyond. Absolutely indispensable reading for every person who has ever wondered about the inner Light, or experienced some form of it within. This book is comprehensive and eclectic, inclusive and clarifying, fascinating and inspiring. Dip into it or study it, use it as a guide, a workbook, or a companion on your search for truth. This unique work will lead you unerringly forward, inward, and upward. Drs. Vidich and Stein's book is far and away the definitive study of this fascinating subject, the new gold standard.

This single book actually contains a small sheaf of several free-standing books, one each on the inner Light as it forms the basis of a major world religion...Updated *translations and interpretations, a leavening of tales to move the heart to tears of love, a satisfying breadth, a full bibliography to deepen the search, plus a great index to sharpen it, and exercises to make it all practical—this new book is a complete gift, which I hope to enjoy for many years.*

—Marshall Zaslove, MD, psychiatrist, author of the medical productivity handbook, *The Successful Physician,* and contributing author of *Meditation as Medication for the Soul*

In a world rampant with sectarian religious dogmatism, the unifying esoteric core underlying most spiritual traditions—the mystic experience of inner Light—is too often forgotten. Using multiple evidential lenses, which include science, theology and the exploration of historical religious canons, authors Stein and Vidich examine the lives and teachings of authentic "spiritual luminaries of inner Light" as represented in the major world religions.

The authors' scholarly rigor is tempered with their conviction that even in our sometimes dystopian world, the transformational power of the experience of inner Light is still accessible to humanity-at-large—and not only to the select few, as a way to achieve lasting inner and outer peace. Let There Be Light *will be an important contribution to academia as well as to the individual seeker of knowledge and spiritual truth.*

—Eliot Jay Rosen, author of *Experiencing the Soul—Before Life During Life After Death*

While the mechanisms involved in our outer vision are appreciated by modern-day medical scientists, it is our spiritual scientists who have described the experience of the Light that is within each of us. In a compelling presentation on the "Inner Light," Drs. Stein and Vidich provide an authoritative study of the teachings of the great mystics and sages of the world's wisdom traditions. Let There Be Light *is destined to be a classic in Comparative Mysticism and spirituality, an inspiration for those of us who yearn for the map and guideposts of the journey within.*

—Louis A. Ritz, Ph.D., Department of Neuroscience, University of Florida, College of Medicine, Director, University of Florida Center for Spirituality and Health and contributing author of *Meditation as Medication for the Soul*

Let There Be Light *celebrates the splendor of supernal light (and sound) as it has been known, realized, embodied and taught by mystics, sages and saints across the world's wisdom traditions. The authors display a wealth of knowledge, as well as a keen sense of appreciation for the beauty which is at the heart of the mystical life. This is a book which seekers and students will enjoy for its insight, as well as its message of hope: that the Light is available to all who seek it with humility and grace, and those who bask in its radiance are not only transfigured, but empowered to change the world.*

—Carl McColman, author of *Answering the Contemplative Call*

Let There Be Light *by Dr. Art Stein and Dr. Andrew Vidich is a truly wholesome and enlightening book. Their innovative research and prolific writing is a generous and timely contribution towards interfaith kinship, to defuse misunderstanding and infuse deeper understanding of the world's sacred traditions. Believers and non-believers alike can learn, relate and build genuine friendship among each other based on the inspiring universally shared values which the authors highlight, to let more light and happiness blossom on our earth.*

—Thupten Tendhar, Tibetan Geshe, teacher of Buddhism, nonviolence and peace studies, poet—*Peace: Rhythm of My Heart*

It was a rare privilege for me, to be given the opportunity to preview this gem. It is not an exaggeration that I would wake up each morning looking forward to reading the next chapter of the book. The adjectives that come to my mind to describe these writings are "luminous, elegant, comprehensive, and breathtaking in their scope and depth." Readers are invited to "enter into the silence of your soul, where the real journey begins."

—Celina Pereira, physician (MD, FAAP), educator and meditation teacher

*The world is awash in spiritual books, but it's rare to find one so richly alive with both wisdom and experience. Whether you are a student of the interfaith vision or a seeker looking for the common mystic thread connecting our human history, look no further—*Let There Be Light *is the comprehensive companion you've been looking for. With clarity, humor and an abundant ability to find the precious contributions of all traditions, Arthur Stein and Andrew Vidich have made* Let There be Light *a must-read for the interspiritual seeker. Highly recommended.*

—Rev. David B. Wallace, Dean and Senior Instructor, One Spirit Interfaith Seminary, NYC

Truth, even that created long, long, ago and hidden so very well, will ultimately be revealed. With their new book: Let There Be Light: Experiencing Inner Light Across the World's Sacred Traditions, *Drs. Stein and Vidich have illuminated spirituality's true heart for all to understand. The essence of the mystical Inner Light and Music, whose pulse infuses life into the creation, is now demonstrated to be an accessible Path that all souls ultimately travel.*

—Dr. Alan R. Post, chiropractic physician and health care consultant, contributor to *Meditation as Medication for the Soul*

The Divine is far above the comprehension of the human mind, but Let There Be Light *assists us in our quest to come closer to God and to gain insight into spiritual reality. The book presents a rich compilation of humanity's spiritual experiences from a wide variety of historical religious and cultural perspectives. I found it fascinating to read how spiritual reality can be perceived and expressed in so many positive ways, each seeking to illumine the shared goal of building human unity in today's troubled world.*

—Christine Muller, author of "Scientific and Spiritual Dimensions of Climate Change—an Interfaith Study Course," International Environment Forum

The quest for inner light imbues the world's sacred traditions and can be a powerful unifying force within humanity. When we find our inner light, darkness and egoism diminishes. As we discover within ourselves the light of life and of love, our spirit flourishes.

Using the metaphor of being in a caravan in the company of mystics, sages and storytellers, the authors of Let There Be Light *invite readers to join in what could become an insightful extended journey. All are welcomed to refresh at the numerous oases of peace and lovingkindness along the way.*

—Anne Mimi Sammis, sculptor, artist, peace educator, PBS creativity programs

Let There Be Light *has undertaken and beautifully succeeded in creating an anthology of the relationship that various religions have to the Light. However, the book is more than information. It is also inspiration. In addition to the detailed histories, scriptural references and commentaries, the authors also provide a practical "how to" section at the end of each chapter. So, the reader is able to delve deeply into not just an understanding but also an experience of the Light through each of these different faiths. It is a wonderfully inspiring and illuminating book, a book about light and also a book of light.*

—Sadhvi Bhagawati Saraswati, humanitarian and author of *By God's Grace* and *The Encyclopedia of Hinduism*

Let There Be Light

Experiencing Inner Light Across the
World's Sacred Traditions

by

Arthur Stein, PhD & Andrew Vidich, PhD

Integral Horizons

Let There Be Light
Experiencing Inner Light Across the World's Sacred Traditions

Publisher's Cataloging-In-Publication Data
(Prepared by The Donohue Group, Inc.)

Names: Stein, Arthur Benjamin. | Vidich, Andrew, 1953-
Title: Let there be light : experiencing inner light across the world's sacred traditions /
  by Arthur Stein, PhD, & Andrew Vidich, PhD.
Description: Revised edition. | [Wakefield, Rhode Island] : Integral Horizons, [2016] |
  Includes bibliographical references and index.
Identifiers: ISBN 978-0-692-73102-4
Subjects: LCSH: Inner light. | Light--Religious aspects. | Spirituality. | Mysticism.
Classification: LCC BL624 .S74 2016 | DDC 204.2—dc23

Cover design by Karin A. Kinsey
Copyediting by Stephanie Marohn
Typesetting by Karin A. Kinsey

Revised Edition
Printed in USA

With deep gratitude to Spiritual Masters,

Teachers, Sages and Saints

Both known and unknown,

Lamplighters of Compassion, Humility and Love,

Who illumine life's Pathways

For All of Humankind.

Contents

Acknowledgments

Having the opportunity to work together on this project over the past decade has been an ongoing learning experience, a time of intense research, editing, writing and shared fellowship. There were, of course, challenges that emerged as we recognized more fully the scope, breadth and complexities of the journey we had embarked upon.

First of all, we gratefully acknowledge the great pioneers in the realm of human consciousness—the honored Teachers in whose name religious and spiritual traditions have developed around the world. For millennia until the present day, these masters, saints, manifestations, sages, prophets, teachers and their students have been major benefactors of humankind. Having themselves discovered and experienced the sustaining and guiding Light within, they have taught by word and example that truly humane beings have the innate capability to live harmoniously in peace with justice, dwelling in beloved community on our beautiful mother earth.

In the inspired words of the Prophet Isaiah: "...and they shall beat their swords into plowshares, and their spears into pruning hooks: nation shall not lift up sword against nation, neither shall they learn war any more." What would it take to build transformative, sustainable bridges of lovingkindness, social justice, and compassion in today's world, linking diverse peoples together, inspired by such meaningful ideals of sages past and present?

Since we began research on this book, there have been many persons who have been supportive and encouraging of our endeavor. Their participation and expertise has been essential in bringing the manuscript to completion.

Foremost, we would like to acknowledge our copy editor Carl McColman, who not only provided superb editing, but a valued substantive critique. His scholarly knowledge and compassionate perspective helped bring this book to its present form. We would also like to thank Dr. Dawson Church for his initial feedback and astute eye at several stages in the book's process. His insightful comments helped guide us in the right direction at key junctures. A long-time supporter, his publishing experience and generous sharing of his contacts have been invaluable in bringing all the threads of this tapestry together. We would like to thank Karin Kinsey for her design of the front and back cover and interior design, and excellent work on chapter revisions and final typesetting of the entire book. It has been a joy working with her as she was able to translate conceptual language into brilliant visual images. Also, we thank Stephanie Marohn for her proofreading and steadfast attention to detail. As we headed down the homestretch towards publication time, our friend, IT computer specialist Kevin Bell, patiently helped keep our burgeoning manuscript in some sem-blance of order. Finally, thanks to Elishka Kocendova for her design of the Timelines within the book. Her fine work in getting a large amount of information and graphics into small spaces adds to the overall feeling and readability of the book.

We want to thank Brian Toomey for his valuable contributions to the project since its inception. His research skills were especially helpful in providing conceptual frameworks and initial drafts for several of the book chapters. Art also wishes to thank his colleagues and successive generations of his students at the University of Rhode Island over the past half-century, noting that there is indeed much truth in the expression, "In teaching I'll be taught."

We extend our gratitude to many persons who provided their knowledge, suggestions and feedback as our study progressed. Especially we'd like to thank those who reviewed individual chapters from a scholarly, a teacher's, a practitioner's, a mystic's point of view—in many instances from a combination of these various perspectives. They include Dr. James Morris, Huston Smith, Dr. Barbara Von Schegel, Carl McColman, Dr. Bernard McGinn, Paul Sherbow, Lama Surya Das, Dr. Donald Smith, Dr. Michael and Debbie Purdy, Rev. Robert V. Thompson, Rev. John Hall, Rabbis Jim Rosenberg, Aryae Coopersmith and Yossi Laufer, Christine and Dr. Gerhard Muller, Dr. Stephen Silverman, Dr. Neil Tessler, Venerable T. Kenjitsu Nakagaki, Dr. Patricia Hunt-Perry, Barbara Schugt, gesha Thupten Tendhar, Arran Stephens, Dr. Dan Campbell, Bob Gallagher and Rev. Donald Williams. We are appreciative, both for the ways you helped improve the manuscript and for your ongoing interest in this project. Also, we give heartfelt thanks to our spouses, Clare Sartori Stein and TAMIR, for their insights, editorial skills, and encouragement as we approached completion of this endeavor.

In closing, we are very grateful for mentors who, by the authenticity of their personal example, teach by treating everyone with lovingkindness and by embodying the quality of spiritual equipoise in every-day living.

Note to the Reader

Our study quotes extensively from the scriptures of many of the world's major religious and spiritual traditions over several thousand years, and also from many masters, mystics, saints, teachers and sages, including all of those in whose name these faith traditions came to be later known and practiced. Those inspired teachers, enlightened though they were, generally spoke in the common parlance of their times and which did not often reflect today's growing gender sensitivity.

Hence, you'll often see the original term "man" in direct quotations instead of the more inclusive word "humanity," and the masculine pronoun "He" used to refer to God, Divine Presence or similar terms. Also, since there are multiple names used for the divine creative power, we have respectfully used the term "God" in many places throughout this work to refer to the power that created all. We therefore suggest readers to kindly "edit in" for oneself any appropriate gender-based or other present-day refinements of language you may deem necessary.

The title, "master" may conjure up negative connotations inherent "in a master–slave" relationship or the concept of a master race. In great contrast, the term also has the very positive connotation of mastery of one's vocation. For example, to be known as a master carpenter, poet, or an esteemed conductor of an orchestra such as Maestro Toscanini, is an acknowledgment of one's skill level and accomplishments in these endeavors. As used in our book, the term "master" refers to one who has achieved a very high level of self-understanding and "realization" of the *Light of God* within them, also known in various traditions by many other names.

Introduction

We live in this night ocean wondering,
What are these lights?
—Rumi

Within the world's religious scriptures, many significant passages involve light—be it the "burning bush" experience of the lawgiver Moses on Mount Sinai, the "light brighter than a thousand suns" of which the Bhagavad Gita speaks, or the teaching of Jesus of Nazareth, "If thine eye be single, thy whole body shall be filled with light" (Matthew 6:22, KJV). Numerous esoteric references to inner Light appear not only in the scriptures of the distant past, but also within the personal experiential accounts by mystics, sages, and seers across the centuries from many of the world's cultural and ethnic traditions.

These experiences have variously been called the Inner Light, Divine Presence, effulgent luminosity, ringing radiance, and other similar descriptive terms. Such phenomena are found or referred to within the scriptures of virtually all of the world's religious and spiritual traditions, and are also present in the accounts of individuals' personal experiences in meditation and other contemplative practices. References to various expressions of light and enlightenment are also found in "teaching stories" that can often convey levels of deep understanding and appreciation to a broader range of listeners.

We have sought to identify effective practices, techniques, and disciplines related to inner Light that great mystics, masters, and teachers have made accessible over several millennia to their disciples, committed students, and other seekers of truth. We also draw attention to a number of significant related references and accounts by teachers and practitioners of the closely related phenomenon of Inner Sound, which is also known within various teachings as "audible sound current," *Naam, Word,* "celestial music," or other descriptions.[1] We also provide testimonies from persons who have experienced aspects of inner Light and Sound in a variety of circumstances outside of formal religious or spiritual contexts. These may be precipitated, for example, by being profoundly moved by uplifting music or Nature, sudden personal epiphanies, near-death experiences (NDEs), out of body experiences (OBEs), and during the dying process itself. Primarily because they have not been adequately understood or fully comprehended as a part of the mystical experience, these experiences have attracted relatively little scholarly inquiry. We hope that this book will contribute to thoughtful questioning, appreciative listening, and openhearted dialogue— qualities most welcomed when seekers after truth meet, sit together, and share.

In the words of the 16th century Indian mystic known as Dadu Sahib, "While others narrate only hearsay, Dadu says what he actually sees."[2]

We seek to highlight in this book those who, based on credible testimony, have experienced this divine light. They attest that accessing this esoteric knowledge is not just a matter of intellectual understanding, logical deduction, feelings or emotions, but rather that one actually "sees with inner spiritual vision." Such persons, whenever and wherever they may live, do not speak from hearsay, but from firsthand, critical investigation of their inner reality. Whether a person be called sage, satguru, saint, or some other term, depending upon his or her cultural context, matters very little in this regard. Drawing upon their own direct experiences, these visionaries attest that inner Light is at the true core of all human beings, and that this Light in its essence is the conveyor of pure and unconditional Love from its source.

How might one communicate this human search for deeper knowledge, wisdom, and understanding? In Hindu philosophy, for example, this search is expressed by two Sanskrit terms *apara vidya* and *para vidya*. The former connotes knowledge which is gained through the five senses, mind and intellect. It is knowledge which enables a person to gain the basic theoretical understanding. The second, is integral in nature, and enables a person to see things as they truly are, through knowledge gained beyond the use of the intellect alone. This deeper spiritual knowledge leads to enlightenment and liberation *(moksha)* based in *para-vidya*, understanding attained in meditation and contemplative practice.

Our research for this project covers a period of about four millennia, the first half of which (c. 2000 BCE–100 CE) marked the emergence of four major world religions—Hinduism, Judaism, Buddhism and Christianity. Because of the scope and breadth of the research involved we felt that the most effective organizational way to proceed was to focus primarily in this book on these four religious/ spiritual traditions, from their times of origin in antiquity through the present day. We anticipate a subsequent publication to follow upon completion of our research within the time-frame of the Common Era (CE).

* * * *

Throughout the ages, this ever-living current of Light and Sound has gone by many names. Among the Kalahari Bushmen, it is known as n/om, and among Iglulik Inuits, it is the *qaumaneq,* a light within the skull. In the Greek and Hellenistic worlds, it was the *phos* of Plato's allegory of the cave and the Greek mystery cults, the music of the spheres *(musica universalis)* of Pythagoras, and the *Logos* (Word) of Heraclites.

In the Abrahamic traditions, within the Jewish Torah in the book of *Bereshith*/Genesis, God said, "Let there be Light" *(Aur).* From this emanated the *Aur Ein Sof* (Infinite Limitless Light), so prominent over the millennia in the mystic quest for Kabbalah, meaning "that which is revealed," and in the *Nar Tamid* (eternal light). In Christianity, Christ is the *phos alethinon* (true light) and Jesus is the *logos sarx* (Word made flesh), for St. Gregory of Palmas it was the Taboric light of the Transfiguration, and for Dante it was the *empyrean* (literally, "on fire"). In Gnosticism, we find the region of pure light *(pleroma)* and emanations of light *(aeons).*

Moving east, the Vedas teach that *Purusha* (Absolute Self) is *jyotirmay purusha* or "made of light," and is the *jyotir uttamam* (supreme light). The Vedic universe springs forth from *naad* (vibration) or *vak* (Word), and is followed in the Bhagavad Gita, where we find *brahma-tejas* (the effulgence of the absolute). In the Upanishads, we have *atmajyotis* (light of the Self), and Patanjali's yogins are *jyotismati* (shining light). The nondual Kashmiri Shaivites have the *spanda* (vibration) that appears as *prakasa* (consciousness as light) at the core of their scriptures.

The Buddha speaks of the brightly shining mind (Pāli, *pabhassara citta*) and clear light of awareness (Tibetan, Ösel; Sanskrit, *prabhasvara*) that resides as the *bhavanga* (Pāli, "ground of being"). Taoism tells us to cultivate our celestial, positive light energy *(yang)* to enter into the dynamic and unadorned supreme way *(Tao).* Other terms common in India include: *anahad shabd* (unstruck melody), *naam* (creative vibration), *bani* (divine song), and *jyoti* (light). We find a similar language in near-death testimonies, with repeated use of terms such as living, loving, warm, brilliant, sparkling, dazzling, and effulgent light.

Our study on celestial inner Light also makes reference to what may be termed inner Sound. This sound has been known/called variously as *Naam, Shabd,* and/or Audible Sound Current and *Word* by some Christian mystics. Inwardly experienced, mystical sound is most often experienced as part of inner Light. Mystics often describe such experiences as occurring primarily within (but not exclusive to) meditative practices, transcending barriers of time, location, and cultural setting. In addition to detailed accounts of such experience within formal meditative and other contemplative practices, numerous other testimonies come from a variety of sources, such as sudden epiphanies, OBEs, NDEs, and pre-birth and after-death experiences.

To the most receptive of practitioners, the various manifestations of inner Sound Current and Light are held ultimately not to be separate from each other. From the rarified perspective of spiritual masters and adepts, these phenomena are perceived as inextricably linked together—as One. Such mystics often employ poetic language to describe what is ultimately ineffable or indescribable.

Our research encompassing many major religious spiritual traditions from widespread geographic regions, and spanning several millennia in historic time, dramatically attests that interior Light is universal and a deeply meaningful mode of human experience.

Jalalu'ddin Rumi, the great 12th century mystic poet and teacher mused, "We live in this night ocean wondering, / What are these lights?"[3] His question points to nothing less than the luminous splendor of the divine presence flowing into expression within the physical realm. Half a millennium later, George Fox, the founder of the Society of Friends (Quakers), spoke of his personal experience of both inner Light, and the "small still voice" that dwells within the sacred core of all persons.

A characteristic common to each of the world's major religions is two distinguishable aspects or "sides": an exoteric side, concerned with social and ethical norms, cosmologies, and rituals; and an esoteric side, comprised of disciplined inner practices designed for deeply penetrating into the nature of reality. A perennial question asked by many religious seekers and scholars—"Is there a universal core of potential mystical experience?"—is answered in the affirmative by the vast majority of mystics. The core experience of luminous inner Light and Sound, as explored in this book, is not incidental but fundamental to this esoteric quest and represents a universal category of human spiritual and religious attainment.

The 20th century Master and poet saint Sant Darshan Singh writes:

> He is hidden in every instrument, in every song and melody.
> All creation reflects His glory.
> There exists not a sparkling wave nor a fiery star
> that does not owe its radiance to His Light.

In our present study of inner Light from an inter-spiritual perspective, we are beneficiaries of substantial research over the past half-century, of improved translations of original texts, numerous archeological finds, accessibility to global travel, increased scholarly communication, advances in the study of integral consciousness, and the power (if judiciously used) of the Internet.

What is the relationship between Light in its spiritual sense, and physical light as understood in our everyday physical use of the term? Science in general, and the field of quantum physics in particular, has much to say about the nature and cosmological role of light. Light is an absolute; it was present with explosive force when space first emerged from singularity/nonduality at the Big Bang. As Albert Einstein demonstrated a century ago, light always travels at 186,000 miles per second, indifferent to material bodies, with no passing time from its perspective. Light appears within all material bodies and is seen at fine resolutions as energy "moving" in perhaps more than a dozen dimensions.

In the broadest sense, light is the *sine qua non* essential for all terrestrial life forms. For example, through the process of photosynthesis, plant growth takes place. Additionally, without the presence of light from beyond and within our Earth there would be no such thing as human creativity manifesting itself in such endeavors as music, poetry, painting, and architecture.

Light also serves as a metaphor for mindfulness, goodness, and a sense of responsibility toward not only our fellow human beings, but indeed toward all the beings with whom we share our planet. One does not need to be spiritually minded to recognize that many social, economic, and environmental challenges face humanity today. As a collective species, we need to "return to the Light"—to return to a shared commitment to peace, justice, stewardship, and caretaking of our planetary Garden. Only by recognizing our need to reaffirm all the positive qualities and values that the Light represents—compassion, community, care for creation, and commitment to the greater good—will humankind be able to resolve the great challenges.

Light is the energy by and through which coarser matter can be changed to finer matter. In spiritual terms, light is the means by which an individual's consciousness is brought to a higher frequency, one that allows the mind and heart to be better attuned to the underlying "truth of that which is"—and can even lead to transcending the limitations of the ordinary human ego. In terms of light and inner vision, the poet Johann Goethe was delighted by his insight that the physical eye evolved "so that light could see, and not the reverse. Light," he posited, "is what gives us our sense of luminous reality, a cosmos whose divine purpose is made visible."[4]

In *Why Religion Matters*, Huston Smith refers to light as the "very foundation of matter, and the underlying process of nature, spirit and consciousness." He points out, as have several other scholars, that "light is a universal metaphor for consciousness. It's all over our vocabulary—for instance we say 'the light dawned' when we see a point clearly....The same word light, universally and cross-culturally, is the word that we use for understanding."[5]

Any exploration of the inner Light and celestial Sound must eventually consider another quintessential spiritual quality: Love. Terminology for divinely inspired Love can be found in the spiritual lexicons of virtually all the major wisdom traditions. Such language is often closely related to the language of the inner Light or Sacred Sound. Imagine a stool supported and balanced on three legs: three pillars of truth known as Light, Sound, and pure, unconditional Love. In an inclusive mystic sense, a profound unity exists within and between these "pillars of truth"—sonorous Light and ringing radiance are permeated with luminous Love. Love itself takes multiple forms, a truth explored by the Christian writer C. S. Lewis. Among the forms of love are *eros*—the love of physical attraction; *philos*—the love of friendship, family ties, and community bonds; and *agape*—the love of the Divine, a love that is unconditional and self-giving. Embracing these distinctive forms of love can help us to find a fuller and richer understanding of life itself. A popular biblical passage testifies to the centrality of love, both in life in general and in the spiritual quest: "If I speak in the tongues of men and angels, but have not love, I am only a resounding gong or a clanging cymbal" (1 Corinthians, 13:1).

In the individual chapters of our study we draw attention primarily to recurring themes and practices that emerge in the experience of many advanced practitioners, especially in such areas as the centrality of meditation to accessing inner Light, and the nature and qualities of divine presence as encountered within meditative practice. We also consider how such deeper understandings and expansive consciousness positively affect the quality of life of an aspirant, as well as positively impacting the broader society. As a primary goal of this book is to provide practical and heartfelt guidance in utilizing the wisdom of the great mystics, every chapter concludes with a summary of core teachings and guidelines a practitioner can readily use in her or his daily life.

The book offers a reflection on the nature and universality of light, and then pulls together key themes, contemplative practices, and deeper realizations that have emerged in the individual chapters. Light exists independently before, within, and beyond all cultures and learning, and potentially permeates all aspects of spiritual life. Effulgent luminosity can present itself within disciplined structured spiritual practices, or appear of its own accord as "grace."

Inner Light is a human heritage, foundational to the ongoing journey of the soul. Light, along with Sound, is a universal core mystical experience in humans, sometimes understood in culturally specific ways but universal in its deepest expression. The aspirant's journey begins by first recognizing or understanding this Light.

A personal transformative experience of Light can be accessed through various meditative disciplines. These contemplative practices can form the basis of a personal "laboratory" for the study of spiritual growth. The experience of Light brings with it a new mode of knowing and perceiving reality that transcends the particularities of culture, nationality or class distinctions. Here we will seek to underscore the paradigm shift in awareness that may well accompany the aspirant's quest for spiritual realization. On this phase of the journey, the sincere seeker can learn to understand the prerequisites for gnosis (spiritual insight or knowledge) and the requirements for maturing in the co-creative process of spiritual growth.

The fuller the experience of Light, the greater and more profound the experience of unity consciousness. This points to the fundamental goal of all spiritual endeavor, which is the realization of our *spiritual oneness*. We all ultimately come from one Source and embody one Essence. As such, we form an indivisible fellowship of light, a unified matrix of luminescence, seemingly separate but inextricably bound together. From this state of essential oneness emerges the spontaneous and natural expression of unconditional love, compassion, and forgiveness.

Many sacred traditions of the world's religions describe Light and Love as central to the mysteries of the origins of the universe and the journey of the soul. Love is the meaning and purpose of our soul's journey and its final consummation. This journey, which began in eternity the moment each soul was created, will only end when a soul returns to its Source. This experience of divine love, universal compassion, and loving-kindness marks the realization of the full potential of the human being.

Knowledge of the shared spiritual essence of all humankind can greatly influence one's deeper understanding of one's own and others' belief systems, substantially helping to develop greater harmony and understanding across religious, spiritual, secular, and scientific communities. While many paths lead to one truth, all paths share the profound potential to develop this innate inner knowledge. Therefore, the potential for experiencing the inner Light and Sound current is available to all humankind, and intrinsically important to our very well-being. This potential exists *a priori* within creation itself, and is thus not made by, or dependent upon, any particular culture. It has the capacity to stimulate interest in this knowledge by tapping into wellsprings of deeper contemplative practice. It may also, over time, foster a greater sensitivity and sense of responsibility toward all life forms within our fragile global ecosystem.

The recognition is emerging in today's fragmented world of the need to comprehend what some mystics have called a "tree of life," to find the common trunk and subsurface roots from which spring forth religion, spirituality, philosophy, music, art and science. This reintegration is necessary, not only to ensure our physical well-being, but our mental, spiritual, and cultural revitalization as well. What is called for is a weaving together of very often seemingly disparate strands of knowledge from various fields into a fabric, of rainbow design. This in turn will better enable us to understand ourselves, each other and the life-nurturing support systems which we inhabit.

Recent mind/brain/body research on the extraordinary linkages between neuroscience and human wisdom, such as that detailed in Dr. Daniel Siegel's *Mindsight: The New Science of Personal Transformation,* draws attention to the neurobiology not only of individual growth and development, but also of finding better ways to understand how human beings relate to one another.[6] Such research documents how meditation and other contemplative practices can positively influence building mutual respect and human unity among people throughout the planet. Indeed, recent research and discoveries in the fields of neuroscience, quantum physics, positive psychology, mindfulness, epigenetics, energy medicine, and near-death research have all contributed to a growing body of evidence supporting a new paradigm of the universe that is profoundly intelligent, interconnected, and interdependent.

Today we live in a time filled with tremendous social, economic, and environmental challenges, along with many possibilities for positive transformational responses to these trials. One encouraging development in recent years is the increasing numbers of people of all ages around the world, especially among the younger generation, who are exploring ways to "tap inside," developing their inner resources to more clearly access the innately spiritual side of human nature. We hope that, wherever you may be in your own spiritual process, this book will provide insight and inspiration for experiencing more empathy, friendship, and joy within daily life—and being of service to others wherever the opportunity arises.

Can enough "common ground" be found among persons of good will from diverse cultures to pull together a unifying ethos, a global ethic, for all humanity? Will we meet the collective challenge to draw upon the best legacies of the past to address the issues of our day, so that we may truly live up to the name Homo sapiens (wise people)? What will it take to build a unifying, nonviolent, sustainable bridge of loving-kindness, and social justice—beginning within ourselves, our families, and our communities and expanding throughout the planet?

What is most needed is an opening of the heart, a deepening of insights, and a willingness to listen empathetically to others. Such a "turning" by a substantial portion of the population would be truly revolutionary. In this sense the most lasting social reforms can only be wrought by positive changes inwardly of perception and attitudes.

The concept of *enlightenment* can be understood in a secular sense, for example, in describing the major intellectual movement in 18th century Europe known as the Enlightenment (which had more to do with scientific reasoning than spiritual intuition). By contrast, those whose values, uplifting inward experiences and inspired teachings are described in this book could represent an alternative way of understanding human enlightenment—that it involves direct experience of the Light within one's own being. Literally, when the word itself is broken down into its separate components as *en-lighten-ment,* its three component syllables, "in-the-light," can be seen not only as metaphorical expression, but also as a valuable source for spiritual unification within the luminous core of one's authentic self.

Researching and writing this present book proved a highly integrative experience that has broadened and deepened our understanding in many ways. Coming from different cultural and academic backgrounds, we have over the years learned about and experienced a variety of meditation, mindfulness, and other contemplative practices, East and West. We have each had longtime interests in comparative religion and spirituality, with our current primary interest being the contemplative and experiential core of the world's great mystic, wisdom, and spiritual traditions. We have offered courses in these areas and frequently participate in multicultural, interfaith and inter-spiritual activities, locally and globally. And we have been very fortunate to have had the opportunity to study under several enlightened spiritual Masters, and have profound respect as well for all inspiring Teachers throughout history whose lives have been beacons of Light for humankind.

It is our heartfelt hope that *Let There Be Light* will serve as a useful resource on inner Light teachings and practices from the world's sacred traditions. Inspiration from enlightened teachers and sages, along with teaching stories drawn from many cultures, may well encourage further explorations. It is humankind's oft unclaimed birthright that the hidden treasures of eternal Light and Love can be personally experienced in the "here and now" of our lives. It is our prayer that each person may have the opportunity to become receptive to universal qualities that deepen our levels of basic understanding. And may people everywhere, with mutual respect, experience a world at peace.

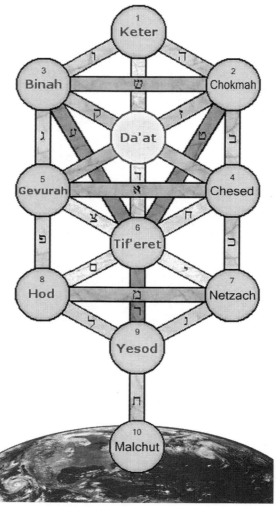

This is a graphic Illustration of Sephirot in Jewish mysticism: (singular sephira). The Sephirot symbolically portray the "building blocks or energy centers of the Creation" and are here structurally depicted on the "Tree of Life." Each represents a Divine attribute emanating from the supernal Light of God (Aur Ein Sof). They are manifested in each of the descending "Four Worlds" and are the sources of the corresponding ten faculties (kochot) of the soul. They descend "downward" from Keter to Malchut, representing at each level: 1-crown, 2-wisdom, 3-understanding, 4-kindness, 5-strength, 6-beauty, 7-victory, 8-splendor, 9-foundation and 10-sovereignty (Public Domain).

CHAPTER ONE

Judaism and the Soul's Quest for Eternal Light

For with You is the source of life; by Your light may we see light.
(Psalm 36:10)

An Overview of the Journey

A story is told of a young American who journeyed to Europe to meet the renowned Rabbi Israel Meir Hakohen Kagan (d. 1933). Reb Kagan was widely known as the *Hafetz Hayim*, "Lover of Life," the title of his first book, which encapsulated his personal outlook as well. When the visitor entered the rabbi's one-room apartment, he was amazed at the simplicity of the furniture—only a bed, a table, and a chair:

"But where are the rest of your possessions?" asked the young visitor.

The sage replied only with his own question. "And where are yours?"

Flabbergasted, the young man answered, "I don't have any here. I'm only passing through."

"Nu?" responded said the *Hafetz Hayim*, "so am I."[1]

Almost four millennia earlier, a man named Abram, son of Terah, living in Ur Chaldea, Mesopotamia, responded to an inner calling, an angelic voice telling him to "go forth" with his family and flocks to the land of Canaan. He and his wife Sarah thus commenced a physical journey westward from the Fertile Crescent, outwardly across the desert, and inwardly culminating in his becoming the first patriarch of what would become a radically new monotheistic religion. His powerful unseen God, YHWH (Yahweh), guided him to his destiny and gave him a new name, Abraham ("father of multitudes"), which reflected the promise that he would become "father of a people" (Genesis 17:5).[2]

Abraham's descendants eventually fell into bondage after they had left Canaan for Egypt, seeking refuge from a famine. After several centuries, the prophet/lawgiver Moses led the people to freedom. They became known as Israelites. After a dramatic escape from Egypt, Moses led the Israelites forth from their captivity through the desert to Mount Sinai, where he encountered the presence of God and received the law (Torah), thereby giving the people a new vision of their religious identity.

On the sixth Day of the creation story, the Torah tells that: "Then God said, 'Let us make humankind in Our image, according to Our likeness'" (Genesis 1:26). Jewish mysticism subsequently has emphasized humankind's divine origins and teaches that generic Man, male and female alike, is blessed with an innate capacity to remain connected (or to reconnect) with the Creator. This tradition conceives the human soul as a divine spark emanating from God. When the soul came (comes) into individual existence, it is "clothed" first in a heavenly, spiritual body, then in an etheric or astral body, and finally in a physical body appropriate for living on the Earth.

A substantial number of Jewish mystics believe that the soul moves through a series of births and rebirths, in its cosmic journey to uncover selfunderstanding of its deepest purpose. The ultimate goal is to return to God, to the ultimate source, the *Ein Sof* (which translates literally as "that which has no end").

Personal testimonies of mystic experience are often an exception rather than the rule in the history of Jewish literature. Why is this so? One traditional explanation held that if a person spoke too openly about highly personal inner experiences, the blessing of having such experiences might be withdrawn.[3] Thus, to the extent that mystical experiences are described, they are often couched in highly symbolic and metaphorical language. Yet where such accounts are found, they provide significant glimpses into the deepest essence of Jewish spirituality. Whatever the precise nature of these experiences, they often proved to be profound and life-changing.

The Jewish understanding of the life purpose of the embodied soul on Earth—if, indeed, such an understanding could be put fully into words—is for the soul to bridge the gap of separation and achieve union with the Creator. To achieve this goal, a condition that in Hebrew is called *devekut,* a disciple would meditate on the divine Names of God given to the disciple by a spiritual Master known as a *Zaddik* (or *tsaddik*). The Zaddikim (plural) were the major conveyors of spirituality for those seeking union with God. Some mystic teachings refer to the Zaddikim as Torah incarnate—living embodiments of the Word of God.

The ideal relationship between Zaddik and disciples encompassed unselfish love and commitment. The loving bond between the disciple and spiritual guide was not unique to the Jewish tradition; it finds its corollary in many other mystical traditions and was a primary means of transformation for the novitiate. In principle, each person can have direct communion with God without going through an intermediary. But fortunate, it is attested, is the person who comes under the guidance of a spiritually evolved teacher, who like a lamplighter lovingly helps to illuminate the path for the aspiring student.

In general, mysticism involves the direct inner perception of spiritual realities. Jewish mystical thought and practices are like an ongoing caravan, its journey bridging three millennia. In the course of this journey, significant landmarks point to the Inner Light, beginning with the Genesis creation story and the biblical origins of the Jewish people. The journey continues through Mount Sinai and the Torah, Moses and Joshua, the prophets and the psalmists, and the vicissitudes of the Kingdom of Israel in 70 A.D. At this point, the biblical record ends, but the caravan has only traversed one-third of its journey.

The first major movement of post-biblical Jewish mysticism begins with the Merkavah tradition (100–200 CE), which harkened back to the chariot visions of the prophet Ezekiel during the Babylonian exile (609–515 BCE). The journey centuries later moves on to Spain and the early Kabbalist movement with Rabbi Abraham Abulafia (1240–1296 CE) and his students, and to the Golden Age of Kabbalah, with its classic, *Zohar (Book of Splendor)*.

The greatest mystics of this period focused on the *Ein Sof* (Creator God) and the emanating infinite Light of God *(Aur Ein Sof)*, which permeates all of creation with its supernal Light, Sound, and Love. Kabbalah, the name of the most widely known school of Jewish mysticism, comes from the Hebrew root *kabal*, meaning "received." Along with the Torah, the higher levels of Kabbalah are traditionally held to have been given at the time of revelation at Mount Sinai, although it was revealed in historic time only in stages appropriate to the capacity of the people at the time to fully receive it.

The town of Safed in the Galilean region of the Holy Land became a great center of Kabbalistic mysticism in the 15th century under the guidance of the Ari, Rabbi Isaac Luria (1437–1508 CE). There the central concepts of *tsimtsum* and *sephirot* were more fully developed, and women took on a greater role in the spiritual life of the community. The next period we will highlight centered in Poland and Russia with the widespread flowering of the Hasidic movement begun by the Baal Shem Tov (1700–1760 CE).

In the post-Holocaust years of the mid-20th century, the Chabad movement centered in Brooklyn, New York, and headed by the Lubavich Rabbi, Menachem Schneerson (1902–1994), sought to be a restorative presence within Judaism worldwide. A number of other contemporary teachers, movements, and communities around the world are seeking in various ways to rekindle the sparks of Jewish mystic tradition and are harbingers of its renewal. The creative practice of the traditional Jewish concept of *tikkun* ("healing" or "repairing") remains a vital resource, bringing hope and Light to the myriad challenges of our times. The process of tikkun addresses the need to bind and heal the wounds in individual persons and within communities, and between the nations and peoples of our shared planetary home.

Eternal Light: Biblical Origins and Monotheism (c. 2000 BCE–150 CE)

In a number of ancient cosmogonies, light is the primal element of Creation. The Jewish Torah has a number of significant references to light and luminosity, beginning with the first Day of the Creation story in Genesis:

> "And God said, 'Let there be light.' And there was light. And God saw the light, that it was good." (Genesis 1:3–5)

Over the millennia, this single passage of Hebrew scripture has inspired untold thousands of pages of interpretations, poetry, and not surprisingly, yet more questions. While seen in modern times by some as mere metaphor, the origin of Light as told in Genesis, as a whole provides the essence of a basic mystical recounting of the primal beginnings of Creation. It tells of the first emanation of the current of divine Light and Sound that pours forth with tremendous force, manifesting in the first moments of creation.

Commenting on the words, "Let there be light. And there was light. And God saw the light, that it was good," the Kabbalist *Book of Splendor (Zohar)* proclaims illustratively: "Let there be light in this world, and there was light in the world to come." One can ask: And what is the relationship here between creation of light on earth, and in the world to come? One explication on the nature of this relationship provided by a leading 20th century Kabbalist, Rabbi Yehuda Lev Ashlag, emphasizes that those who have purified themselves through Torah can develop the capacity to witness the "great light" of the "world to come," even within this lifetime.

> The act of creation brought into being all creatures according to their true nature and in their full stature, in all their perfection and in all their glory. Thus the light that was created on the first day appeared in all its perfection, including even the light of this world, in complete delight and pleasantness....However, in order to prepare a place of free choice in which there exists the potential for spiritual work, the light was then hidden and concealed for the righteous to receive in the world to come.... (Yet) for those who have purified their wills to receive through the way of Torah, then they are worthy of this great light even in this world. Just as the sages have said, "You can see your world during your lifetime."[4]

Another significant biblical passage that speaks of light is Moses' experience with the burning bush prior to leading the Israelites out of their bondage in Egypt. The story of Moses encompasses the entire book of *Shemot* (Exodus). One day while grazing the sheep of his father-in-law, Moses beheld a bush burning in the desert: "An angel of God appeared to him in a flame of fire…, but the bush was not consumed" (Exodus 3:1–17). This verse has traditionally been subject to mystical interpretations of Moses' encounter with YHWH, as Moses witnessed inner as well as external illumination.

The Torah account describes Moses' vision in three different stages. First he was shown a fire that did not consume the bush, exciting his curiosity to investigate. Doing so he realized that a Godly holiness was resting upon the bush in the form of an angel. Then Moses received a revelation in which a "voice" of God called out to him from amid the bush, "Moses, Moses," who in turn responded *"Hineni"* (Here I am) (Exodus 3:1–14).

We will refer here in this passage to God by the modern Orthodox and Hasidic respectful term *Hashem,* meaning "the Name," which designates the ineffable quality of the Merciful One. Hashem then continued, "Do not come closer, remove the shoes from your feet, for the place upon which you stand is holy ground." When Moses subsequently asked His identity, Hashem responded, *"Eheye Asher Eheye"* ("I am who I am" or more literally, "I shall be as I shall be"), and assured Moses that *"eheye emach"* ("I shall be with you").

In time, Moses became a prophetic voice for God and eventually led the Hebrew people during their exodus from bondage, followed by years of wandering in the Sinai desert. As the lawgiver at Mount Sinai, he was said to have been imbued with the *Ruach Hakodesh* (a spirit of holiness). Among the teachings he received on Mount Sinai, the Hebrew people were told to keep a *Ner Tamid* (Eternal Light) burning at all times in the sanctuary that was to be constructed atop the altar (Exodus 27:20).

The Ner Tamid continued to be significant in Jewish religious observance, throughout the biblical period and extending to the present day. Two thousand years later, it is symbolically kept lit day and night in synagogues and temples around the world. A Kabbalistic interpretation of the Ner Tamid relates that the Light of God will never be extinguished, and that Jewish people even in times of darkest tribulations remain connected with the Aur Ein Sof, the eternal Light emanating from the ultimate divine Source. The illumination of the eternal Light lies dormant within each person, waiting to be rekindled and glow figuratively with light. It is a continuous reminder of the covenant established between Creator and creation, the bond between the Sacred Name of God—the Tetragrammaton written as YHWH (right to left: yud, heh, vav, heh)—and the nascent Jewish people at Sinai. (Traditionally, the pronunciation of this Name is forbidden in Jewish religious law.) Beyond the five books of Moses, the scriptural canon of biblical Judaism contains many references to light. In the Psalms (many of which are traditionally attributed to King David, circa 1000 BCE), such references include:

- Raise up over us the light of Thy countenance upon us. (Psalms 4:7)
- Your word is a lamp for my feet, and a light unto my path. (Psalms 119:105)
- Even darkness will not obscure anything from You, and the night will light up as day. (Psalms 139:12)
- For You will light my candle: the Lord my God will enlighten my darkness. (Psalms 18:29)
- The Lord is my light and my help; whom shall I fear? The Lord is the strength of my life; of whom shall I be afraid? (Psalms 27:1)
- For with You is the source of life; by Your light may we see light. (Psalms 36:10)

Here the psalmist understands the intimate connection between eternal life and the divine light of God, the "fountain of light" that is both his source and essence.

- Blessed is the people that know the joyful sound: they shall walk, O Lord, in the light of thy countenance" (Psalms 89:15).[5]

In this psalm, the imagery of sound and light are linked together in the interior life of the mystic. Those who have had the experience of "joyful sound" will be guided by the light of YHVH, "walking" within the covenantal relationship between Creator and created.

While authorship of a number of the psalms is unclear, the psalms collectively embody a poignant, spiritually uplifting quality that has inspired Jews, as well as people of many other religious/spiritual backgrounds across the centuries.[6] These prayer-poems convey a profound sense of ultimate trust in the Light-giver, the "Oneness" who illuminates the darkness. This Light may be understood as both transcendent and immanent. The supplicant seeks to sustain his connection with God through heartfelt prayer. With such a source of help in times of danger, for the truly receptive, there is ultimately nothing to fear.

The short-lived zenith of the Kingdom of Israel took place when the entire land was ruled by King David (c. 1000–960 BCE) followed by his son Solomon (c. 960–929 BCE).

Beginning in the same proximate time frame, over the next thousand years (c. 1050 BCE–50 CE), several new major religions came into being in the continent of Asia, including Buddhism, Jainism, Confucianism, Taoism, and Christianty.[7]

Among the Jewish people this era saw the gradual consolidation of monotheism, marked by a gradual transition to broader perceptions of their God.[8]

Isaiah, Prophetic Voice for Human Dignity, and Rabbi Akiba, Embodiment of Compassion

Through the noble ethical and social justice teachings of such courageous prophetic voices as Isaiah, Amos, and Micah, YHVH implored that compassion be shown to the most vulnerable of society, like widows, orphans, and the strangers within the gates. Faithfulness to the Creator could best be demonstrated through compassion and right action. This most significant "commandment" is brought forth with crystal clarity in the very poignant Torah *Haftorah* reading in synagogues and temples throughout the world on Yom Kippur, the Day of Atonement.

On this, the most central and solemn of Jewish holy days, a day marked with fasting and penitential prayer, the words of Prophet Isaiah, speaking as the "voice" of God, challenge the congregation and, by extension, all of humanity. This is the heart of his message:

> Is this not the fast I [G-d] will choose? To undo the fetters of wickedness, to untie the bands of perverseness, and to let out the oppressed free.... Is it not to share your bread with the hungry, and moaning poor you shall bring home. When you see a naked one, you shall clothe him.... Then your light shall break forth as the dawn, and your healing shall quickly sprout, and your righteousness shall go before you.... Then you shall call and the Lord shall answer, you shall cry and He shall say, "Here I am. And you draw out your soul to the hungry, and an afflicted soul you sate, then your light shall shine in the darkness, and your darkness shall be like noon. And the Lord shall always lead you... and you shall be like a well-watered garden. (Isaiah 58:1–12; Tanakh:Stone Edition).

To those who would faithfully follow the path of righteousness just described, G-d promised, "Your light shall break forth as the dawn..., and your light shall shine in the darkness, and your darkness shall be like noon." For those who selflessly comforted the afflicted, their capacity to receive the Eternal's inner Light shall be constant, shining forth within the inner eye in the midst of the darkest night as well as at noontime.

Isaiah thus connects the experience of compassion to interior illumination on the mystical journey. The qualities of compassion and loving-kindness, arising out of the experience of unconditional love, will flower even more fully as the inner journey of spiritual growth progresses.

Rabbis Hillel and Akiba ben Joseph were revered Rabbis and mystics of the first century CE, whose practical applications of Torah and prophetic teachings are well remembered, and studied through the present day. Once Rabbi Hillel (c. 80 BCE–30 CE) was approached by a skeptic, who challenged him to teach him the essence of Torah while he stood on one foot. Hillel responded by telling the man, "What is hateful to yourself, do not do to your fellow man. This is the essence of the Torah and the remainder is but commentary. Go, study and practice it."

Like Hillel, Rabbi Akiba lived during a very difficult period at the beginning of the Common Era. Yet, he continued to emphasize that God's presence was everywhere, and that holiness could be equally found within the humblest of homes. Akiba taught that "the great principle of the Torah" was "You shalt love your neighbor as yourself." He emphasized that "scripture instructs us that whosoever sheds human blood is regarded as if he had diminished the divine image." According to Akiba, to partake in a scandalous lie about others amounted to denying the very existence of God. The same light of God which is loved and revered in oneself must be loved and revered in others.

Rabbi Akiba died in 132 CE with great equanimity. Though he lived during a tragic time in Jewish history, it was also a period marked by the flourishing of interpretive study dedicated to understanding deeper meanings of the written Torah. The most significant work of that age was the *Midrash* (the root of which, *darash*, means "to search"). According to Midrashic perspectives on the study of Torah, divine revelation was not just a closed book recounting what had happened in some distant time. In a mystical sense, all souls of yet unborn generations were said to be present at Mount Sinai, so that the revealed teachings were the ongoing possession of every Israelite, of every age. Thus, biblical exegesis could go further than the original holy texts, attempting to fathom what was left unsaid and explore even deeper interpretations. As one rabbinic text put forward, "matters that had not been disclosed to Moses were disclosed to Rabbi Akiba and his generation."

Concurrently, this meant that no one had the last word on the subject of God, which was too vast for the human mind ever to wrap around and fully comprehend. As a powerful reminder that any attempt to explain the full nature of God proved so inadequate that it was potentially blasphemous, Jews were forbidden to pronounce the very holiest Name of God. When speaking of God's presence on earth or discussing the divine mystery, phrases, such as the *kavod* (glory) of God or the *Shekhinah* (the divine presence, expressed in a feminine mode), were used. Mystics throughout history have often recognized the futility of attempts to describe their most intimate encounters with God through conventional human language. "This tradition of profound reticence would long continue to characterize Jewish theology and mysticism."[9]

The Merkavah Period: The Chariot and Throne Light Mysticism (c. 1–200 CE)

The earliest period or school of post-biblical Jewish mysticism was known as *Merkavah* (1–200 C.E.), which in Hebrew can mean either a chariot or a throne. The Book of Ezekiel 1 provides a vivid illustration of a prophetic vision, and "the riders of the Chariot" for over a thousand years took their journey on a route provided by the ancient prophet. The prophet Ezekiel had an illuminated vision when he was in exile in Babylon, said to be around the year 593 BCE. Here is an excerpt of the vision when he ascended by chariot to a heavenly abode, and there witnessed upon a throne of sublime light "the likeness of the glory of the Lord."

> I saw something like the appearance of fire, and a brilliance surrounding it. Like the appearance of a bow that would be in the clouds on a rainy day, so was the appearance of the brilliance all around. That was the appearance of a likeness of Hashem [God]. When I saw, I fell on my face and I heard a voice speaking. Then he said to me, "Son of Man, stand on your feet and I will speak to you. A spirit entered into me as He spoke to me, and it stood me on my feet, and I heard that which was being spoken to me...." (Ezekiel 1:27–2:2)

The prophet describes a mystical vision in which the heavens open up to reveal a high cloud of flashing fire surrounded by a radiance, and comes into contact with the "likeness of the glory of G-d." Using Ezekiel's visions as a model, a practice called *ma'aseh Merkavah* (working the Holy Chariot) became the center of a Kabbalistic practice utilizing meditation in seeking to attain the same kind of mystic experience that Ezekiel describes.

Accounts of Ezekiel seeing the fiery chariot and the throne of God are found in a number of other biblical sources.[10] A modern scholar, Aryeh Kaplan, speaks in some detail about the significance of the chariot being a vehicle by which mystic initiates ascended into another level of consciousness. He also notes the significance of repetition of a series of Divine names as a key to facilitation of such inner experiences.

> The *Greater Hekhalot* is one of the most ancient of all mystical texts, dating back to the First Century. It is also one of the few ancient tracts that explicitly describes the methods through which one enters the mystical state. Through the repetition of a mantric formula, utilizing a series of Divine Names one enters the threshold of the mystical Chambers, and then one must proceed from one Chamber to the next. When one

reaches the step before the seventh and final chamber, he is placed in a "chariot" (karon). The general word for this type of mystical experience is *Merkava,* which also means a chariot. The Merkava is a spiritual vehicle that one creates for himself, with which he ascends into the mystical state.[11]

Those practitioners who reached the level of *yored Merkavah* (spiritual initiates) then aspired to become adepts. Through the repetition of the Sacred Names of God, the material world's control over the adept's soul was diminished:

> ...thus free(ing) their souls to experience the Chariot of light that carries the mystical traveler from level to level. This ascent necessarily involves successfully passing by the fierce Angels *(Malakhim)* who guard the entrances of each heavenly level...Having successfully traversed the heavenly levels, the adepts may then aspire to the highest of all sacred realms, that which houses the Throne of Glory, where they may, if so blessed, experience the vision of God's countenance that Ezekiel describes.[12]

Making reference to bright and concentrated light in describing Divine Presence is more than a poetic or imaginative embellishment, and is perhaps the most precise way in which that Reality can be expressed in human language. This descriptive usage of interior light is found later in many mystical texts, and is especially prominent among such "riders of the Chariot" as Abraham Abulafia, Abraham of Granada, Dov Baer of Lubavich, Isaac Eizik of Komarno, and Aaron Roth.[13]

Gershom Scholem, a pioneer scholar of 20th century Jewish mysticism, noted that the major goal for Merkavah practitioners was for their soul to ascend from the earth through the spheres of various rulers of the cosmos. This ascension enabled the soul to return to its divine home in the fullness of God's light. According to an account given around 1000 CE by Hai ben Sherira, the head of a Babylonian academy, there is a "passport procedure" to help one navigate the various obstacles and temptations along the way of the ascension. This involved prayers and fasting, and...

> "lay [ing] his head between his knees and whisper [ing] many songs and hymns whose texts are known from tradition. Then he perceives the interior and the chambers as if he saw the seven palaces with his own eyes...and saw what was there...." Every new stage requires a mystic seal that the "traveler seals himself which puts demons and hostile angels to flight, in order for the soul to continue its journey without danger." All the seals and secret names are derived from the Merkavah itself, where they "stand like pillars of flame around the fiery throne" of the Creator.[14]

A passage like this indicates that, although there was very little written documentation as such, considerable in-depth Jewish meditative and contemplative practices involving inner illumination existed during the Merkavah period.

Kabbalah and Jewish Mysticism

Sometimes Jewish mysticism is equated entirely with Kabbalah, but this identification is neither particularly helpful nor fully accurate. The Kabbalah and its best known work, the *Zohar*, came into the foreground as a great manifestation of religious energy in the 12th and 13th centuries and remained a major factor for centuries. As scholar Louis Jacobs puts it:

> The Kabbalah was indeed produced by mystics, and it contained the fruit of profound religious meditation and the instruments used by later mystics to attain their aim of encountering the Divine. However, there were many mystics who flourished before the "kabbalistic era," and the Kabbalah deals with many matters that are not mystical.[15]

The study of Kabbalah is seen in various ways. Often it is likened to entering a splendid but potentially dangerous orchard. There are many gates into the orchard, some leading to sensual delights, and sometimes awesome experiences such as entering the world of disembodied sound, where the soft beating of wings announces you have reached the realm of *Ofanim* where angelic beings in the shape of wheels reside. Successful pilgrims, having integrated their psychological, ethical, and spiritual selves, will continue until they reach a clear space.

Here grows a tree, whose branches (the Sephirot) are portrayed in ten differently colored spheres, each representing an ascending "world" or level of spiritual perception. Having come upon this "tree of life," the mystic knows that he has reached the point where he is truly ready to climb. The gates have led him into the hidden *Pardes* (an acronym meaning orchard), which refers to the *Gan Eden* (the Garden of Eden). In this orchard grows a sacred tree that marks the mystic's ascent to God.[16]

The story is told of four sages who, in the first century, CE, entered the "orchard" of Jewish mysticism, seeking to fully embrace the four levels of Pardes. The first three levels of understanding biblical scripture (simple, allegorical, midrashic/interpretative) culminate in the fourth level, *Sod* (mystical), where the secret or innermost meaning of Torah is revealed. Only one of the four sages, Rabbi Akiba, is said to have fully integrated the esoteric teachings, so he alone emerged from the Pardes in fully peaceful equipoise. He had attained the heights of interior illumination and lived until the age of 90.

Thoughts, words, and actions become interconnected for those rare Kabbalists who complete the journey. Believing that humankind is created in the image of God, the mystic works to polish himself (or more accurately, become polished) until he becomes so clear that he reflects nothing but the light of YHVH. Union with the Absolute in this case is a matter of "like attracting like." The godlier a person becomes, the more divinity shines through him or her. As his sensibility is further refined, he will become conversant with the ethereal world of angelic beings and pure light and sound, until finally he reaches the unmanifest level of awareness called *devekut,* cleaving to God, the highest state attainable by human consciousness.

The "Golden Age" of Spain and the Early Kabbalists

By the tenth century, such cities in Spain as Cordova and Granada rapidly became renowned as leading centers of cross-cultural creativity and religious tolerance. Seeds were sown that were instrumental in laying a foundation for what became known as the "Golden Age" in Spain. It was a time of flourishing expression in the arts, literature, poetry, architecture, and in the realm of spirituality, especially mysticism. For several centuries thereafter many practitioners of the three Abrahamic traditions, Judaic, Christian, and Muslim, not only coexisted with but also learned from each other, becoming mutual beneficiaries of the personal, religious, and cultural interchanges that took place.

Rabbi Abraham Abulafia (1240–1296) and His Students

Abraham Abulafia was born in the province of Aragon in Spain in the year 1240. After the death of his father who was also his religious teacher, at age 20 he traveled to the land of Israel in search of the mythical river Sambatyon. He returned to Europe via Greece and then Italy, where he studied philosophy, especially Maimonides' *Guide to the Perplexed.* During this time, he also began a serious study of Kabbalah. Over the years, Abulafia became a sought-after teacher by people of many backgrounds.

Abulafia eventually went to Sicily where he lived most of his remaining years, developing a circle of committed students and admirers and writing prolifically. His teachings of Ecstatic Kabbalism included the traditionalist proponents of halakhah, the collective body of Jewish religious law derived from Torah and expounded upon over many centuries by sages and rabbis.[17]

In his preachings and writings, Abulafia held that the most advanced stage of mysticism was the mystical-prophetic experience.[18] One of Abulafia's students, the anonymous author of the *Shaare Tzedek (Gates of Justice)*, described his first mystical experience as follows:

> The third night, after midnight, I nodded off a little, quill in hand and paper on my knees. Then I noticed that the candle was about to go out. I rose to put it right, as oftentimes happens to a person [who is] awake. Then I saw that the light continued. I was greatly astonished, as though after close examination, I saw that it issued from myself. I said: "I do not believe it." I walked to and fro throughout the house, and behold, the light is with me. I lay on a couch and covered myself up, and behold the light is with me all the while.[19]

After a few more days of meditation, Abulafia's student noted that he made additional progress in the meditation practice then known as the Kabbalah of Names. Through the utilization of *gematria* (the search for hidden meaning within Torah, utilizing analysis of letter and word placement and numerical values), he sought higher meanings and mystical secrets hidden within the text of the Torah. He reported witnessing illumination of the various letter-combinations of the Divine Names within a setting of light.[20]

Abulafia was very interested in the transmission of the "voice" of the Divine in human affairs. The emergence of Jewish philosophy that could no longer accept the corporeal doctrine of the Divine made it necessary to reinterpret such biblical verses as "Moses spoke and G-d answered him with a voice." He concluded that the source of the Divine voice and speech came from the inspiration within a person's heart and not in the fire of the bush. Humankind is likened to a *kinnor* (harp) on which God makes music. And the Shekhinah, like a blowing wind, moves through the attuned human vessel when the musician is attuned to the Divine melodies reverberating within the instrument.[21]

According to Abulafia, meditation lead the disciple to and through the higher spheres until he or she reached the state called the "Exalted Man," and became one with the Creator. Such souls were then called "Masters of the Divine Name," and Abulafia believed they fully aligned with God when they entered these states of union. Such a *tzaddik*, or spiritual master, though fully engaged in the world, is inwardly never separate from God. The primary purpose of the tzaddik was to assist his fellow beings to achieve the same level of spiritual elevation that he had attained.

The Zohar (c. 1286–1300) and the Sefirot Tree of Life

The *Sefer Ha-Zohar*, commonly known as the *Zohar, The Book of Splendor*, was compiled and written in the Castile region of Spain, around the years 1286–

1300. Although its origins are still somewhat disputed, the Zohar is attributed primarily to Rabbi Moses de Leon. Its fame can be gauged by the fact that, for a period of several centuries, it alone, among the whole of post-Talmudic literature, was ranked as a canonical text along with the Bible and Talmud.

For a growing number of leading medieval Kabbalists, the older Merkavah mysticism, with its celestial throne and its heavenly household and palaces through which the traveler passes, was no longer of supreme importance. The new Kabbalistic *gnosis* or cognition of God, an "inner Merkavah," as it were, concerned God Himself. Medieval Kabbalists, along with nonreligious philosophers such as the ethicist Baruch Spinoza, became deeply interested in such questions as why God (Ein Sof) created the world. What is the relationship between Ein Sof, existing outside of time, and the created temporal world? How does eternity interact with temporality?

In an attempt to penetrate the celestial glory, not only externally but within the human being himself, Kabbalists developed meditative and contemplative practices to delve into the hidden inner worlds where the divine light is mysteriously refracted into itself. Hence the adoption of new symbols, foremost of which were the Ten Sefirot written in the *Zohar.*

Sefirah (plural *sefirot*) derives from the Hebrew root *sefer* meaning "to count" or the verb meaning "to number." They are not actual numbers, though, and have no intrinsic physical properties or substance. Sefirot can be more accurately conceived of as "ideal concepts or intelligence...that constitute the Attributes of G-d."[22]

In a mystic sense, sefirot can also connote the "the shining one." It serves as a means through which God's light is contained and transmitted throughout the world. In the words of of Rabbi Yehuda Lev Ashlag:

> The whole spiritual universe is divided generally speaking, into five worlds, which are called [in descending order] *Adam Kadmon, Atzilut, Briyah, Yetsirah* and *Assiyah*. Each one of them composed of endless sub-worlds....The lights that are enclosed within these five worlds are called *Yechidah, Chayah, Neshamah, Ruach* and *Nefesh*. The light of *Yechidah* shines in the world of Adam Kadmon.... [and filters down to the most.... material world of *Assiyah*, where the light is known as *Nefesh*.] These five worlds contain all the spiritual reality originating at the level of the *Ein Sof* and continuing right down to this world. Now each is included within the others, so that each world contains within it all the aspects of the five worlds....[23]

It is important to understand that while different names are given to these five major categories of consciousness or "worlds," they are not separate universes. They can be better conceived as concentric, one within the other, ranging from *assiyah,* the world of physicality, to *adam kadmon,* the primordial source. Ashlag notes that in the "three lower worlds" the pure light of Ein Sof has "covers" that "limit and put a measure on this light for those who receive it, in order that the person may only receive light according to the degree of his or her own purity." From the moment a person is born, "he or she has a [holy] soul" whose full capacity has not yet been activated. Yet, by leading an aware and wholesome life, the individual person has the ever-present potential to come into increasingly fuller contact with the eternal light of the Divine Source.[24]

At the human level, the Ten Sefirot of which the Zohar speaks are symbolically configured in the form of a "Tree of Life." They can be seen as an ascending ladder, with each level corresponding to a certain quality of the Divine. The lower seven sefirot represent aspects of the physical universe, the milieu in which a person's ordinary consciousness operates. The three highest sefirot in Kabbalah are translated as *binah* (understanding), *chokhmah* (pure awareness), and *keter* (crown).

Binah consciousness occurs when a person is able to be still and notice the inner workings of the mind that arise in ordinary thinking. He or she can experience the difference between binah awareness and all the other feelings that arise with ordinary thought. The practitioner feels alert, mindful, and lucid. Integrating with everything happening around him or her, feeling connected, whole, and relaxed brings a new sense of calmness and a greater sense of equanimity to his or her life. The practitioner can see things more clearly and have more refined discernment and more balanced appraisal of how things will unfold.

Chokhmah represents the element in which the first spark of a thought is initiated, and binah represents the element in which the thought is actually formed. In this state of mind there is only the experience of each moment as it arises. Each sound is exquisite, each visual impression unique. This practice of sitting quietly and observing one's physical experience is a generic meditation practice found in a wide variety of traditions, with the major objective being to attain full presence to what is happening in the present moment.

The keter (crown) sefira is also the "connective point" to the next level of sefirot ascending into higher realms of consciousness, until it is said to be connected, ultimately, to the Adam Kadmon, the highest realm of the "spiritual universe." Keter is an ephemeral state of which very little can be said—it can be experienced but not easily spoken about. There are meditative techniques to develop awareness of the "qualities" represented with each sefira. The sefirot do not exist in a spatial continuum, and therefore it is impossible to differentiate them except through metaphorical language. This can be done when we use colors to represent their being differentiated. The Chokhmah-Wisdom is seen as "a color that includes all colors," and the Keter/Crown, for example, is seen in a "blinding invisible white."[25]

Chokhmah consciousness is far more subtle than binah. The early Kabbalists called it *ayin,* nothingness or "no-thingness." Actually, that no-thing is really "something" that can be experienced. It is an experience of pure awareness that can be perceived, but not with the cognitive mind. There is "nobody" or [or "no-body"] to notice, no identification with the self, and therefore no one to react. It is attested that one cannot "will" chokhmah, but that it comes only through grace. We cannot force it, but we can invite it in. Once chokhmah is brought together with binah, then, as Rebbe Shneur Zalman of Liadi (founder of the Chabad movement in 18th century Russia) innovatively put it, we have *daat* (knowledge), a conscious integration of almost everything we do in life.[26]

Attaining this state of mind is a Jewish way of realizing a significant degree of enlightenment. Many sages consider this "attainment" of chokhmah awareness to be a prerequisite for developing *devekut,* constant awareness of the Divine, which is the goal of almost all contemplative practices in Judaism.[27] With the practice and blessing of devekut, each succeeding generation has the potential to encounter the holy ancient One of old.

YHVH and Holy Temple Mysticism

Many treatises and practices within Kabbalistic writings relate to the Tetragrammaton, the four Hebrew letters—yod, hay, vav, hay—which together form the unpronounceable holy name of Yahweh (God), the Source of all Sources, the Cause of All Causes. In the work *Berit Menuhah* (Covenant of Rest) attributed to Abraham ben Isaac of Granada in the 14th century, the text speaks of *orot* (illuminations), which are spiritual influences on the material world coming from on high. This harkens back to biblical days of the great temple in Jerusalem. After meticulous spiritual and ritualistic preparations, the high priest entered the Holy of Holies on Yom Kippur (the Day of Atonement). Upon uttering the divine name, he was granted a vision of the Shekhinah, within the entire sefirotic Tree of Life. It was said that "if the High Priest saw the gate of the Ark filled with white light he rejoiced exceedingly."[28]

An illustrative excerpt from the *Berit Menuhah* speaks to the mystic qualities of light and sound experienced by the high priest when he meditated at the Ark and supplicated for the forgiveness of sins, both his own and those of all the children of Israel:

After this he would hear a voice, saying: My son bless Me. Then would the High priest know that it was a time of grace. He would then shake his garments and the sound of the bells would be heard outside and Israel would know it was a time of grace. Then the High Priest would pronounce the name as it is written YHWH, together with its vowels, and gently and mysteriously he would meditate on it. Then the threshold of the Temple would tremble... and be filled with a celestial light.[29]

Such descriptions of the ecstasy of the high priest in the Holy of Holies were said to be an inspiration for those seeking mystical ecstatic experience for many successive centuries.

Rabbi Isaac Luria (1534–1572) and the Safed Mystic Community

Not long after 1492, a rising current of messianic interest appeared in the Mediterranean world. Among the most influential advocates of an emerging messianic viewpoint was Isaac Abrabanel (1437–1508) whose written works expressed hope for redemption. He declared the coming of the Messiah Age, and the personhood of the Messiah would soon be revealed.

Though an ongoing Jewish presence had remained in the region since biblical times, a rather extraordinary community began to develop in Safed in the Galilean hills from about 1530 on. The small town of Safed emerged in the mid-1600s as a thriving economic and spiritual center, attracting an unusual array of scholars and rabbis, and religious life flourished with renewed vitality. In the study houses, synagogues, and academies, spirituality and intellectuality flourished.

The relatively stable political situation, along with a healthy economic base, provided the conditions under which a rather extraordinary community began to develop around 1530 onwards. Safed attracted an unusual array of scholars and rabbis, and religious life flourished with a vitality that the Jewish community in Palestine had not experienced for centuries. In the study houses, synagogues, and academies, religious life and intellectuality flourished.

In 1536, Spanish-born Joseph Caro, who was both an attorney and an inspired mystic, arrived in Palestine from Constantinople. The *yeshiva* (institute for Jewish study) he established in Safed drew a number of illustrious *haverim* (communitarian associates), such as the teacher-scholar Moses Cordovero. Rabbi Cordovero innovated a daily practice based on the 13 divine attributes or qualities of God that were recited in the Jewish daily prayers. He urged his students to make humility "the key tool." Using the imagery of the Tree of Life, the students focused on aspects of Godliness throughout the day. For example, at midnight, the practitioner arose, washed, and contemplated the spiritual substance of the Torah in the form of the "bride of G-d," the Shekhinah. Cordovero's conviction that in this world the mystic's heart is God's true dwelling place, was fully congruent with the concepts already present in Safed's Kabbalist tradition.

In 1570, Rabbi Isaac Luria (1534–1572), known as the Ari (lion), arrived in Safed. Earlier, as a young man in Cairo, Luria had come into contact with the Zohar, after which he became an ascetic and diligently studied, prayed, and meditated upon the Book of Splendor for two years. One day while in meditation, the prophet Elijah appeared to him in a vision and gave him a "spiritual initiation." Every night after that for the next eight years, the Ari was said to find himself in the company of angelic hosts and great departed sages. Then, directed inwardly by his celestial master Elijah, he moved his family to Safed.[30]

Soon recognized as the leader among the Safed mystics, he became a great catalyst for change in the practice of Jewish mysticism. Personally embodying the traits of simplicity, humility, and charity, the Ari became renowned for his generosity and personal kindness. As a spiritual master, he imparted wisdom to his disciples, providing each with mystical knowledge pertinent to their individual soul. He is reputed to have the ability to tell each student the "ancestry" of their soul and the transmigration through which it had gone. (Though the idea of transmigration was rarely discussed publicly, it was nonetheless very much a part of Jewish mystical tradition.) Significantly, the Ari gave detailed meditation instructions whereby students could progress at their own pace in their personal spiritual journey.

In explicating on the relationship of God, creation, and human beings, he further refined the earlier doctrine known as *Tsimtsum*. Rabbi Luria taught that, in initiating the process of Creation, God first had to become an "exile into Himself." Thus, the first "act" was not an act of revelation but one of limitation. Only then, after "stepping back" to create what was known as *tsimtsum,* a void from out of which to emanate, did God send out a ray of light and begin His unfolding as God the Creator. The first being that emanated from the light was *Adam Kadmon,* archetypal Man.

The Ari, like so many others over the ages, struggled with the question of why God permits human suffering. How could the Creator God, as portrayed in the creation story in *Bereshith* (the book of Genesis) permit these injustices to happen to the descendants of those with whom He had made a Covenant? Perhaps, it has been opined, the very creation itself had some inherent flaw that needed to be repaired.

In the allegorical process of the Creation, "good" elements of the emerging cosmic order became mixed with "negative" ones. It is a tale of a shattering—a *shevirat ha-kelim*. The divine light entered into the 10 vessels that were waiting to receive it and some were shattered, the shards falling into the abyss from which the world arose, carrying sparks of the light that were trapped within.

From the moment of its first being then, the benignly conceived world was not entirely as it ought to have been. For example, the mythic expulsion from Eden, was seen by the Ari as symbolic of the light that was scattered by the disruption and displacement brought about by the *shevirah*. The restoration of the original wholeness and the mysteries of this reintegration—this divine *tikkun* (Hebrew for "binding up" and, by extension, healing of the wound)—became the chief theoretical and practical concern of the Ari's theosophical system. This linking of spiritual attunement to enlightened ethical conduct, individually and collectively, proved to be very significant in this process. Over time, a belief became rooted in Safed that collaborative spiritual/religious activity and positive social conduct could help restore order in the cosmos, and to repair a "fabric" that had tragically been torn.

Within the realm of humankind, the restorative process of *tikkun* is mercifully present to bind up the wounds of the world, and help humanity to be drawn toward the inner and outer source of Divine Light. It thereby becomes the responsibility for each person to be receptive to the process of tikkun, and its healing potential for oneself and all one's relationships.

In Lurianism, the historic notion of "exile" became a cosmic symbol. This exile could be redeemed, however, through *tikkun ha-olam*—healing the world—which in mystic terms meant gathering up the shards of the broken vessels and helping to restore the scattered light within them. This restoration would ideally also take place concurrently within individual men, women, and children in the human community. When all is restored to its rightful place, it was believed, the Messiah will come: "His arrival will not deliver our redemption to us, but rather signal that redemption has, through Man's co-creative spiritual efforts, been achieved."[31]

Accordingly, the task of the Kabbalist in private meditations now encompassed the whole world, beginning with purifying one's own thoughts, words, and actions. Once a humbled mind had become consciously attached to the divine source, it could assist in the overall process of the redemption of humanity. For this purpose of tikkun, Rabbi Luria developed elaborate mental/spiritual exercises, sometimes referred to as practical Kabbalah in the form of *kavannot* (contemplative symbols denoting specific visualizations), contemplating the letters, words, and phrases of the daily prayers. He taught his "lion cubs" (students) to pray continuously for the well-being, not only of themselves and their family, but

2000 BCE	1500 BCE
• First Hebrew patriarch, Abraham, and Matriarch Sarah depart Mesopotamia, for land of Canaan, c. 1800 - 1700	• Moses leads Israelite Exodus from Egypt, receives Decalogue and Torah at Mount Sinai, 1400

1-200 CE	500 CE
• Merkavah (Throne) and Hekhalot Mysticism - 1-200 • Hekhalot Rabbatai (The Greater Palaces); • Merkavah Rabbah (The Great Chariot); are published. • Rabbi Akiba, d. 132	• Completion of transition of the Oral Law, the Mishnah, into writing by Rabbi Judah ha Nasi in 3rd century CE • Amorai (rabbis) complete editing of Jerusalem and Babylonian Talmuds; 220 BCE-550 CE • Sefer Yetzirah (Book of Creation) - 200-500

1000 BCE	500 BCE
• David, King of Israel, composes Psalms, c.1010-970 • King Solomon, c. 967-928 • Prophetic Judaism Isaiah, Amos, Elijah, etc. 800-500 • Rabbinic mysticism	• Exekiel's Chariot vision c. 6th century • Torah fully constituted c. 435 • Rabbi Hillel - c. 80 BCE - 30 CE Canonization of Tanach 200 - 100 BCE

700-1000 CE	1000-1100 CE
• Sa'adia Gaon (882-942) • Influx of Jews into Spain and Portugal, 700-1000	• "Golden Age" in Spain (11th-13th centuries) • Solomon ben Isaac (Rashi) (1040-1105) • Judah Ha-Levi (1075–1141) • Bahya ben Joseph ibn Paquda

1100 -1200 CE	1300 CE
• Abraham ben David (– Rabad) (1125-98) • Moses Maimonides (–Rambam) (1135-1204) • Rabbi Abraham Abulafia, 1240-1296	• Early Kabbalists - 1175-1220 CE • "Sefer ha Bahir" (Book of Illumination) • "Sefer ha Zohar" (Book of Splendor) c. 1286-1300 CE • Moses Maimonides writes "Guide for the Perplexed".

1600 CE	1700 CE
• First Jewish settlers arrive in North and South America	• Baal Shem Tov (Master of the Good Name),1700-1760 CE, founder of Chasidus emphasizing meditation and joy • Schneur Zalman of Liadi, first Lubavich Chabad Rabbi, publishes his classic, "the Tanya." • R. Nachman of Bratzlav

1400 CE	1500 CE
• Many Jews settle in Netherlands, Turkey, and Eastern Europe, 1343–1500 • Rishonim provided spiritual guidance during turmoil.	• Lurianic Kabbalah (1534-1730) Mystic community of Safed under guidance of Rabbi Isaac Luria (The Ari). 1437-1508 • Chaim Vital; "Safer Etz Cheyyim", (Book of the Tree of Life) • Francesca Sarah and Rachel Aberlin, 16th century Safed

1800 CE	1900 - 2015 CE
• Revival of Hebrew as spoken language and literature • "Golden Age" of Yiddish literature and theater in Europe and USA • Emergence of Reform • and Conservative Judaism movements • Martin Buber, 1878-1965	• Rabbi Abraham Kook, 1865-1955 • Albert Einstein, 1875-1955 • Movements for Social Justice • R. Yisrael Meir Kagan, 1838-1933 • Gershom Scholem, "Major Trends in Jewish Mysticism", 1941 • Aryeh Kaplan 1934-1983, • Adin Steinsaltz, b.1937, • Chabad Lubavicher Rebbe • Menachem Schneerson, 1902-1994 • Rabbi Zalman Schachter-Shalomi • (1937–2014) • Abrahamic Reunion, 1990's-2010

also their neighbors, broader community, and, ultimately, all people throughout the entire world.

Five centuries later the current Chief Rabbi of Great Britain, Jonathan Sachs, has written cogently about the nature and significance of the concept and practice of tikkun olam:

> A single life, said the sages, is like a universe. Save a life and you save a world. Change a life and you begin to change the world... There is a name for this idea in Judaism: *tikkun olam,* mending or perfecting the world. Of all the ideas in Judaism's ethics of responsibility it is the least *halakhic,* the least rooted in law. Its origins, we will see, are mystical. *Tikkun olam* is something each of us does differently. It is an expression of the faith that it is no accident that we are here, in this time and place, with these gifts and capacities, and this opportunity to make a positive difference to the world. This belief is known as divine providence (in Hebrew, *hashgahah peratit*): the idea that God is operative in our lives *as individuals,* not only, as the Greek philosophers believed, concerned with universals. We are here because someone wanted us to be and because there is a task that only we can fulfill. No two people, places, times and circumstances are the same. Where *what I can do* meets *what needs to be done*—there is God's challenge and our task.[32]

Loving all of creation without exception, the Ari himself carefully avoided harming even insects and worms, insisting that these too would evolve through the course of transmigrating souls. It was said that Rabbi Luria, through his spiritual gnosis, had the secrets of the nature of reincarnation revealed to him. He "was a mystical master in the strict sense. To his formal disciples he imparted esoteric wisdom, to each of them mystical knowledge pertinent to their particular soul."[33] On meeting people he could see their entire past and present moral state. Legend has it that his spiritual competence became such that he could know where, and how high, on the cosmic *Etz Hayim* (Tree of Life) each soul was located. In this vein, he explicated verses from the Torah for each of his students at the moment when he felt the student was intuitively ready to receive the meaning behind the verse. Through these specific practices, he was able to reconnect his students to the Light within themselves, and to nurture the positive qualities of compassion, wisdom, and love within the sefirot of their own soul.

The Ari held that there were optimal ways to approach each aspect of one's life. Indeed there were as many "formulas" for contemplative purposes as there were life experiences. He is reported to have taught: "Everything depends on the intensity of your concentration and your attachment on high. Do not remove this from before your eyes." Although Luria was reluctant to record his teachings in writing, Chaim Vital (1543–1620), his leading student among an inner circle of disciples, kept careful notes that were published after both men died. Vital's most significant account of his master's teachings is the multivolume *Shemonah She'arim* (Eight Gates).

Among the many people the Ari influenced was the rabbi and author Elijah de Vidas, who, although not a formal disciple, had met and highly respected the Ari. His Reshit Hochmoh (Beginning of Wisdom) is considered by many to be a "crown jewel" of the Safed Kabbalist literature. Its wisdom teachings are divided into five "Gates." The Gate of Love begins with the recognition that "Our devotion to God, May He be blessed, must be performed with love. As Scripture says, 'And thou shall love the Lord the God with all thy heart, and with all thy soul, and with all thy might.' This passage is the gateway to our reverence for G-d." The practitioner is reminded that "genuine love" means serving God "without seeking a reward." This same attitude of selfless service is to be upheld as well in one's relationships with fellow human beings.

One very notable aspect of the Safed community was the relationship between men and women. In her book The *Receiving: Reclaiming Jewish Women's Wisdom,* Rabbi Tirzah Firestone notes that, unlike other contemporary religious communities, Jewish and non-Jewish alike, a considerable number of women in Safed played significant roles in the spiritual life in a community that was appreciative of feminine sensibilities. There "the lives of Safed's women bespeak a whole that is born of bringing together sides of life that were traditionally separate, even exiled from one another, such as masculine and feminine modes of spirituality, orthodox religious observance and nontraditional mystical practices."[34] Women who wished to study Torah supported one another and, over time, generally prevailed in their struggle to gain the respect of their male counterparts.

Francesca Sarah is one of the women of Safed whose lives were illuminated by wisdom and mystic insight. Little is known of her personal life, including the dates of her birth and death in the 16th century.[35] What is known is that as a young woman she went to the House of Study along with the men and became a scholar. Also recognized as a visionary, she became a teacher in her own right who sometimes spoke quite freely at the behest of her *maggid* (angelic guide). In doing so, she shared prophetic guidance, especially when it pertained to the well-being of the citizenry. She was tested by the sages and rabbis of her day as to the substance of her words, and was not found wanting. Her ability to attune herself to what was considered to be Divine Will was exceptional. She could align herself with the higher dimensions of her soul, the *chaya* and the *yechidah,* while remaining grounded in the common-sense *(sechel)* skills that enable one to live a balanced life in the everyday material world. Rachel Aberlin, another female luminary in Safed, came to northern Israel with her husband in 1564, and later in her life, after the death of her husband, became the spiritual companion of Chaim Vital (1543–1620), the leading student and documenter of the Ari. She was known to see the Divine presence around her, "without needing to refer to a textual source" for explanation of spiritual phenomena, and deeply understood the esoteric nature of numinous light in dreams and visions. According to Rabbi Firestone, "Rachel knew that all the holy books in the world could not equal the true and manifest experience of the Divine Light itself. Sacred texts were guides and pointers to the light of spirit, not the light itself."[36]

Ba'al Shem Tov (1698–1760) and the Rise of the Hasidic Movement

In the mid-1700s, a new and popular mystical movement, Hasidism, emerged in Eastern Europe. At its peak, this movement had millions of followers. The word *Hasid* in Hebrew means "righteous," and in the Bible, referred to those leading especially holy lives. Its founder, Israel ben Eliezer (c. 1700–1760), became known as the Ba'al Shem Tov, which literally meant the "Master of the Good Name," and was also sometimes referred to by the acronym Besht.

Israel ben Eliezer was born in 1698 in a village on the Polish-Russian border. Both his parents died when he was a young boy. Adopted by the village synagogue, he received an education common to Jewish communities at the time. The youth "had a brilliant mind as well as a deep spiritual nature but at an early age he learned to keep his gifts a secret" (Kaplan, 1982, p. 269). He also developed a strong love of nature. At the age of 18, he received a leadership role in the Society of Nistarim, a secret society of Kabbalists that had been strongly involved in rebuilding impoverished Jewish communities in Eastern Europe. After his marriage, Israel and his bride settled in a small village in the Carpathian Mountains where, for several years, he spent his days and nights studying, praying, and meditating. He emerged spiritually as a gifted teacher who began to make known some of the insights that had come to him in his prayer and meditation.

The Ba'al Shem Tov (Besht) years later penned a remarkable letter to his brother-in-law, Rabbi Gershon of Kitov, a famed Polish scholar who was then living in Palestine. The epistle was lost in transit but resurfaced and was published 20 years after the Besht's death. As the Besht was primarily a teacher in the oral tradition, he left very few formal writings, and so this letter has considerable historic value in providing insights into his mystic experiences. After greeting his relative, the Besht confided that on the day of Jewish New Year, 5079 (September 1746),

> I engaged in an ascent of the soul, as you know I do, and I saw won-
> drous things in that vision that I never had before seen since the day I
> had attained to maturity.... I went higher until I entered the palace of
> the Messiah wherein the Messiah studies the Torah together with all the
> *tannaim* and the saints and also with the Seven Shepherds (Adam, Seth,
> Methusalah, Abraham, Jacob, Moses and David).... I asked the Messiah:
> When will the Master [the Messiah] come?" and he replied, "you will
> know of it in this way; it will be when [your wellsprings spread forth]
> and your teaching becomes famous and revealed to the world, and when
> that which I have taught you and you have comprehended will spread
> abroad so that others too, will be capable of performing unification and
> having soul ascents as you do. Then will all the *kelippot* [forces of evil] be
> consumed and it will be a time of grace and salvation.[37]

The scholar Aryeh Kaplan noted that "one of the Baal Shem Tov's most
important accomplishments was to reveal a universal form of meditation which
could be used by even the simplest person." The Way of Prayer focused around
the regular prayer service, which is to be recited three times daily by every Jew. In
his teachings, the Besht gives explicit reference to the importance of focused concentration of both mind and heart in the meditative recitation of prayer. Harking
back to the words of Rabbi Jacob ben Asher (1270–1343) in his *Tur,* a major code
of Jewish Law: Thoughts and intentions in prayer must be pure, focused concentration. Saints and men of deed would meditate *(hitboded)* and concentrate
in their prayers until they reached a level where they divested themselves from
the physical. The transcendental spirit would be strengthened in them until they
would reach a level close to that of prophecy.[38]

The method of the Ba'al Shem Tov could be used by anyone, from the greatest Kabbalist to an unschooled villager. An inspired prayer itself becomes as a
mantra, when the mind is fully focused on the words. It was taught that "while
praying, one then rises mentally from one universe to the next, from chamber to
chamber, until [reaching] the highest level":

> Place all your thought into the power of your words until you see
> the light of the word. You can see how one word shines into another, and
> how many lights are brought out in their midst. This is the meaning of
> the verse, "Light is sown to the righteous, and joy to be upright in heart."
> (Psalms 97:11) The lights in the letters are God's chambers, into which
> He transmits his emanations.[39]

The renaissance in Jewish mysticism inaugurated by the Ba'al Shem Tov, and
the Hasidic movement that he founded, utilized a number of contemplative practices. Not only did Hasidism bring meditation back into the forefront of Jewish life,
but it also infused the broader community with new energy and commitment. The

Besht did much to bring hope and joy back into the lives of many. He emphasized to his *talmidim* (students of Torah) how important experiencing *simcha* (joy) was for developing a Kabbalist outlook on life. For people to lovingly and selflessly serve Hashem (God) and one's fellow human beings, without thought of personal gain or recognition, was held to be a sacred privilege that would, of its own accord, bring happiness to one's heart and upliftment to the community.

After Ba'al Shem Tov's passing, Rabbi Dov Baer known as the Maggid of Mezritch, continued to impart his mentor's teachings. While known for his conceptual understanding, the most brilliant young scholars of the day were drawn to the Maggid (teacher of mystical Judaism), as they believed the Torah was vibrantly alive in him. Two of his most accomplished students were the great mystics Rabbi Nachman of Bratslav (1772–1810) and Rabbi Schneur Zalman of Liadi (1745–1812).

Rabbi Nachman felt that virtually everything you study, every time you learn Torah, what you learn, could and should be translated into a prayer. He often used as his focusing prayer, *Ribbono Shel Olam,* meaning "Lord of the Universe." If he were going to study the meaning of the Sabbath or if the time of the beginning of Sabbath were approaching, he invoked, "Oh, *Ribbono Shel Olam,* let me merit to have at least one hour in my life where I would experience what Sabbath truly means. Please make it real for me." Such heartfelt prayer would lead to deeper insight and beyond ecstasy, becoming a portal to vistas within.

In his distinguished opus, the *Tanya,* Reb Schneur Zalman (known to his followers as the Alte Rebbe) spelled out "the way of *Chabad*—the utilization of the human faculties of wisdom, understanding and knowledge as they reside in the inner core of the soul." The acronym "Chabad" combines the first syllables of the three Hebrew words meaning *chokhmah* (wisdom), *binah* (understanding), and *da'at* (higher knowledge).

The Alte Rebbe and his descendants made the Russian town of Lubavich their main center, hence their movement rapidly became known as Lubavich Hasidism. The qualities of the Chabad principles became the hallmark of Lubavich Hasidism, underpinning its method for a way of life combining service to God and community upliftment. Though numerous Hasidic groups emerged over the next century, the Lubavich rabbis remained the most widely known.

Beginning in the late 18th century, the Jewish Enlightenment movement, a secular counterpart to the more general Enlightenment movement within the broader European intellectual community, ironically contributed to an incipient decline of Jewish mysticism. Aryeh Kaplan notes, "Until the rise of the Jewish Enlightenment, mysticism and intellectualism had equal status within Judaism.

The ostensible goal of the Enlightenment, however, was to raise the intellectual level of Judaism, and positive as this may have been, it was also done at the expense of other Jewish values....[From an extreme secular perspective] anything that touched on mysticism was denigrated as superstition and occultism and was deemed unworthy of serious study."[40] The practice and public expression of Jewish mysticism declined thereafter, and renewed interest did not substantially re-emerge within the worldwide Jewish community until after World War II.

Chabad Teachings in the Twentieth Century

Today, Chabad is the largest and most significant movement within contemporary Hasidic Judaism. Remaining strictly observant in their own lifestyle and *halachic* practices, Chabad members strive not to be judgmental, but helpful wherever possible to those co-religionists who seek to be reconnected to more traditional aspect of Jewish learning and observance.

The highly respected seventh Lubavicher Rebbe, Menachem Mendel Schneerson (1902–1994) served as the spiritual guide of the worldwide Chabad Hasidic community for 53 years. As a student in pre-war Europe he studied mathematics, physics, and engineering. Settling in the Crown Heights section of Brooklyn, in 1941 he accepted the role of Chabad leadership and soon became affectionately known simply as the Rebbe.

With his legendary understanding of Torah along with his strong interest in scientific inquiry, he served as a bridge between the two cultures of religion and science for generations of modern young Jewish Yeshiva students. Rebbe Schneerson's seeking to reconcile religion and science follows a tradition that goes back at least to the Ba'al Shem Tov, who lived at the beginning of the "Age of Enlightenment," a period of European history marked by significant advances in the physical sciences and the triumph of a secular philosophical worldview. The Ba'al Shem Tov understood the nature of this development, and encouraged Jews to develop an understanding of the beneficial aspects of the new science and metaphysics of his day. He urged, however, that this secular knowledge become leavened with the study and practice of Torah.

In his book *On the Essence of Chasidus*, Rabbi Schneerson brought forward the basic teachings of the Chabad movement as they have evolved in the last decades of the 20th century. He pointed out that Torah is derived from the word *hora'ah* (teaching) because its purpose is to teach people a pathway "in which they should strive to purify and refine the world, which indeed is the very purpose of the soul's descent into the world." Contemporary generations are charged with a greater responsibility and their service must be of higher quality than that of previous generations and periods of exile—their calling is to transform the "redoubled darkness" to "redoubled light."[41] The best means for achieving these lofty goals is for persons to do their very best to live exemplary lives in accord with the guidance of the Torah and the wisdom teachings of sages and prophets over the ages. The rebbe described many practical applications and stories about "walking the talk" in his book *Toward a Meaningful Life: The Wisdom of the Sages.* In short, upright ideals put into daily practice would greatly accelerate the coming of the Messiah, the harbinger of a Messianic Age.

For the rebbe, to be able to see the extraordinary within the ordinary customary is itself a miracle. Once when asked about miracles happening he responded:

> Someone will say, "if only I saw, then I would believe, then I would change my life!" What are we waiting for, the parting of the sea? Miracles are happening around us every moment. Life itself is a miracle; consider the sheer wonder of human birth. In fact, we do often refer to birth as a miracle; why, then, do we so easily forget that every person on earth is the product of a miracle?...It's not that we don't believe in miracles, we simply stop taking the time to appreciate them. To see a miracle means to appreciate the uncommon within the common, the extraordinary within the ordinary.[42]

Like his predecessors, Rabbi Schneerson underscored the special role of the Ba'al Shem Tov in the prophesized Messianic Age to come. The Ba'al Shem Tov had regarded the world as in a state of spiritual unconsciousness, and through the teachings of Chassidus sought to arouse the world from this condition.[43] Chassidus, he held, created the possibility for all people to be able to comprehend Godhood, by explaining the esoteric parts of the Torah and "making them accessible to the intellect through examples and analogies corresponding to the faculties and characteristics of the soul."

Light is a "favorite metaphor" in Kabbalah and Chassidus, seen by adherents "to represent and describe the various manifestations and emanations radiating out from the ultimate source, the Ein Sof." In his book *Mystic Concepts in Chassidism,* scholar Jacob Schochet, who had worked closely with Rabbi Schneerson, quotes the rebbe's cogent observation:

> Of all physical phenomena, light is that which most closely approximates what is spiritual and freed from the limitations of matter. For example, it is not corporeal; it delights the soul; it enables one to see. It is also analogous to the nature of Divine emanations, insofar as light is never separated from its source, spreads itself instantaneously, irradiates all physical objects, does not mix and mingle with any other sub-

stance, never *per se* changes, is essential to life in general, and is received and absorbed relative to the capacity of the recipient, etc.[44]

According to Chabad thought, the presence of inner light animates the human soul in its pristine sense. Each soul receives the life-giving Aur Ein Sof, the pure manifestion of Light emanating from the Ultimate Source. Nothing can exist apart from this Light and nothing exists except for the Light.

It is the presence of "foreign substances" that manifest as layers or coverings that prevent the soul from experiencing its own natural brilliance. Ideally, the task of the individual, with the help of appropriate guidance, involves healing such blockages through the practice of self- introspection, purification, and right action. Moving toward "Loving one's neighbor as oneself" is a good place to begin.

The Sabbath Light Throughout the Ages

Jewish esoteric writings link the Sabbath Day to the Light of God, and acclaim that Sabbath's special covenant relationship between Creator and Creation. The fourth commandment received at Mount Sinai instructs: "Remember the Sabbath day to sanctify it. Six days shall you work and accomplish all your work, but the seventh day is a Sabbath to your G-d.... Therefore G-d blessed the Sabbath and sanctified it" (Exodus 20:8–11).

For centuries, Jewish families have observed the beginning of the Sabbath, on Friday evening at sunset, with the blessing over the candles, generally by the mother and daughters of the household. This lighting and reciting the blessing marks the passage from "ordinary time" to "sacred time," symbolically representing the incoming, ever-present light and love by the Divine Presence. In Judaism, candles can represent the eternal human soul, which is why, once kindled and lit, the Sabbath candles are not blown out.

The *Nar Tamid* (eternal light), a perpetually lit lamp replenished by the purest oils, dates back to biblical times, when it was suspended above the Holy Ark. Today representations of the Nar Tamid are found perpetually lit in thousands of Jewish synagogues and temples around the world. This lamp serves as a continuing remembrance of the Light and Love emanating from the Creator, that cannot be extinguished, and serves as a symbol of the covenant between the Creator and humankind.

Safed Kabbalists of the 16th century, like rabbis and sages of old, likened the Sabbath to a Queen and a bride. The Sabbath Bride was joyfully welcomed each week with joy and the singing of psalms at sundown. The most popular of the hymns on this theme that has come down to the present day is *Lechah*

Dodi (Come my beloved to welcome the Sabbath Bride). This Queen of the Days, affectionately greeted in song, is the presence of Shekhinah, whom Kabbalists and many other mystics came to regard as the revealed feminine aspect of God.[45]

Rabbi Abraham Heschel (1907–1972), a 20th century prophetic voice and scholar/activist, called the Sabbath the "greatest cathedral of Judaism."[46] The Sabbath provides a sanctified time for healing and growth within the individual person and for renewing the spiritual integrity of the community, a day to experience tranquility and inner peace. The Hebrew word for Sabbath rest is *menuha*, a blessed time and space for repose. Within the stillness can be experienced joyfulness and harmony, which is perceived by the faithful as a foretaste of *ha'olam habah*, the "world to come."

One of the most distinguished words in the Torah is "holy" (*kadosh* in Hebrew), which represents the mystery and majesty of the Divine. This word is introduced for the first time in the book of Genesis at the end of the story of Creation. It is significant that it applies to time, "And G-d blessed the Sabbath day and made it holy." Six days of the week, we live under the dominion of material things in the limited world of space. On the Sabbath, humankind is enjoined to become attuned to holiness within this world, a taste of that which exists in the "higher realms." We are called upon to share that which is eternal, to turn from the results of creation to the deeper mystery underlying creation.

Metaphysically, Jewish tradition conceives the physical world as a world of space that is rolling through the infinite expanse of time. "Spiritual time" is beyond the division of past, present, and future. In the realm of spirit, there is no difference between a second or a century, an hour or an age. The Sabbath provides a periodic opportunity to be immersed in the holiness that is at the heart of time. It provides an opportunity to focus on at-one-ment with God and the soul's ultimate reunion with its Creator.

Hanukkah, the Festival of Ever-Present Light

Among the Jewish holidays, Hanukkah, also known as the Festival of Lights, is generally considered to be, spiritually speaking, a relatively minor holiday. The festival is observed by the kindling of the lights of a special candelabrum, the Hanukkah Menorah, over a period of eight days.

According to I Maccabees 4:36–59, its origins date back to the 2nd century BCE and the restoration of the holy Temple in Jerusalem. It commemorates the story of how one small remaining cruse of pure oil was found to light the sacred lamps in their temple, seemingly sufficient to light the lamps for only a day. Yet the lamps burned brightly for eight days.

News of this "miracle" rapidly spread throughout the land.[47] Today, over two millennia later, Hanukkah menorahs are lit for eight days in celebratory remembrance, and benedictions are recited, one for the lights and one for the miracle. The mystical significance of the menorah lighting derives from the remembrance of the engaged presence of YHWH within human history and the light of God emanating ultimately from the Aur Ein Sof, the unending light. To bring light into the darkness, observant Jews seek to find that symbolic cruse of oil, the divine source of the innermost core of the soul—the *yechidah*—that perpetually remains pure. Significantly, that cruse cannot be touched, for it is one with its Divine source. The lighting of the Hanukkah menorah signifies lighting up the spiritual darkness of the soul's exile, by accessing its infinite essence. That is why it is lit after the sun goes down, in the "domain of the many" where the darkness is most present.

Interestingly, a traditional belief maintains that the sacred lights kindled with pure intention on Hanukkah and the Sabbath can ascend from the material world up to the "heavenly realm" of the *Ein Sof*.

> The *Ohr Chozer* is a "returning" or "reflective" light. [It] comes into existence when the illuminating radiance from the *Ein Sof* is returned with Godly intention from Creation, such as a light from a Chanukah menorah or Shabbat candlelight that reaches the heavenly realm with the *Brachot* (blessings) that are spoken."[48]

This Jewish imagery of a returning or reflective light parallels one of the profound mysteries how when the soul's light meets the Creator's Light, we have Light upon Light.

Jewish Conceptions of the Soul

Most Jewish mystics hold that the soul is immortal and survives beyond physical death, but within this consensus there are a considerable number of views as to the nature of the soul's odyssey beyond mortality.[49]

Because of its intangible, incorporeal nature, the human soul typically eludes attempts to define it. Recognizing this, in his book *Does the Soul Survive?* Rabbi Elie Kaplan Spitz observes:

> Although there are a variety of understandings of soul in the Jewish tradition, the common starting point is that soul is no less than an extension of God.
>
> In the crafting of Adam, the Torah says, "God formed Adam out of the dust of the ground and breathed into his nostrils the *neshamah* of life; and Adam thus became a living creature."(Genesis 2:7). In Hebrew there

are three terms used for breath—*Nefesh, ruach and neshama*—words that in the Jewish mystical tradition describe facets of the soul. The image of breath conveys the idea that soul is intangible, animates life and links us to the source of creation.[50]

Elaborating on the link between the soul and its source, the rabbis of the Babylonian Talmud (mainly completed in the fifth century) concluded:

> As God fills the whole world, so also the soul fills the whole body. As God sees, but cannot be seen, so also the soul sees but cannot be seen. As God nourishes the whole world, so the soul nourishes the whole body. As God is pure, so also the soul is pure. As God dwells in the innermost part of the Universe, so also the soul dwells in the innermost part of the body.[51]

Characterizing soul as an extension of God helps us understand why the soul is so hard to define, for God is neither object nor person. To experience God and soul entails detachment from our customary self-absorption. The more fully we encounter soul, the more our attachment to the "I" or the limited self recedes.

In the story of Creation, when God said, "Let us make Adam in our image and our likeness" (Genesis 1:26), we can see the divine Poet at work. This first created human, Adam, is endowed with a divine spark, made in the image of the Imaginer.[52] The flame emanating from the spark is an image that the Zohar uses to express the multifaceted nature of soul. Conceived as divine spark, soul possesses qualities of Light, described as a pure dynamic tool of awareness that enables human enlightenment.

Rabbi Isaac Luria of Safed spoke of two additional elements of soul—chayah and yechidah. These two higher spheres depicted within the Sefirot might be called "spirit," as distinguished from soul, because of their intrinsic link to the Divine. Making this verbal distinction between soul and spirit could lead to some confusion, but the key point is that, as the soul rises, it concurrently sheds any dross it may have attracted during its sojourn in the lower spheres.

Among Hasidim such as the Maggid of Mezritch (Rabbi Dov Baer), the development of the soul moves in stages, during a lifelong process. How we conduct our lives, and the quality of our awareness, contribute to the dynamics of this development. The soul, as it identifies with its spiritual dimension, begins to reflect its purity in all aspects of daily life, as expressed by rightful thought, words, and actions. When such thoughts, words, and deeds align with an inner consciousness that reflects a Godly integrity, then we are acting in a way that can be called soulful or authentic.

Soul also has been described as a flame comprised of multiple bands of color. The inner flame (blue) enables the other bands of color to flourish. Life challenges us to cultivate our inner flame so that it burns brightly. Rabbi Spitz's experience leaves him more keenly aware that a unique part of each person, a divine spark, enlivens all aspects of our lives, and unites humanity with the source of Oneness:

> Our past has meaning and our future relevance only if we live with awareness and compassion in the present moment. When we are fully focused, that moment is a sacred window through which we may catch a glimpse of our soul's source, the Divine.[53]

We began this chapter on Jewish mysticism with a little story about the young American scholar who had traveled over to Europe to meet with the revered Rabbi Israel Kagan, known as the Hafetz Hayim (Lover of Life). When questioned by his guest about the sparseness of furniture in his host's tiny apartment, the Rabbi's gentle response was that he, like his visitor from abroad, was also "just passing through."

This story brings to mind Rabbi Rami Shapiro's *Open Secrets: The Letters of Reb Yerachmiel ben Yisrael*, a remarkably poignant book of letters by a fictional Hasidic master to his former Hebrew school student who had left their village in Eastern Europe to begin a challenging new life in America. The rabbi responds over several decades to a wide variety of philosophical and practical questions with empathy and compassion, ranging from human relationships and what it means to be Jewish to whether all religions are true, finding a teacher, and more. Many years passed and finally the subject of the beloved rabbi's imminent death arose. The rabbi, now in his frail last days, warmly began, "I write now only to say goodbye and to thank you for your love. There is nothing a rabbi cherishes more than a student who trusts enough to question." He then continued:

> Listen my dear Aaron Heschel, death is real in this world. Do not cover it over...with denial of death's simple reality. When we look at the world from the perception of Yesh, we see birth, we see death. When we look at the world from the perspective of Ayn, we see no birth and no death. Both are true. Yesh and Ayn are poles of a Greater Unity: Only G-d is real, for only G-d is whole and complete....What we truly are, is G-d manifest in time and place. Know this and live well until you die.[54]

> You have been a blessing to me beyond anything words can convey. Remember, "love is stronger than death." (Song of Songs 8:6).... Shortly I will be no more. Let out love grow ever stronger.[55]

Present-Day Movement Toward Rekindling the Light

A number of individuals and groups who in recent decades have done, and continue to do, creative work involving Jewish contemplative practices, both in their personal lives and their vocational endeavors. They share in common a mindful and heartfelt desire to rekindle and nurture the inner light within contemporary Judaism.

Eclectic Scholars: Rabbis Adin Steinsaltz (b. 1937) and Aryeh Kaplan (1934–1983)

Modern Jewish learning has been enriched by such authentic voices as Rabbi Adin Steinsaltz, a highly respected Israeli scholar, teacher, social critic, and mystic who serves as a much-needed bridge between religious and secular communities locally and internationally.

Born to secular parents in 1937, he excelled in his studies of mathematics and sciences at Jerusalem University in addition to his rabbinical studies. He became committed to exploring the relevance of classical Judaism, seeking, for example, to make the Talmud more accessible within the context of present-day concerns. His monumental study, *Opening the Tanya,* provides a valued exposition of the moral and mystical teachings of the great Hasidic Master, Reb Schneur Zalman of Liadi (1745–1812). In addition to his scholarly work, he also strongly supports numerous humanitarian causes.

In *The Thirteen Petalled Rose: A Discourse on the Essence of Jewish Existence and Belief,* Steinsaltz posits a vast system of "worlds" that exist within different dimensions, including a world of physical action and one of spiritual action. "Various worlds interpenetrate and interact in such a way that they can be seen as counterparts of one another."[56] Four worlds emerge—emanation, creation, formation, and action—that are characterized as higher or lower based on the degree to which they are transparent to the "divine light," which is their very light and subsistence. Reb Steinsaltz, supported by his personal meditation practice, attests experientially that approaching the Divine presence is available to all of humankind.

Rabbi Aryeh Kaplan (1934–1983) was born in New York City into a Sephardic Jewish family with longtime rabbinical roots in Salonika, Greece. As a young man he developed parallel intellectual interests in science, specializing in physics, along with his Jewish studies. Shortly after receiving *smicha* (ordination), Rabbi Kaplan became known as an original thinker and scholar for his interpretive studies on the Torah, Talmudic teachings and ethics. His specialty became Jewish mysticism, especially in the areas of Kabbalah, Hasidism, and meditation, where he exhibited a seemingly innate capacity of being able to reconcile and integrate scientific and religious worldviews in positive ways.

A student and practitioner of meditation himself, he sought to reconstruct traditional Jewish contemplative and meditation practices, aware of a need to make them accessible to the contemporary world. He saw both deep prayer and focused practices involving meditation as building blocks to develop, through regular daily routines/practices, an "intimate relationship with the Divine." In studying meditation practices and methodologies from other great religious and spiritual traditions, he selectively drew upon some practices for teaching purposes while remaining faithful to his Orthodox Jewish roots. He explained that "the best known form of meditation today is mantra meditation, and since there is no adequate generic Western term for this type of meditation I shall use the Eastern term 'mantra'...."[57]

For sitting meditation, Reb Kaplan recommended being in a familiar, quiet space that helps create a sense of calm and well-being. Some key aspects of his meditation guidance include the following instructions:

- With eyes closed lightly and totally relaxed, repeat a meaningful mantra in a soft voice or silently with the "tongue of prayerful thought."
- Reciting the mantra very slowly will help limit extraneous thoughts. Focus attention on light or visual images you see within.
- As the meditator becomes more advanced in this practice, control over (or reception of) these images will improve considerably, and their vividness will intensify. "If this indeed happens, guard against ego-inflation, receiving such experiences with humility and gratitude."[58]

It is interesting to note here the similarity with other esoteric contemplative traditions. The essential elements of turning inward, mental stillness through recitation of God's Name, and absorption or concentration on the inner Light are a powerful reminder of the steps to inner ascension.

The Jewish Renewal Movement

Beginning in the late 20th century, the Jewish Renewal movement sought to reinvigorate contemporary Judaism by reintroducing Hasidic, Kabbalist, and meditative practices drawn from a variety of traditional sources. It self-described as "a worldwide trans-denominational movement grounded in Judaism's prophetic and mystical traditions." Following its emergence in the 1960s and 1970s, Jewish Renewal gradually spread to many parts of the United States, as well as Canada, Latin America, Europe, and Israel.

Rabbi Zalman Schachter-Shalomi (1937–2014)

The movement's most prominent leader has been Rabbi Zalman Schachter-Shalomi, a Hasidic-trained rabbi ordained in the Lubavich movement. His major writing includes *Wrapped in a Holy Flame: Teachings and Tales of the Hasidic*

Masters. His warmhearted manner as a teacher and consummate storyteller has connected many seekers to finding ways to explore Jewish mysticism.

Many leading teachers and scholars identify with the Renewal movement.[59] Its innovative activities are evident in the support of and participation in *haverim* (literally, "friends") movement, which encourages smaller groups of people meeting, praying, studying together within or independent of formal congregations. This also helps facilitate increased engagement in uplifting cultural and socially relevant activities.

Beginning in the 1960s, a number of Jewish spiritual seekers, especially young adults, began to turn eastward in their quest to learn about and practice meditation and other inner growth disciplines. Many benefited from these contemplative practices, which over time have became the primary spiritual identification for some. Yet others have recognized the deep esoteric side within their own Jewish root tradition, about which they had little or no knowledge. A considerable number of young Jewish spiritual seekers responded to such mentors as Reb Zalman and storyteller/balladeer Rabbi Shlomo Carlebach, who helped pioneer the revitalizing Baal Teshuvah (Return to Judaism) movement.

When Reb Zalman passed away at age ninety-two in early July 2014, his longtime friend and colleague Rabbi Arthur Waskow spoke for the Jewish Renewal movement and many others:

> Does the death and burial of a Great Teacher mean his light has gone out? We are taught, *"Or zarua latzaddik*—the light of a tzaddik is buried in the fertile soil like a seed."—It sprouts again and again; and in Zalman's case, has already and will often again give birth to new seeds of light.[60]

He continued: "No one else in the twentieth/twenty-first century brought such new life, new thought, new joy, new depth, new breadth into the Judaism he inherited—and transformed."

Rabbi Tirzah Firestone

Known for her significant work on Kabbalah, depth psychology, and the reintegration of the feminine wisdom tradition within Judaism, Rabbi Tirzah Firestone believes that the legacy drawn from Jewish mystical and Hasidic teachings can contribute to redressing the great imbalances facing the world's people in the twenty-first century. In the mid-1980s, she responded to an inner calling to explore her Jewish spiritual roots. Studying with Reb Zalman Schachter-Shalomi and others in the Jewish Renewal movement led to her rabbinical ordination. Her book *The Receiving: Reclaiming Jewish Women's Wisdom* focuses on seven exceptional women mystics and sages whose lives spanned the second through twentieth centuries. Following in the spirit of pioneering researchers and teachers such as Rabbi Leah Novick, Tirzah Firestone's work offers a woman's lens to further understand age-old esoteric teachings in a way that is psychologically and spiritually relevant today. "It is time for women and men [together] to avail ourselves of these teachings at long last," she writes. "We must study them, be healed by them, and reclaim them as our own."[61]

> The time has come for the Jewish tradition to receive the gifts that women's wisdom contributes in order to regain its wholeness and awaken Judaism's message to the world—a vision of oneness that is desperately needed in our fragmented times.[62]

One quality highly valued by many Jews is best known by the Yiddish expression *menschlishkeit*. To be a *mensch*, a decent person, includes being balanced in one's approach to life and being considerate of others' needs. In fact, the prerequisite of becoming an enlightened human being, literally to be "in-the-light," includes developing the qualities of humility, compassion, and attunement to one's truest self.

Quietly providing service to others, genuine acts of loving-kindness, and selfless acts of mercy and forgiveness are hallmarks of true enlightenment within Judaism. These acts of selflessness are beneficial not only for the persons directly involved, but additionally for the well-being of all creation.

Jewish lore, especially in Kabbalistic and Chasidic literature, is replete with the stories of righteous acts by saintly individuals known collectively as *lamed vav tzaddikim*. Kabbalah elaborates on a concept that first appears in the Babylonian Talmud around 600 C.E. During every given generation, it is said there are 36 (*lamed vav*) truly righteous individuals, (*Tsaddikim*) "hidden" in the world by simply appearing as regular hard-working people of no special status.... During grave and dangerous times, they emerge to rescue people from peril.... Upon completing their redemptive task they return to their hidden, humble lives...."[63] Inwardly, they remain gateful for the opportunity to have selflessly rendered assistance for the well-being of another.

Ever-Present Light

Creation stories—tales of the origin of the cosmos, the earth and of humanity—by necessity are mythological in nature. This in no way detracts from their significance and the great mysteries of life itself, of which they speak. It is human nature to ponder the puzzles of life's existence as did our primordial ancestors, and to question its meaning.

In the archetypal Jewish Creation story as told in the book of Genesis, God existed alone in majestic oneness, but eventually decided to create an "Other" with which to relate. Central within the creative process was the Divine Light. Without its effulgence, the whole of Creation and the perpetuity of the earth's life forms, including Humankind, the "Crown" of creation, could not exist.

The Jewish mystical tradition inextricably links living consciously as a humane being within the world with the Divine or Inner Light. This is evident in Judaism's creation stories, beginning with "Let there be Light," and the emanation of God's perfect Light (Aur Ein Sof), which permeates and sustains all that exists. Light is central in the formation of covenant, from the promise of the rainbow after the flood, to the revelation when Moses received the Torah at Mount Sinai. Light shines in scriptures, psalms, prayers, and prophetic teachings, and in building optimal human relationships based on principles such as "Love your neighbor as yourself," and the recognition that the "Light of G-d is present within each person."

Thus it has continued over many centuries until the present day. The effulgent Light remains ever present, to be potentially tapped into and experienced by all peoples. Widespread discovery of this hidden treasure is a *sine qua non* for basic human unity and peace within a sustainable world.

The words of the aforementioned Rabbi Rami M. Shapiro point to the importance of recognizing this unity as well as our own uniqueness in the everyday moments of life. He contrasts two Kabbalistic concepts: *ayin* (emptiness) and *yesh* (manifestation), to illustrate his point. "Doing everyday things with a clear and attentive mind awakens us to the fact that we are both apart from and a part of everything else. We discover that from the perspective of *yesh,* we are unique, irreducible, irreplaceable manifestations of God. We discover from the perspective of *ayin* that we are totally interconnected with and dependent upon all other manifestations of God. We are awake to our being and our emptiness simultaneously. And from this we awake to God, the Source and Substance of both."[64]

Within this context, it is appropriate here to recall the experiences of Rachel Aberlin, a leading luminary in 16th century Safed. Having reached an understanding of the nature of numinous light within her dreams and visions, "Rachel knew that all the holy books in the world could not equal the true and manifest experience of the Divine Light itself. Sacred texts were guides and pointers to the Light of spirit, not the light itself."[65]

Guidelines at the Heart of the Teachings

1. The Light that was created on the first day was a manifestation of God and mirrored God in its goodness. Let There be Light and the Light is Very Good.

2. This Holy Light of God can never be extinguished and every soul remains eternally connected with the Aur Ein Sof, the eternal Light. We are all beings of Light and life.

3. Man is created in the image of God, therefore the mystic humbly seeks to become polished to increasingly reflect the light of YHWH. Become Light to Attract the Light.

4. It is the responsibility of every soul to kindle and shine this light. Shine your light in the darkness, and your darkness shall be like noon.

5. To bring light into the darkness, the soul has the capacity to turn to its innermost core—the yechidah—through prayer and contemplative practices.

6. "All the holy books in the world cannot equal the true and manifest experience of the Divine Light itself. Sacred texts are guides and pointers to the light of spirit, not the light itself." Live in the Living Light of the Spirit.

7. The restoration of the soul's original wholeness is the divine tikkun, or healing of the wound of separation from the Source. To be able to do one's own small part in the ongoing process of "tikkun olam," healing of the world, is truly a blessing.

8. Redemption comes when, with a spirit of lovingkindness, we do our best to comfort the afflicted, bring compassion to the downtrodden, and work selflessly for the well-being of all. Wish for others what you would wish for yourself.

9. Meditation and prayer can open us to the source of calmness deep within, which help us respond constructively to whatever each passing day may bring.

A Contemplative Practice

Serve others selflessly for it is in service to others that we truly serve God.

"You shall love the Lord your G-d with all your heart, with all your soul, and with all your capacity...And you shall love your neighbor as yourself." Love of God is, in its essence, loving and serving God's creation:

"Have compassion for each humble life form, and truly hear the plaintive call of those in need." All great religious and spiritual traditions have emphasized that the litmus test of real love is the degree to which it is exemplified and practiced in daily living. As we engage in the service of God's creation we are urged to do so, with the purest motivation in one's heart, To do otherwise, we may outwardly impress others, but cannot fool the living presence of God within ourselves.

- Begin by practicing *conscious acts of kindness* whenever the opportunity arises.

- Slowly extend this by assisting others, even if some considerable expense may be involved.

- Extend this further by recognizing and acting upon others' needs, without any thought of public recognition or reward.

- Finally, commit to doing one's very best in every circumstance, to be of service lovingly and fully.

Drawing of Hildegard of Bingen entitled *The Universe*. Hildegard was educated at the Benedictine cloister of Disibodenberg and became prioress there in 1136. She had experienced visions since a child, but kept them to herself until, at the age of 43, she heard a command to make her visions known to others. She later described how disobeying this command made her ill, so she consulted her confessor, who in turn reported the problem to the archbishop of Mainz. Hildegard was then subjected to inspection by a committee of theologians, who confirmed the authenticity of her visions. A monk (Volmar) was assigned to help Hildegard record her visions in writing. The result was *Scivias,* a collection of twenty-six visions dealing with topics such as the church, redemption, and the relationship between God and man (public domain, from *Scivias.*).

CHAPTER TWO

The Transfigured Presence: Christianity and the Gospel of Light

Believe in the light while you have the light, so that you may become children of light.

John 12:6 (ESV)

The light of the body is the eye: if therefore thine eye be single, thy whole body shall be full of light.

—Matthew 6:22 (King James Version)

From humble origins in a Bethlehem manger, Christianity is now the largest and most widespread religion in world history. The dramatic story of the triumphs and vicissitudes of Jesus' life has touched countless millions, and many still feel his life journey is "the greatest story ever told."

Who indeed was Jesus of Nazareth, whose presence even after death so inspired a devoted community of early believers? The New Testament Gospels (the word "gospel" means "good news") begins with a wondrous tale of a new-born infant, greeted by shepherds and barnyard animals, while descending angels heralded and brightened the midnight darkness. Magi from the East soon arrived, having followed the light of a bright star that guided them from afar to the manger where the baby lay.

Jesus and the Good News of the Light

The Christian religion that emerged thereafter centered on the life, death, and "afterlife" of Jesus, who would have been known in Nazareth, where he grew up, by his Hebrew name, Jeshua ben Josef—Jesus son of Joseph. As comparative religions scholar Huston Smith aptly notes, the actual biographical details drawn from Christian scriptures of his all-too-short lifetime are indeed meager:

He was born in Palestine, probably around 4 B.C., and grew up in Nazareth. He was baptized by a prophet, John, who was electrifying the region with his proclamations of God's coming judgment. In his early thirties Jesus had a healing-teaching career that lasted between one and three years. Minimally stated, Jesus was a charismatic wonder-worker who stood in a tradition that stretched back to the beginnings of Hebrew history. The prophets and seers that comprised that tradition mediated between the everyday world, on the one hand, and the spirit world that enveloped it.[1]

Jesus, following in the Hebrew prophetic tradition, was an advocate for the dispossessed. He also taught the need to live a life of prayer and contemplation.

The Gospels, especially John, portray Christ as the archetypal Man of Light, the *axis mundi* (world axis) of an illuminated cosmos.

> In the beginning was the Word, and the Word was with God, and the Word was God. He was in the beginning with God. All things came into being through him, and without him not one thing came into being. What has come into being in him was life, and the life was the light of all people.
> The light shines in the darkness, and the darkness did not overcome it. There was a man sent from God, whose name was John. He came as a witness to testify to the light, so that all might believe through him. He himself was not the light, but he came to testify to the light (John 1:1–9).

The light shines in the darkness, and the darkness did not overcome it. There was a man sent from God, whose name was John. He came as a witness to testify to the light, so that all might believe through him. He himself was not the light, but he came to testify to the light (John 1:1–9).

Thus, an explicit identity is drawn in this gospel between God and Light. God's Light is itself the Word that called forth creation. "This is the message we have heard from him and proclaim to you that God is light and in him there is no darkness at all" (1 John 1:5). God is named "the Father of lights" (James 1:17). Likewise, Christ says of himself, "As long as I am in the world, I am the light of the world" (John 9:5), and Christ is identified as the "true light, which enlightens everyone...coming into the world" (John 1:9).

This statement of the mystic identity between God the Father, Light, and Jesus is repeated in Corinthians 4:6:

> For it is the God who said, "Let light shine out of darkness," who has shone in our hearts to give the light of the knowledge of the glory of God in the face of Jesus Christ.

As the mystic Light made flesh, Jesus' life is unsurprisingly replete with visionary light. At Jesus' initiation into the life of the spirit by John the Baptizer, "the heavens were opened to him and he saw the Spirit of God descending like a dove and alighting on him" (Matthew 3:16). In the mystic sense, with his immersion in flowing water, Jesus' spiritual vision was intensified, enabling him to experience the ineffable gifts of the spirit. Seeking more clarity and inner direction, Jesus then entered the desert for forty days of prayer and fasting. Within the pristine quietude of the wilderness, his life's mission defined itself, and he subsequently began his public ministry.

The Gospel of Matthew quotes the prophet Isaiah (9:1–2), stating that despair will fall away. Christ writes Matthew, fulfilling his Messianic role as a light-bringer:

> The people who sat in darkness have seen a great light. and for those who sat in the region and shadow of death light has dawned. (Matthew 4:16, repeating the same passage in Isaiah 9:2)

Later in his essentially three-year ministry, Jesus is said to have taken aside the disciples Peter, James, and John and led them to the summit of Mount Tabor. There he "transfigured before them, his face shone like the sun, and his clothes became dazzling white" (Matthew 17:1–2). Jesus' appearance underscores his spiritual transcendence, away from worldly identity and into a more universal Christ consciousness. According to some mystic traditions, much spiritual illumination and advanced guidance is given through this light form.[2]

The Christian scriptures stress repeatedly that all sincere seekers are meant to partake of this divine Light. Irrespective of identity and past transgressions, all are meant to stand illuminated. We see this when Christ addresses common folk as "the light of the world" and Paul exclaims to them, "For once you were darkness, but now in the Lord you are light. Live as children of light" (Ephesians 5:8). The faithful are called, for "the night is far gone, the day is near. Let us then lay aside the works of darkness and put on the armor of light" (Romans 13:12).

This participatory mystical calling for Christians to move into the light appears throughout the New Testament, including exhortations such as "Sleeper, awake! Rise from the dead, and Christ will shine on you" (Ephesians 5:14) and "be blameless and harmless, children of God without blemish in the midst of a crooked and perverse generation, in which you shine like stars" (Philip 2:15).

Saul [Paul], on the Way to Damascus

One of the first "ordinary" persons to lay aside the darkness and take up the light of Christ was Saul of Tarsus. While some were lenient and friendly toward the first Christians who gathered together in Jerusalem after Jesus' death, Saul expressed hostility toward those connected to Jesus.

Then, while traveling north from Jerusalem toward Damascus, Saul had a startling revelation that would change his life forever. As written later in the Acts of the Apostles, he testifies to having experienced a penetrating vision of divine Light that transformed his deepest core:

> Now as he was going along and approaching Damascus, suddenly a light from heaven flashed around him. He fell to the ground and heard a voice saying to him, "Saul, Saul, why do you persecute me?" He asked, "Who are you, Lord?" The reply came, "I am Jesus, whom you are persecuting. But get up and enter the city, and you will be told what you are to do."
>
> The men who were traveling with him stood speechless because they heard the voice but saw no one. Saul got up from the ground, and though his eyes were open, he could see nothing; so they led him by the hand and brought him into Damascus. For three days he was without sight, and neither ate nor drank (Acts 9:3–9).[3]

The "blinded" Saul was then led to a follower of Jesus named Ananias, who prayed over Saul and implored:

> "Brother Saul, the Lord Jesus, who appeared to you on your way here, has sent me so that you may regain your sight and be filled with the Holy Spirit." And immediately something like scales fell from his eyes, and his sight was restored (Acts 9, 17–18).

Made fresh by his radiant epiphany and faith healing, Saul (whose name in Greek is Paul) in subsequent years proceeded to travel through Asia Minor, and on to Greece and Rome, shaping Christianity as a distinct faith open to all people.

Both Faith and Spiritual Works

Paul emphasized the importance of faith as a corner stone to the edifice of salvation. His theology holds that humans cannot by their own strivings alone achieve redemption. It is only through God's grace and Christ's sacrifice that salvation is possible. As Paul himself once put it:

> For by grace you have been saved through faith, and this is not your own doing; it is the gift of God—not the result of works, so that no one may boast (Ephesians 2:8–9).

This faith-centered strand in Pauline theology developed, by way of Augustine, into Martin Luther's passionate call for *Sola Fide* (Latin for "faith alone"). But Paul's faith was not a faith based upon blind or passive belief but filled with sincere striving as well. The apostle James affirmed that "faith by itself, if it has no works, is dead" (James 2:17). The Greek word Paul used for faith is *pistis,* which often relates more closely to persuasion or assurance and not faith devoid of works or blind faith. Pistis, then, may be understood as a persuasive conversion experience that descends upon a person of its own accord, just as the Light blinded an unprepared and unseeking Saul.

While visionary experiences may descend upon anyone, regardless of how holy or sanctified they may be, Christian mystical tradition has embraced disciplined contemplative practice as key to spiritual illumination. The mystical dimension of Christianity has understood the value of spiritual practices like meditation and contemplation—since its inception. The necessity of rigorous inner work through prayer, solitude and self-examination is a powerful theme in the theology of the New Testament, including the teaching of Paul. On occasion Paul was known to even invoke metaphors of athletic discipline to explain the importance of a regular practice in developing the spiritual life, such as.

> Train yourself to be godly. For physical training is of some value, but godliness has value for all things, holding promise for both the present life and the life to come (1 Timothy 4:7–8).

Together the two cornerstones, faith in God's unconditional love and the spiritual training endorsed by Paul and James, weave the fabric of an exquisite tapestry of a Christian mysticism of Light. Through the mysterious union of committed spiritual work and revelatory grace one is born into the Light. The Christian mystics we survey in this chapter are often eloquent in their writings on these themes of grace, surrender, and gift—that when the Light does descend, it is a gift of unimaginable worth, and, through Christ, all are invited to receive that gift, in contemplative silence.

The Eye of Light in Christian Scripture

Throughout the Christian scriptures, believers are called to see with and through the Light, and are repeatedly entreated to renounce any false sense of separateness or unworthiness. Instead, they are called to reach toward the illumined stature of its most revered adepts, "giving thanks unto the Father, who has enabled you to share in the inheritance of the saints in light" (Colossians 1:12). The luminous splendor of mystical attainment is not only an abstract possibility, but is also expressed to be our shared human birthright and responsibility. The Epistle to the Ephesians equates such illumination with the highest purpose of life, "so that, with the eyes of your heart enlightened, you may know what is the hope to which he has called you, what are the riches of his glorious inheritance among the saints" (Ephesians 1:18).

Jesus' teachings on "the light of the body" (Matthew 6:22–23, Luke 11:34) have, like so many other scriptural passages, been translated and interpreted quite widely. Notice how various translations of the Bible render this passage in markedly different ways.

King James Version: "The light of the body is the eye: if therefore thine eye be single, thy whole body shall be full of light. But if thine eye be evil, thy whole body shall be full of darkness. If therefore the light that is in thee be darkness, how great is that darkness!"

Mark, New Revised Standard Version: "The eye is the lamp of the body. So, if your eye is healthy, your whole body will be full of light; but if your eye is unhealthy, your whole body will be full of darkness. If then the light in you is darkness, how great is the darkness!"

New International Version: "The eye is the lamp of the body. If your eyes are good, your whole body will be full of light. But if your eyes are bad, your whole body will be full of darkness. If then the light within you is darkness, how great is that darkness!"

Contemplative perspective holds that Jesus was clearly referencing interior mystical experience, that he may well have been referring to an inner spiritual eye which when opened revealed interior worlds of light. The Greek word variously rendered as single, good, and healthy is *Haplous,* which means "unfolded" or "single," thus saying that the eyes that work together (i.e., unitively, nondually) are those that fill the body with mystical light.

Doubting Thomas and Gnosis of Light

In addition to the four New Testament Gospels of Matthew, Mark, Luke, and John, early Christian writings include various additional accounts of the life of Christ, including the Gospels of Mary Magdalene, Philip, Judas, and Thomas. The Gospel of Thomas, arguably the most important of the alternative gospels, was lost to modernity until an ancient manuscript copy was discovered in a cave outside Nag Hammadi, Egypt, in 1945. Whereas the New Testament Gospels focus on a narrative account of Jesus' birth, life, and death, the Gospel of Thomas opens with a bold assertion that it contains "the hidden words that the living Jesus spoke." The text is comprised of 114 pithy sayings from Jesus to his disciples, and some believe the gospel documents a mystical oral tradition in early Christianity.

The gospel is attributed to the apostle Thomas, whose most famous biblical appearance is in the Gospel of John, which criticizes him for his doubt—his demand to experience the resurrected Christ directly.

But Thomas, one of the twelve, called Didymus, was not with them when Jesus came. The other disciples therefore said unto him, "We have seen the LORD." But he said unto them, "Except I shall see in his hands the print of the nails, and put my finger into the print of the nails, and thrust my hand into his side, I will not believe...."

Although the doors were shut, Jesus came and stood among them and said, "Peace be with you." Then he said to Thomas, "Put your finger here and see my hands. Reach out your hand and put it in my side. Do not doubt but believe." Thomas answered him, "My Lord and my God!" Jesus said to him, "Have you believed because you have seen me? Blessed are those who have not seen and yet have come to believe" John (20:26–29).

In distinction to this well-known parable, Thomas' Jesus cajoles his disciples to skillfully probe and penetrate their own latent divinity. Indeed the only mention of belief in Thomas is in verses 91–92 when the disciples say to Jesus, "Tell us who you are so that we may believe in you." Evoking a Zen-like rhetorical style, Jesus' words pointedly ignores their request for intellectual propositions that one can either accept or reject. Jesus answers them by invoking a deeper truth in his teachings, and instead calls them back to the present moment in which they can experience his wisdom and encounter him directly.

You examine the face of heaven and earth, but you have not come to know the one who is in your presence, and you do not know how to examine the present moment. Seek and you will find. In the past, however, I did not tell you the things about which you asked me then. Now I am willing to tell them, but you are not seeking them (Thomas 12).

Jesus' teaching is simple and direct: He calls his disciples to see how abstract or propositional knowledge (i.e., language "about" God) can be a veil that obscures the reality of direct mystical presence. Throughout the Gospel of Thomas, Jesus identifies this deeper level of encounter with inner illumination, and urges the disciples to seek, with heartfelt devotion, the already-present Light. What Jesus calls the "Kingdom of God" is not a distant afterlife promise—it is the core of the living present, and the pith of our deeper selves.

Repeatedly in the Gospel of Thomas, Jesus evokes the Light:

When you are in the light, what will you do? (10)

Jesus says: "I have cast fire upon the world, and see, I am guarding it until it blazes" (10).

His disciples said: "Show us the place where you are, because it is necessary for us to seek it." He said to them: "Whoever has ears should hear! Light exists inside a person of light, and he shines on the whole world. If he does not shine, there is darkness" (24).

Jesus says: If they say to you: "Where do you come from?" (then) say to them: "We have come from the light, the place where the light has come into being by itself, has established [itself] and has appeared" (50).

"Therefore I say: If someone becomes like God, he will become full of light. But if he becomes one, separated from God, he will become full of darkness" (61).

"I am the light that is over all. I am the All. The All came forth out of me. And to me the All has come. Split a piece of wood—I am there. Lift the stone, and you will find me there" (77).

Jesus says: "The images are visible to humanity, but the light within them is hidden in the image. The light of the Father will reveal itself, but his image is hidden by his light" (83).

Biblical scholar Marcus Borg has written about the tension between doctrine and spirituality so prevalent throughout Christian history. Borg notes that, prior to the modern era, the doctrinal aspects of the faith were so ubiquitous that belief as *assensus* (from the Latin for "assent") was taken for granted; the concept of belief as fidelity, confident trust and deep spiritual connection has always been and remains a critical aspect of the faith of many Christians.

In the modern era, the word "belief" has come to have a strictly cognitive definition: to believe is to accept a propositional statement as true ("I believe in God" means "I accept the idea that God exists" rather than "I love God with all my heart"). But historically, belief meant far more than mere intellectual certitude. The word for belief in Latin, *credo,* implies the giving or trusting of one's heart to the object of belief; its Greek equivalent, *pistis,* traces to a sense of inner conviction and trust that is as much affective as it is cognitive. When Jesus says "believe in me" (John 14:1), to fully grasp the intent of his teaching, we might render his words like this: "When you give your heart wholly to me, you will be blessed." Not only does this provide a fuller understanding of Jesus' teachings, but it also points to the intrinsically mystical nature of his words.

This richer, more heart-centered understanding of belief within Christianity finds a balance between faith (opening one's heart to God in love) and experience (the graced, direct encounter with the living Light "hidden in the images" of the world).

The Gnostic Gospel of Philip, another apocryphal gospel unknown until its discovery at Nag Hammadi, captures this sentiment poetically:

A harvest is gathered into the barn only as a result of the natural action of water, earth, wind, and light. God's farming likewise has four elements—faith, hope, love, and knowledge *(gnosis)*. Faith is our earth, in which we take root; hope is the water through which we are nourished; love is the air through which we grow; gnosis is the Light through which we become fully grown.[4]

Gnosis, a Greek word for knowledge, is often misunderstood. It represents knowledge arising from direct experience, unlike *epistamai* (from which we get the English word "epistemology"), which refers to knowledge as cognitive understanding. The knowledge in "God's farming" that the previous passage refers to is the experiential knowledge of directly encountering the Light.

The Desert Hermits and the Spiritual Eyes of Early Christian Mystics (200–550)

After the New Testament period, a wide proliferation and great diversity of Christian teachings emerged. In the early fourth century, increasing numbers of Christians retreated from civilization to become hermits in the caves in the deserts of Egypt, where they sought ascetic lives of inner discipline. These figures became known as the Desert Fathers and Mothers.

Their outposts were positioned remotely, while remaining near enough to urban areas to have access to civilization when needed. Individuals continued to be drawn toward desert Christianity, with its disciplines of prayer, fasting, and solitude. Eventually, Desert Fathers such as Saint Paul the First Hermit (c. 230–341), Saint Anthony the Great (251–356), and Saint Pachomius (292–348) began to introduce communal aspects into the lives of the hermits, including common prayer and meals.

Over time, these early experiments in communal, intentional spiritual living blossomed into the first Christian monasteries. Compendiums of the wisdom and teachings of the early Desert Fathers were recorded. These early ascetical writings focus more on practical and ethical parables and instruction than on divulging the content of their inner experience to others. This spiritual climate of the desert proved a fertile ground for the Christian seeker of the ancient world, including three of the most highly revered fathers of the Christian tradition: Saint Augustine of Hippo (354–430); St. John Climacus (579–649); and the "Lamp of the Desert," Pseudo-Macarius of Egypt (300–391).

Gifted with a brilliant philosophical mind, Augustine of Hippo was a man of worldly tastes who converted as a youth to Manichaeism, and then later in life came to Christianity. Many scholars regard his *Confessions* as the world's first autobiography, and a model for much later Christian writing. It is also a masterpiece of Christian mystical literature.

St. John Climacus lived in St. Catherine's monastery at the base of Mount Sinai, the same mountain where Moses was purported to have received the Law. His *Ladder of Divine Ascent,* which compared the practice of a holy life to a graduated climb up the rungs of creation toward beatific union, remains one of the most revered books in the Orthodox Church to this day.

These early Christian writers experienced an influx of Divine Light, and all emphasized that contact with this Light was mediated through a mode of knowing (gnosis) that is wholly distinct from that mode of knowing (epistamai) by which we look upon the physical world.

Augustine's *Confessions* recounts his initiation into inner illumination, during which the Light communicates directly to Augustine. The Light proclaims that it is "the food of strong men; grow and you will feed on me; nor will you change me like ordinary food into your flesh, but you will be changed into me." Then Augustine reports:

> I entered into my inmost part...and saw, with my soul's eye (such as it was), an unchangeable light. It was shining above the eye of my soul and above my mind, not that ordinary light visible to all flesh nor something of the same kind, only greater as though it might be our ordinary light shining more brightly and with its greatness filling all things. Your light was not that kind but another kind, utterly different from all these...it was higher than my soul because it made me, and I was below because I was made by it. Whoever knows truth knows that Light, and whoever knows it, knows eternity.[5]

Similarly, in their 1982 translation of John of Climacus' *Ladder*, scholars Colm Luibhéid and Norman Russell provide an explicit commentary on John's place among the "'light mystics' of the Christian East," along with a catalogue of the references to Inner Light found in Climacus.[6]

With chastity, says John Climacus, the lust in our souls "receives that non-material *(aÿlon)* light which shines beyond all fire." Purity of heart leads to "enlightenment" or "illumination." This "is something indescribable, an activity [or energy *(energeia)*] that is unknowingly perceived and invisibly seen...The truly obedient monk often becomes suddenly radiant and exultant during his prayers."[7]

John writes of the purifying agency of the light that releases the soul from the stranglehold of old habits and destructive behavior:

> You will know that you have this holy gift within you...when you experience an abundance of unspeakable light...For the perfect there is increase and, indeed, a wealth of divine light...A soul, freed of its old habits and also forgiven, has surely seen the divine light.[8]

Each of these mystics recognize a distinction between spiritual and material knowing—that the eyes with which we look upon the incorporeal Light of God are distinct from those through which we gaze upon the physical. This suggests that we must learn (or remember, in the Platonic sense of recollecting archetypal knowledge that we have forgotten) how to see by means of our spiritual faculties. The following passage from Pseudo-Macarius illustrates the mystical nature of the spiritual eyes:

> For the soul that is thought worthy to partake of the spirit of his light, and is irradiated by the beauty of his ineffable glory, (he having by that spirit prepared her for his own seat and habitation) becomes all light, all face, and all eye: neither is there any one part in her but what is full of these *spiritual eyes of light;* that is, there is no part in her darkened: but she is all entirely wrought into light and spirit, and is all over full of eyes, having no hinder part, or any thing behind; but appears to be altogether face, by reason of the inexpressible beauty of the glory of the light of CHRIST, that rides and sits upon her.[9]

Thinkers from the medieval era (Saint Bonaventure) to the postmodern age (Ken Wilber)[10] have explored how these different ways of knowing allow us to view each domain and understand the value of each respective mode appropriately. Scientists see truth with the eyes of the body, while mathematicians and philosophers see with the eye of the mind, and mystics, imbued with divine grace, see with the subtle spiritual eyes of light. For the mystic, the eyes of the spirit embody a higher order of perception that is distinct, all-inclusive, and not subject to the limitations of time, space, and causality.

This division of labor with respect to truth and evidence cuts both ways, of course, with scientists needing to remain nonjudgmentally open on the reality and significance of what by definition they cannot see with their material tools: for example, the incorporeal Light of God. Likewise, mystics whose inner eyes are truly open do not refute the truths uncovered by modern science, but often corroborate them through their own mystical experiences.

Indeed, such a defense of science and common sense rationalism informs the theology of both Augustine and Bonaventure (1221–1274), each a champion of the validity and utility of empirical truth in a prescientific era. In the 20th century, Christian mystics like Raimon Panikkar or Pierre Teilhard de Chardin have sought to heal the at-times hostile relationship between science and religion. Some, like the Cypriot mystic and healer Daskalos, see themselves as researchers seeking after truth and treat their own inner life as a type of laboratory. Daskolos maintains that the method of leaving the body and traveling into the beyond is a practical science that can be performed and replicated with reliable results.[11]

The Mystical Theology of Pseudo-Dionysius

An enigmatic Syrian theologian, Pseudo-Dionysius the Areopagite (flourished c. 500), lived at the time of transition between Christian antiquity and the Medieval era. His *Corpus Areopagiticum* was falsely attributed to the obscure biblical figure Dionysius the Areopagite, who is mentioned only once, in Acts 17:34. Accordingly, no authentic biographical details of this shadowy figure are known. What we do know was that his writings, which comprised a novel, syncretic blend of neoplatonism and Christian theology, became profoundly influential in the development of medieval Christian mysticism, and Western thought in general.

Pseudo-Dionysius was a grand thinker, who, in his theorizing about the heavens and earth, coined the term "hierarchy," from the Greek *hieros* (sacred) and *archia* (rule). He saw a system of governance in the heavenly spheres, with Godhead at the apex and a succession of archangels and angels beneath. The ecclesiastical church hierarchy, he argued, formed an imperfect mirror of the celestial hierarchy above.

For Pseudo-Dionysius, a link with the celestial hierarchy, and indeed with God Himself, is mystically possible. When our "understanding [is] carried away, blessedly happy, we shall be struck by [God's] blazing light. Marvelously, our minds will be like those in the heavens above."[12] This passage contains several key themes in his writings: God, though ultimately beyond all distinctions, is approached through divine Light; however, we must shed all intellectual knowing, cognition, understanding, and symbols before we can truly apprehend this Light.

Pseudo-Dionysus strives to make transparently clear that this Light is beyond everything, beyond the beyond, saying:

> Since the union of divinized minds with the Light beyond all deity occurs in the cessation of all intelligent activity...[they] praise it most appropriately through the denial of all beings. [They discover] it is not a thing since it transcends all things in a manner beyond being...No. It is at a total remove from every condition, movement, life, imagination, conjecture, name, discourse, thought, conception, being rest, dwelling, unity, limit, infinity, the totality of existence.[13]

He spent much time, emphasizing what Hindus and Buddhists refer to as *neti-neti,* or simply "not this, nor that." In so doing, he would become the father of a school of thought known in the West as apophatic theology. Here, focal attention is given to the idea that God is beyond all possible positive assertions, beyond the Good and the Bad, the existent and nonexistent, serving as the ground beyond all pairs and all dualities. True seekers are called to "hunger for an unending, conceptual, and true communion with the spotless and sublime light of clear and splendid beauty."[14] Once in this Light we come into a single, eternal unifying knowledge. This light, like Christ itself, is both the means of illumination and the path to the Absolute Godhead.

> The Good which is above all light is given the name "light of the mind," "beam and spring," "overflowing radiance." It fills with its light every mind that is above and beyond the world, or around it or within it. It renews all the powers of their minds. It steps beyond everything inasmuch as it is ordered beyond everything. It precedes everything inasmuch as it transcends everything. Quite simply, it gathers together and supremely anticipates in itself the authority of all illuminating power, being indeed the source of light and actually transcending light. And so it assembles into a union everything possessed of reason and of mind... It returns them from their numerous false notions and, filling them with the one unifying light, it gathers their clashing fancies into a single, pure, coherent, and true knowledge.[15]

The Visionary Light of Medieval Catholicism

Hildegard of Bingen (1098–1179), Poet, Healer, Musician, Visionary

Hildegard von Bingen (1098–1179), an amazing and gifted Benedictine abbess (leader of a convent), was an artist, playwright, counselor, linguist, naturalist, scientist, political advisor, philosopher, physician, herbalist, poet, activist, visionary, and composer. She composed one of the earliest liturgical dramas, which (because it is almost entirely sung) is considered by some scholars to be the first opera. Renowned as a visionary, she was consulted widely as an oracle on both secular and spiritual matters. From a very young age a sickly child, she began to receive intense spiritual visions when only three years old. When she was eight, her parents delivered her into the care of the church.

She was reticent to publicly reveal her visionary life until experiencing inward, repeated instruction from God to do so. In reference to her writing, she opens by saying that her words did not flow from humanness or volition, hers or otherwise. Rather, she claims that they emanate from her contact with a supernal *Lux Vivens* or "Living Light."

> The light that I see is not local and confined. It is far brighter than a lucent cloud through which the sun shines. And I can discern neither its height nor its length nor its breadth. This light I have named "the Shadow of the Living Light," and just as the sun and the moon and stars are reflected in water, the words I see and hear in my vision are not like

the words of human speech, but are blazing like a blazing flame and a cloud that moves through clean air. I can by no means grasp the form of this light, any more than I can stare fully into the sun. And sometimes, though not often, I see another light in that light, and this I have called "the Living Light." But I am even less able to explain how I see it than I am the other one. Suffice it to say that when I do see it, all my pain and sorrow vanish.[16]

As with other mystics, Hildegard reveals the nonlinear, nonreductionist nature of intuitive revelation. There is light within light within light, each wave of which has neither a beginning nor end. The Living Light of which Hildegard spoke was a wave from an infinite sea of illumination cascading down from the inner sky of the soul.

This Living Light would guide her in all of her works, providing the visionary material for her famous *Scivias,* a series of twenty-six visions providing spiritual interpretations on the sacraments; the origin, nature, and end of creation; and the process of sanctification. Intellectually and spiritually, Hildegard was one of the most significant persons in preindustrial Europe, remarkable for her ability to unite faith with naturalistic observation of the world of nature, for her forward thinking about the status of women, and for her ability to reconcile a respect for tradition with a longing for social justice.

The Beguine Mystics: Mechthild and Marguerite

During the 13th and 14th centuries, a movement of Catholic lay religious women's communities known as the Beguines emerged on the outskirts of towns and cities in Northern Europe, often in regions that had lost many men to the Crusades. These women dedicated themselves to a holy life of simplicity, community, service, and prayer. Interestingly, their communities were only loosely linked to the church hierarchy, and the women took no formal vows and had no central abbess or leader. Although later in their history they sometimes turned to begging, they primarily lived off of their own manual labor on the outskirts of town.

They are known to history primarily through the works of their female visionaries, who wrote beautifully on the mysticism of love. Of the great Beguine mystics, here we will focus on two: Mechthild of Magdeburg (1210–1285) and Marguerite Porete (d. 1310), although interested readers may also wish to explore the writings of the 13th century Flemish poet Hadewijch of Antwerp and Christina of Stommeln (1242–1312).

Mechthild was born in Magdeburg in 1210 to a noble Saxon family, and began receiving religious visions at the age of five. At fifteen, she left home to become a Beguine lay mystic, and received spiritual guidance from nearby Dominicans. Mechthild claimed theological insight stemming from her visions, and affirmed a new theology of light. She eventually moved to a Cistercian nunnery in Helfta (home of another renowned mystic, Gertrude the Great).

At the repeated behest of her confessor, she compiled a record of her inner experiences in her work, *The Flowing Light of Godhead.* She reports that during a spiritually arid and trying experience, she drew up her will and found the strength to persevere in praising God: As I thus praised, a great light appeared to my soul, and in this light God revealed himself in great magesty and indescribable brightness.[17]

The light in this vision guided her throughout her spiritual life, which she lived and wrote of with an ardent passion. Light formed the heart of Mechthild's spiritual awakening, "Our lady, the soul, has slept since childhood. Now she has awakened in the light of open love."[18] This light awakened in her a notable spiritual intensity, causing her to exclaim, "My eyes are brightened in your fiery light."[19] One in whom this illumination arises becomes a living flame of divine love drawing all souls into its intimate divine embrace.

> The blessed, who now live so blissfully in heaven hovering weightlessly, are all suffused with light and are permeated with love flowing through them and are united in one will. The choirs each have a special light illuminating them and heaven has its own as well. The light is so extraordinarily glorious that I cannot and may not describe it.[20]

> God lets his fiery spirit shine forth unceasingly from his Holy Trinity into this loving soul, just like a bright sunbeam shining forth from the hot sun lights up a new golden shield. The radiant light of God and the loving soul that so delightfully sparkles forth from both of them, has such great power and shines so brightly for all who are in heaven, purgatory, and hell that the highest angels, Cherubim and Seraphim, feel an intimate closeness to the loving soul, and in this same light, on fire with boundless love, they descend to the soul as it flames with love.[21]

Details of Marguerite Porete's life are known from *The Mirror of Simple Annihilated Souls and Those Who Only Remain in Will and Desire of Love.* The text detailed the ascent of the soul through the falling away of personal will in seven successive stages.

In her quest to find complete unity through the love of God, Marguerite tells us that, "God gives Himself through the ardor of light into the heart of a creature."[22] Like other Christian mystics, she understood this light to be a dissolver of mysteries, dispeller of darkness and source of rapturous love. It was a mode of knowing which turned chaos into cosmos and brought order in all things.

The true [inner] Sun shines in their illumination, they see the little specks in the rays of the Sun by means of the splendor of the Sun and of the rays. Thus when such a Sun is in the Soul, and such rays and such dazzling brightness, the body is then no longer feeble and the Soul is no longer fearful.[23]

The Divine Goodness pours out from [His] bosom in one rapturous overflow of the movement of Divine Light. Such movement of Divine Light, which is poured into the Soul by light, shows to the will of the Soul the rightness of what is and the understanding of what is not in order.[24]

Her book continued to be circulated anonymously and became regarded as a mystical masterpiece.

Meister Eckhart (c. 1260–c. 1328), from Whom God Hid Nothing

Johannes Eckhart, OP, was born in Thuringia, Germany in 1260. Eckhart entered the Dominican order as a youth, received ordination to the priesthood, and completed his studies in Paris in 1302. The term "Meister" (German for "master") refers to the title *Magister in theologia,* an academic honor he received while in Paris. Over time, he developed a strong mystical perspective based on his inner experiences, which were reflected in his philosophical writings. He held that God indeed is the only Being, and that we human creatures derive our limited, contingent being from God at all times. Striving to become fully conscious of this divinity within oneself is the soul's entire focus for the mystic's life.

Because of our ultimate nothingness, Eckhart maintains, if we were to detach from all of our creaturely attributes and turn away from the nothingness of time and space, we would immediately experience union with God. Eckhart uses the Biblical metaphor of rebirth to characterize this breakthrough to God who lies obscured beneath distinction and dualism, and discusses its luminosity:

It is the peculiar characteristic of this birth that it always brings new light. It constantly introduces a strong light into the soul since it is the nature of goodness to pour itself forth wherever it may be. In this birth God pours himself into the soul with light so much that the light gathers in the being and ground of the soul and spills over into the faculties and the outer self. This happened to Paul too when God bathed him in his light as he journeyed, and spoke to him. A likeness of the light in the ground of the soul flows over into the body, which is then filled with radiance.[25]

The answer to the obscuring spiritual darkness most of us face, Eckhart teaches, is to rid ourselves of our "creaturely will" and rest solely in God. We must strive to move beyond even the state of willing to carry out God's will, because even here our will exists as a copy of God's, thus creating a layer of mediation preventing complete intimacy.

Simply and wholly, we must obliterate completely our sense of personal volition. Doing this requires the systematic and total cultivation of *abgeschiedenheit* (disinterestedness), a stripping away of all identification with finite and limited qualities.

Eckhart was also a dedicated spiritual mentor, helping others undergo this birth into the light. Several of his students themselves became contemplatives of note, most notably Henry Suso (1300–1366), Johannes Tauler (1300–1361), and the lay mystical group the Friends of God. Suso was a lyric poet inspired by the troubadours who lived Eckhart's wisdom with a devotional intensity.

Early Medieval Italian Mystics (1250–1350):
Dante, Angela, and Catherine

The *Divine Comedy,* by the Italian literary genius Dante Alighieri (1265–1321), culminates in a resplendent vision of Divine Light. The third *cantica, Paradiso* (Paradise), recounts Dante's ascent through the heavens to the Empyrean, a supra-physical sphere of existence where beatific souls partake of varying levels of communion with God. As he reaches this region, the poet recounts his experiences:

> And I saw light that flowed as flows a river, pouring its golden splendor between two banks painted with the wondrous colors of spring. From that torrent issued living sparks.[26]

Roughly contemporary to Dante, Blessed Angela of Foligno (1248–1309) was a married householder with children. Within several years of her initial spiritual yearnings, all of the members of her immediate family had died. Within this personal tragedy emerged an opportunity. She sold her belongings, distributed them among the poor, and entered into religious life. After initial skepticism, her Franciscan friar confessor came to trust the validity of her visionary life and served as her scribe as she dictated some of her mystical and visionary experiences. In her writings, Angela recounts an experience of the divine as a fiery illumination engendering both spiritual certainty and resolute faithfulness.

> This embrace of God sets ablaze a fire within the soul with which the whole soul burns for Christ. It also produces a light so great that the soul understands the fullness of God's goodness...The effect then of this fire within the soul is to render it certain and secure that Christ is within it. And yet, what we have said is nothing in comparison to what this experience really is.[27]

Angela became increasingly resolute in her belief in the necessity of experiencing the Inner Light. Reflecting on her own experience, she emphasizes the cathartic role that this interior light played in her own spiritual development.

> No one can be saved without divine light. Divine light causes us to begin and to make progress, and it leads us to the summit of perfection. Therefore if you want to begin and to receive this divine light, pray. If you have begun to make progress and want this light to be intensified within you, pray. And if you have reached the summit of perfection, and want to be super illumined so as to remain in that state, pray.[28]

Saint Catherine of Siena (1347–1380), one of the most renowned of the Italian mystics, was the 23rd of 25 children. She is one of only four women (all mystics) to be declared a Doctor (exemplary teacher) of the Roman Catholic Church. Extremely pious and spiritually introverted as a young child, she became a Dominican tertiary at sixteen. Three years later, she underwent what she termed a "Spiritual Marriage" to Christ. Subsequent to this, she became much more outwardly oriented, and began to serve the sick and the poor with great vigor.

In addition to a voluminous personal correspondence, she composed a lengthy book, *The Dialogue*, comprised of a series of questions and answers between herself and God. Herein she addresses God and tells Him that:

> You, eternal Trinity, are a deep sea: The more I enter you, the more I discover, and the more I discover, the more I seek you. You are insatiable, you in whose depth the soul is sated yet remains always hungry for you, thirsty for you, eternal Trinity, longing to see you with the light in your light.[29]

She goes on to address a theme common in Medieval Christian visionary mysticism, and in the mysticism of light in general, which is the idea that the Light of God is a purifying fire whose light cleanses selfishness and illuminates God's truth.

> You are a fire always burning but never consuming; you are a fire consuming in your heat all the soul's selfish love; you are a fire lifting all chill and giving light. In your light you have made me know your truth: You are that light beyond all light who gives the mind's eye supernatural light in such fullness and perfection that you bring clarity even to the light of faith. In that faith I see that my soul has life, and in that light receives you who are Light.[30]

The Spanish Carmelite Mystics (1515–1591): St. Teresa of Avila and St. John of the Cross

Saint Teresa of Avila (1515–1582) and her assistant, Saint John of the Cross (1542–1591), founded the Discalced (barefoot) Carmelites as a reform to the existing Carmelite order, which Teresa believed to be in spiritual decline. The Carmelite Order began in 12th century Palestine on Mount Carmel (located in today's Haifa, Israel), the same mountain historically associated with the Hebrew prophet Elijah, the Christian Desert Fathers, and Bahá'u'lláh, founder of the Bahá'í faith. The order focused on contemplative prayer, which Teresa sought to reinvigorate in her reform, starting with herself. Despite long periods of spiritual dryness, she persevered in her prayer discipline, and dedicated herself to two hours a day of silent prayer, one in the morning and one in the evening. This daily period for silent prayer complemented the spoken and sung prayers of the liturgy, and was instituted as part of the daily life of the reformed order.

Teresa often described contemplation with an admirable tenderness and lack of pretense, writing that "mental prayer is nothing else than a close sharing between friends; it means taking time frequently to be alone with him who we know loves us." Her masterpiece of mystical literature, *The Interior Castle*, detailed the ascent of the soul through the interior rooms of the castle of the soul. The notion of an interior world divided into many planes, sub-planes, levels, or worlds is a consistent theme in the cosmologies of the various spiritual traditions. Teresa frames her inner journey using the Gospel of John 14:2, "In My Father's house are many dwelling places." As the soul undergoes this ascent, she writes, "the brilliance of this inner vision is like an infused light coming from a sun covered by something as sparkling as a properly cut diamond."[31]

Teresa writes about her experience of this radiant Light in some detail, noting that there can be no mistaking this experience with physical light.

> It is not a dazzling radiance but a soft whiteness and infused radiance, which causes the eyes great delight and never tires them; nor are they tired by the brilliance which confronts them as they look on this divine beauty. The brightness and light that appear before the gaze are so different from those of earth that the sun's rays seem quite dim by comparison, and afterwards we never feel like opening our eyes again...Not that the sun or anything like sunlight enters into the vision; on the contrary, its light seems the natural light, and the light of this world appears artificial. It is a light that never yields to darkness and, being always light, can never be clouded.[32]

In the peak of her revelation, she reveals that this light makes the physical sun's rays appear "dim by comparison." Here she differentiates between the degree and intensity of the light she is experiencing. Saint Teresa experienced many difficult moments in her life, but the certainty of her illumination "never yielded to darkness."

Saint John of the Cross (1542–1591), Teresa's protégé and younger contemporary, is, like Teresa, one of the 35 Doctors of the Church. Aside from being a renowned mystic, he is also one of the most respected poets in Spanish and World literature. Living outside of Avila, he studied at the recently formed Jesuit academy and considered joining the Carthusian Order before Teresa persuaded him to aid in her reform movement. He then used a period in solitude to work on mystical poetry, which included his famous poem, the *Spiritual Canticle.* Then he returned to his activities in service of the Carmelite Order for the rest of his life.

The suffering which John experienced within his own life led him to speak of the "dark night of the soul," an expression for which he is widely known. St. John mirrors Eckhart in both content and language in concluding that darkness in the soul results from continued attachment to the things of this world: "Darkness, an attachment to creatures, and light, which is God, are contraries and bear no likeness toward each other."[33]

John's formula is simple and precise: Divest yourself from all attachment to this world, and you will be filled with the Light. This Light flows from God's being as an expression of His nature and serves as a path back to Him.

> The soul on which the divine light of God's being is ever shining... is like [a] window...A soul makes room for God by wiping away all the smudges and smears of creatures, by uniting its will perfectly to God's; for to love is to labor to divest and deprive oneself for God of all that is not God. When this is done the soul will be illumined by and transformed in God.[34]

The darkness of the dark night of the soul is also particularly associated with the periods of dryness, spiritual distance, and relative darkness that punctuate the lives of all seekers, even the greatest saints, after they have already experienced periods of inner illumination. The spiritual darkness, John teaches, proves particularly intense after one has already seen the light. While undeniably anguishing, John maintains that these trials serve a great purpose on the path. They humble us and intensify our longing for God, both prerequisites for the serious, mature spiritual life. John further comments on the structure of the spiritual darkness, noting the paradoxical result that, in many ways, the brighter the light God shines upon us, the more the anguish of separation fills us whenever our inner focus is diminished.

> The more pure and simple the divine light when it beats upon the soul, the more does it darken it, empty it, and annihilate it...and also the less pure and less simple the light, the less is the soul darkened and annihilated.[35]

The pure and unadulterated light of God, John says, is too powerful for us to bear directly while living within the confines of earthly attachment and the egoic self. Were God to mete out a full dose of His love to us, we would be like a blown fuse, completely annihilated and unconscious, robbing God of His desire to give the infinite gift of His Love and Light. Understanding this is the key to understanding the "dark nights" and spiritual trials in our lives.

The New Orthodoxy of Light: The Eastern Orthodox Church

The Eastern Orthodox Churches today comprise roughly 240 million Christian believers who claim an unbroken line of direct apostolic succession to Jesus. Distinct from the Vatican City in Catholic Rome, Orthodox Constantinople emerged in the first Christian millennium as a second great religious and cultural power within the Christian world.[36]

Eastern Orthodoxy has historically supported and venerated its mystics, developing a rich literature on contemplative prayer and religious experience. This may stem in part from the focus in the Christian East of a doctrine of deification, which in the West had been theologically tempered as "sanctification."[37] Also, Orthodoxy did not undergo the theological and philosophical shifts of the 16th and 17th centuries that led to the marginalization of mystical theology in Western Europe, affecting both Catholic and Protestant spirituality.

The most significant collection of Eastern Orthodox mystical writings is the multivolume anthology called the *Philokalia* (literally, love of spiritual beauty), first assembled by Nicodemus of the Holy Mountain of Athos and St. Makarios of Corinth toward the end of the 18th century.

The Philokalia compiles writings by masters of the Eastern Orthodox *hesychast* tradition composed between the 4th and 15th centuries. *Hesychasm*, from the Greek "to keep stillness," is a method of contemplative prayer utilized widely by Orthodox mystics and ascetics. Practitioners strip themselves of all thoughts, images, and awareness of the outside world. The prayer fructifies through grace into a direct experience of the uncreated Light of Godhead, thereby trans-

1-100 CE	*100-200 CE*
• *Jesus of Nazareth (c. 5 BC/BCE – c. 33 AD/CE)* • *Four Gospels 70-125* • *Gospel of John c. 80–95* • *Gospel of Matthew c. 70 and 100* • *Paul of Tarsus c. 5 BC - c. 67* • *Paul's Letters 50-56*	• *First Roman Account of Christians 110* • *Formation of New Testament 125-130* • *Early Christian Gnostics Basilides, Satornilos, Valentinus, and Marcion 135-140*

400-600 CE	*600-800 CE*
• *St. John Climacus ca. 579 - 649* • *Pseudo-Dionysius the Areopagite c. 5th* • *Benedictine Monte Casino Founded 525*	• *St. Gregory 1, founder of medieval papacy, 540 - 604*

200-300 CE	300-400 CE
• *Beginning of Coptic Christian Era 284* • *Saint Paul the First Hermit c. 230* • *Saint Anthony the Great ca. 251 – 356*	*Council of Nicea, 325* • *Beginning of Christian Monasticism in Egypt 320* • *Macarius of Egypt ca. 300 - 391* • *Augustine of Hippo 354 - 430*

900-1200 CE	1200-1400 CE
• *Monastery at Cluny founded 909* • *Establishment of Russian Orthodox church 1054* *St. Symeon the New Theologian 949-1022* • *Hildegard von Bingen 1098-1179*	• *Catholic Scholasticism 12-13th* • *Meister Eckhart c. 1260–c. 1328* • *Mechthild of Magdeburg 1210 – c. 1285* • *St. Gregory Palamas, 1296 - 1359* • *Marguerite Porete d. 1310* • *Dante Alighieri 1265 –1321* • *Angela of Foligno c. 1248-1309* • *Catherine of Siena 1347-1380*

1400-1600 CE	*1600-1800 CE*
· *Gutenberg Bible 1453* · *Martin Luther 1483-1546* · *Beginning of Renaissance 1500 CE* · *Beginning of Reformation 1517-1521* · *John Calvin 1509-1564* · *Anabaptists formed 1500* · *Teresa of Ávila 1515-1582* · *Beginning of Unitarianism 1538* · *John of the Cross 1542-1591* · *Jakob Böhme 1575–1624* · *Beginning of Congregationalism 1582*	· *Formation of Baptists 1609* · *George Fox 1624–1691* · *Formation of Society of Friends Jesuits order 1665* · *Emanuel Swedenborg 1688 - 1772* · *Formation of Shakers 1747* · *Formation of Methodism 1784* · *Formation of Seventh Day Adventist 1844* · *Formation of Jehovah's Witnesses 1881*

- *Evelyn Underhill 1875 – 1941*
- *Thomas Merton 1915 – 1968*
- *Bede Griffiths 1906 – 1993*
- *Cypriot healer and mystic Daskolos 1912–1995*
- *Bro. Wayne Teasdale 1945-2004*
- *2nd Vatican Council 1962 – 65*
- *Brother Stendhal-Rast Christian Contemplative Community*
- *Mathew Fox Formation of Creation Christianity 1980-2000*
- *Pope Francis, b. 1936*

forming the supplicant into a humble servant of God. St. Hesychios the Priest stresses that:

> Just as he who looks at the sun cannot but fill his eyes with light, so he who always gazes intently into his heart cannot fail to be illumined.[38]

In this section, we look at the experience and theology of two pioneers of Orthodox spirituality, St. Symeon the New Theologian (949–1022) and St. Gregory Palamas (1296–1359), and at their elaboration and defense of the hesychast tradition.

St. Symeon (949–1022), the New Theologian

St. Symeon the New Theologian was born and raised in Asia Minor by a family of Byzantine provincial nobles and received a Greek primary school education until the age of eleven. His title of "theologian" does not carry a scholastic or academic sense in the Orthodox Church, but rather signifies a tremendous veneration as "a person of prayer, who speaks about the vision of God on the basis of his own immediate experience."[39] The title has been bestowed only three times and is shared with St. John the Evangelist and St. Gregory of Nazianzus. He is called the "new" theologian because, living in the 10th and 11th centuries, he comes much later than the previous Orthodox "theologians" from the first and fourth centuries.

At the age of fourteen, he met a holy monk named St. Symeon the Studite who became his spiritual father or elder. At this point, he began his spiritual discipline in earnest. His spiritual father dissuaded him from entering monastic life immediately and encouraged him to seek out spiritual growth in the midst of daily life. During this period, Symeon worked as the manager of a patrician's household and may also have also served as a diplomat, devoting his evenings to spiritual vigil and study.

Symeon received a powerful vision around the age of twenty while engaged in silent hesychast repetition of the Jesus Prayer. One of the most distinctive forms of Orthodox spirituality, the Jesus Prayer (known also as the prayer of the heart) has become increasingly popular even among western Christians in our time. Its most common form is "Lord Jesus Christ, Son of God, have mercy on me, a sinner," which itself is an extension of the gospel parable of the Publican and the Pharisee (Luke 18:10–14). It has been in use since at least the time of St. Diadochos of Photiki (400–486 CE), and is contained in his *Gnostic Chapters,* a work found in the first volume of the *Philokalia.* The Orthodox masters consistently stress that the repetition ought not to be merely mechanical or without meaning, but rather should always be a direct invocation of the grace of the actual mystic presence of Christ.

Speaking in the third person out of humility, Symeon recounts what happened that evening in his room:

> [H]e stood repeating more in his intellect then with his mouth the words "God have mercy on me, a sinner" suddenly a profuse flood of divine light appeared above him and filled the whole room. As this happened the young man lost his bearings...for he saw nothing but light around him and did not even know that he stood upon the earth. He had no fear of falling, or awareness of the world, nor did any of those things that beset men and bodily beings enter his mind. Instead he was wholly united to non-material light, so much so that it seemed to him that he himself had been transformed into light. Oblivious to all else, he was filled with tears and inexpressible joy and gladness. Then his intellect ascended to heaven and beheld another light, more lucid then the first. Miraculously there appeared to him, standing close to that light, the holy, angelic elder of whom we have spoken (e.g. St. Symeon the Studite).[40]

This luminous appearance of his deceased spiritual mentor, St. Symeon, in a light "even more lucid" parallels the inward ascent of mystics in many traditions. The experience of loss of awareness of the world, the nonmaterial surroundings, and lack of fear of falling all echo common features of many modern-day near-death testimonies.

After a period of lapses, struggles, continued contemplative practice, and earnest contrition, Symeon became firmly rooted in his relationship with this divine Light and found that:

> when the visible sun set,...its place was taken by the tender light of spiritual luminosity, which is the pledge and the foretaste of the unceasing light that is to succeed it. And this was as it should be; for the love of that for which he was searching took him out of the world, beyond nature and all material things, filling him wholly with the Spirit and transforming him into light.[41]

Symeon went on to enter into monastic life, becoming a renowned, but also controversial, saint and writer. He was a strict ascetic, a reformer, and a self-described "enthusiastic zealot." He insisted that the monks in his charge "never go to communion without tears."[42] For Symeon, a life of deep, intense, heartfelt yearning for freedom from sin and impurity was a necessary prerequisite for divine illumination.

> The person inwardly illumined by the light of the Holy Spirit... though he pours forth incessant tears that bring him some relief, the flame of his desire kindles all the more. Then his tears flow yet more

copiously and, washed by their flow, he becomes even more radiant... totally incandescent, he has become like light.[43]

St. Symeon synthesized the teachings of previous Orthodox masters, teaching a direct and simple version of hesychast prayer. He instructed those with an earnest desire to approach and know God, to sit alone in their cell in the corner with the door closed, striving to be free from anxiety and full of humility and gratitude.

> Search inside yourself with your intellect so as to find the place of the heart, where all the powers of the soul reside. To start with you will find there darkness and an impenetrable density. Later...the heart beholds itself entirely luminous and full of discrimination.[44]

The method integrates the repetition of the Jesus prayer, sometimes subsequent to, or concurrent with, controlled breathing. Sometimes utilizing a range of postures or prostrations, the specific modes were dependent on the individual needs of the novice as determined through the direction of their spiritual father. Symeon, like all of the Orthodox masters, stresses the great need for direction from a living teacher or elder (Russian, *starets;* Greek, *gerontas*). He recommends that monks should look upon their teacher in the most reverent of ways and goes so far as to say that one should not even take a drink of water until the spiritual father says to. The depth with which St. Symeon venerated his teacher was seen by some of his contemporaries as well beyond the norm of Orthodoxy.

Despite the controversy surrounding his alleged excesses, St. Symeon's honoring of the significant role that a living guide can have in the spiritual evolution of a disciple is consistent with the teaching of most mystical traditions. St. Symeon certainly displayed an astonishing degree of loving surrender, and considered his teacher's guidance to be of irreplaceable importance, saying:

> If you entrust all of the care of your soul and body to God and to your spiritual father, no longer living for yourself or desiring the good opinion of others, what anxiety can distract you?[45]

Symeon repeatedly stresses that if we are to know God through contact with the Divine Light, then we must carefully guard the heart from being engulfed by all passions, attachments, anxieties, thoughts, or images:

> Worldly thoughts or material concerns blind the mind, or eye of the soul, like a cloth that covers the physical eyes: so long as we are not free of them, we cannot see. But once they are removed by mindfulness of death, then we clearly see the true light, that which illumines everyone who attains the spiritual world.[46]

Despite his own strict discipline, St. Symeon had a surprisingly affirmative and prophetic vision, relevant to those who read his writings even a thousand years later. Although a monk himself, he stressed that no form of religious life was superior to another, and that the uncreated Light of God proved equally available to a married city dweller as to a desert hermit. Symeon insisted that the Light of God was available now, to every single soul regardless of their past or the time in which they live, asserting "even now, living in our midst, there are people who are dispassionate and saintly, filled with divine light."[47] As he so aptly states:

> Do not say that it is impossible to receive the Spirit of God. Do not say that it is possible to be made whole without Him. Do not say that one can possess Him without knowing it. Do not say that God does not manifest Himself to man. Do not say that men cannot perceive the divine light, or that it is impossible in this age! Never is it found to be impossible, my friends. On the contrary, it is entirely possible when one desires it.[48]

St. Gregory Palamas, Defender of Hesychasm [Contemplative Prayer]

The mystical theologian St. Gregory Palamas (1296–1359 CE) was perhaps the most widely recognized teacher within the Orthodox tradition during the medieval period. Born into a well-connected family in Constantinople, as a youth he studied philosophy and theology, and enjoyed spiritual counsel from Theoliptos of Philadelphia. Drawn increasingly toward asceticism and contemplation, at the age of twenty, he entered the cloistered life on Mount Athos, the center of Greek monasticism. By 1052, Mount Athos had become a self-governing monastic republic, a collective of 20 Orthodox monasteries occupying a portion of a remote peninsula in northern Greece. It has functioned as an ongoing center of Orthodox mysticism and monastic life from that time until the present day.

As a monk, Gregory typically spent at least five days a week in total seclusion, joining the rest of the monastic community only for the weekly liturgy. During a six-year period, he retreated to a cave on the outskirts of Veroia, an inland city in Greece. In 1335–1336, after twenty years, Palamas emerged from his monastic seclusion to defend the contemplative prayer illumination known as Hesychasm, which he and his brethren held so dear.

Gregory maintained the hesychast prayer and those who practice it enjoyed profound personal experiences of *gnosis*. These practitioners. he noted, become infused with deep personal spiritual knowing; second, he noted that those partaking of the Light enjoy the company of the procession of Orthodox saints stretching back to the Christ Himself.

Whoever partakes of this divine illumination partakes of it to a certain degree, and to a proportionate degree he also possesses a spiritual
knowledge of created things. All who assiduously study the writings of
the divinely wise theologians know...that this illumination is uncreated
but is not of the divine essence.[49]

In establishing the central spiritual importance of the divine Light, St.
Gregory identifies it explicitly with the Light of Christ's Transfiguration upon
Mount Tabor:

When (Christ) ascended Mount Tabor He shone like the sun and
his clothes became as white as light. When the disciples could look at
it no longer or, rather, because they lacked the strength to gaze at the
brightness, they fell prostrate to the earth. Nonetheless, in accordance
with the Savior's promise they did see the kingdom of God, that divine
and inexpressible light.[50]

Gregory goes to considerable length to demonstrate that the light is not
only his own personal experience and theology, but rather is and reflects the
substance of the whole of the Orthodox tradition stretching back to Christ himself. On this basic point, he paraphrases St. Maximos (580–662) speaking on the
illumination of prayer:

[T]he deifying grace of God is uncreated...eternally existent, proceeding from an eternally existing God," and notes that Maximos teaches
that grace flows as "a light, ungenerated and completely real, that is
manifested when the saints become worthy of receiving it."[51]

He also identifies the light of contemplative prayer as one with the Light
experienced by Paul on the way to Damascus, by Adam prior to the Fall, and within the personal experience of, among others, St. Gregory of Nazianzos, St. Basil
the Great, St. John Damaskos, St. John Chrysostom, and Pseudo-Dionysius the
Areopagite. Gregory emphasizes that the divine light is essentially eschatological
(that is, dealing with the final culmination of God's creative plan) in character.
It anticipates and provides a foretaste of the more permanent union with God
toward which every soul is destined. To behold the light prepares the way for the
internal spiritual appearance of the Christ Light within us.

St. Gregory challenged those who would minimize the significance of the
Light to the status of a mere natural object or some other intellectual knowledge
acquired by imitation tantamount to delusion.

If anyone declares that perfect union with God is accomplished
simply in an imitative and relative fashion, without the deifying grace
of the Spirit and merely in the manner of persons who share the same
disposition and love one another, and that the deifying grace of God is

a state of our intellectual nature acquired by imitation alone, but is not a supernatural illumination and an ineffable and divine energy beheld invisibly and conceived inconceivably by those privileged to participate in it, then he must know that he has fallen unawares into delusion.[52]

Not only does St. Gregory refute his critics' claim that the light a hesychast receives in prayer is both natural and created, he also rebuts the charge that he posited two Gods, a visible and an invisible. Drawing on Trinitarian theology, St. Gregory affirms a "distinction-in-unity" between the energies (Greek, *energeiai*) and the essence (Greek, *ousia*) of God, and asserts "the divine and deifying illumination and grace is not the essence but the energy of God."[53] Moreover, God is "indivisibly divided and united dividedly, and yet in spite of this suffers neither multiplicity nor compositeness."[54] This parallels the distinction drawn in some other mystical wisdom traditions between God Absolute and the Light of God emanating from the Source. St. Gregory continues:

> God both is and is said to be the nature of all beings, in so far as we partake of Him and subsist by means of this participation: not, however, by participation in His nature—far from it—but by participation in his energy. In this sense He is the Being of all beings, the Form that is in all forms as the Author of form, the Wisdom of the wise and, simply, the All of all things. Moreover, He is not nature, because he transcends every nature; he is not being, because he transcends every being; and He is not nor does he possess a form, because he transcends every form. How, then, can we draw near to God? By drawing near to his nature? But not a single created being has or can have any communication with or proximity to the sublime nature. Thus if anyone has drawn close to God, he has evidently approached Him by means of His energy (e.g. his Light).[55]

St Gregory maintains that the *nous*, the faculty of spiritual apprehension (as distinct from discursive reasoning) is imbued with *eros*, the essential desire for loving union with God's luminous energies. Furthermore, this *nous* experienced inwardly as a never escalating desire for union, was the heart and soul of divine revelation.

> Our *nous* because it is created in God's image, possesses likewise the image of this sublime Eros or intense longing—an image expressed in the love experienced by the intellect for the spiritual knowledge that originates from it and continually abides in it...Yet in the Archetype, in this absolutely and transcendentally perfect Goodness, wherein there is nothing imperfect, the divine Eros is indistinguishable whatever that goodness is.[56]

Following St. Gregory's successful exclamation of hesychasm, a series of synods held by Orthodox leaders declared this method of prayer and teaching on the divine uncreated Light of Tabor to be essential church teachings. The saint wrote *The Declaration of the Holy Mountain in Defense of Those who Devoutly Practice a Life of Stillness*, which was signed by twenty leading monks and abbots from the monastic communities at Mount Athos. Today St. Gregory's feast is celebrated on the second Sunday of the Orthodox Lenten season and is recognized to be "a renewed Triumph of Orthodoxy"[57] firmly establishing the centrality of the role of interior illumination in Orthodox mystical religious life.

Jacob Boehme, George Fox, and Protestant Mysticism

On October 31, 1517, Martin Luther (1483–1546) nailed his *Ninety-Five Theses On the Power of Indulgences* to the door of the Wittenberg Castle Church in Germany and so marked the beginning of the Protestant Reformation. Luther, followed by other reforming theologians such as John Calvin (1509–1564) and Ulrich Zwingli (1484–1531), led to the founding of Protestant churches (Lutheranism, Calvinism, Anglicanism, and the Anabaptists), which, in turn, have led to subsequent movements such as Evangelicalism, Methodism, and Pentecostalism.

The son of German peasants, Jacob Boehme received little formal schooling and was apprenticed to a shoemaker at a young age. One day when tending his master's shop, a "mysterious stranger" of apparently humble means, but possessing a certain spiritual dignity, entered and requested to buy a pair of shoes. Fearing he would upset his master, Boehme resisted naming a price, and begrudgingly suggested an excessive sum. The stranger agreed and departed the store immediately after the purchase. Starting down the street, he turned and called to young Jacob by name. Boehme ran to meet him and then, "the strange man fixed his eyes upon the youth—great eyes which sparkled and seemed filled with divine light."[58] He gave the youth a brief word of spiritual encouragement and departed, never to be seen or heard from again. This experience left a lasting impression on Boehme, enlivening and deepening his spiritual search. Similar stories of the penetrating, light-filled glance of a spiritual master are found within multiple traditions.

Later, when he was twenty-five, Boehme saw a simple ray of sunlight reflect off of a pewter dish. This seemingly ordinary event triggered in him an influx of grace, and an ecstatic vision of Godhead as the Ground of all creation. He chose not to speak or write publicly of his vision, and worked and quietly cared for his family until a second revelation in 1610 prompted him to reveal publicly his visions and spiritual teachings. This led to the publication of his first text, *Aurora*. Thirteen years later, he published his masterpiece, *The Way to Christ*. He then spent the remaining year of his life publishing extensively, including his other major works *Misterium Magnum (The Great Mystery)* and *De Signatura Rerum (The Signature of All Things)*. Then this simple shoemaker—and great soul—died in peace surrounded by his family, with his last words being, "Now I go hence into Paradise."

Boehme left behind a rich set of teachings concerning the experience of spiritual ascension. In the dialogue between Master and disciple found in *The Supersensual Life*, he presents an archetypal method of contemplation for entering into the direct experience of divine Light. By silencing discursive thought, remaining fully attentive at the inner door, and joyously receptive to the ascending and descending lights, one can enter the "supersensual ground of life."

> Master: Cease but from thine own Activity, steadfastly fixing thine eye upon one point, and with a strong purpose relying upon the promised grace of God in Christ, to bring thee out of thy darkness into His marvelous light. For this end gather in all thy thoughts, and by faith press into the Centre, laying hold upon the Word of God, which is infallible, and which hath called thee. Be thou then obedient to this call; and be silent before the Lord, sitting alone with Him in thy inmost and most hidden cell, thy mind being centrally united in itself, and attending His will in the patience of Hope. So shall thy light break forth as the morning; and after the redness thereof is passed, the Sun Himself, which thou waitest for, shall arise unto thee, and under His most healing wings thou shalt greatly rejoice; ascending and descending in His bright and salutiferous beams. Behold this is the true supersensual ground of life.[59]

In 1624, the same year that Boehme died in Germany, George Fox was born in England. A mystic and social radical, Fox, like Boehme, was born to a humble family, displayed a contemplative temperament in his youth, and was apprenticed to a shoemaker. A conscientious worker who lived simply, Fox also spent some time as a shepherd. Throughout his life he felt comfortable in the company of both learned people and simple country folk.

As a young man he experienced, one day while walking home alone, the first of many spiritual visions. The effulgent vision revealed how all actions are accomplished by divine will and not a leaf stirs without divine providence.

> I was taken up in the love of God, so that I could not but admire the greatness of His love, While I was in that condition it was opened unto me by the eternal light and power, and I saw clearly therein that all was done, and to be done, in and by Christ....As the light appeared,

all appeared that is out of the light; darkness, death, temptations, the unrighteous, the ungodly; all was manifest and seen in the light.[60]

Later he questioned why he must be afflicted with self-centered wickedness in his heart, and God responded that it was necessary for him to "know all conditions" so that he might "speak to all conditions." Greatly moved by this message, Fox wrote in his *Journal:*

> [I]n this I saw the infinite love of God. I saw also that there was an ocean of darkness and death, but an infinite ocean of light and love which flowed over the ocean of darkness. In that also I saw the infinite love of God; and I had great openings.[61]

Visions such as these prompted Fox to found the Religious Society of Friends, more commonly known as the Quakers. Traditionally, Friends worshiped without music, formal liturgy, or a presiding minister. They simply gathered to sit, pray, or meditate in respectful silence, trusting that the spirit of God might speak through one or more of those who were present. Inspired by his own visionary experiences, Fox listened for and "tapped into" what he called the "still, silent voice" within. His vision of an "ocean of light" may have provided the basis for the Quaker doctrine of the "inward light" or "inner light," accessible through silent prayer and meditation, and regarded as the indwelling presence of God. In the words of the 20th century Quaker writer Rufus Jones, "The Inner Light is the doctrine that there is something Divine, "Something of God" in the human soul."[62] The Inner Light is present in, and accessible to, all people of good will, as seen in the Gospel of John: "The true light, which enlightens everyone, was coming into the world" (John 1:9).

This cross-fertilizing spiritual and social outlook has remained at the core of the Quaker social vision from Fox's lifetime to the present, and form(ed) a relevant basis for a wide range of ideas and movements that have had a major impact on world history.[63] Indeed, the social implications of the concept of the Inner Light provides a broadened lens for reinterpreting the European Enlightenment, which philosophers like Voltaire saw only as a move away from the darkness of religious superstition toward reason and a limited, materalist empiricism. In contrast, the Quaker understanding of enlightenment arose from a felt experience of non-material superrational interior light.

The Society of Friends, although limited in numbers, provided much inspiration and leadership for the movements to abolish slavery in England and the American British colonies which were to become the United States. Similarly, Quaker women played a major role at the Seneca Falls Convention in 1848, a pivotal moment in the struggle for women's suffrage and the birth of feminism.

Likewise, Quakers drew on Fox's contemplative theology of the Indwelling Light as inspiration for leaders and participants in the movements toward universal education and free public schools, prison reforms, and the recognition of human and dignity based care for the mentally afflicted. In the 21st century, Quakers continue to be leaders in the global movements for nonviolent conflict resolution, social justice, humanitarian assistance for those in need, and sustainable ecological stewardship of Mother Earth.

Modern Christian Experiences of Light and the Revival of Contemplative Practice (1900–2000)

Beginning in the late 19th and early 20th centuries, thinkers like William Ralph Inge, William James, Friedrich Von Hügel, and Evelyn Underhill began to research and write on Christian mysticism, not just as an historical phenomenon but also as a living element of religion. This led to a renaissance of mystical theology and practice in 20th century Christianity, with people such as Pierre Teilhard de Chardin, Thomas Merton, Dag Hammarskjöld, Howard Thurman, and Cynthia Bourgeault contributing to an explosion of interest in contemplative spirituality, not just among priests, monks and nuns, but also among Christian laypersons.

The explosion of popular interest in Eastern spirituality within Europe and North America beginning in the middle of the 20th century led to a rekindled interest within Christianity for practices related to inner spiritual growth. By the mid-1970s, a number of Catholic monks, working independently in England and the United States, began investigating the practice of pure contemplative prayer. For example, William Meninger, M. Basil Pennington, and Thomas Keating developed the "Centering Prayer" method of contemplation at St. Joseph Abbey in Spencer, Massachusetts.

Based on ancient Christian documents such as the 14th century anonymous treatise *The Cloud of Unknowing,* this practice of centering prayer focusing one's attention inwardly, while repeating a "Prayer Word," a sacred word or phrase. In this practice, mystical prayer is viewed as an opening of one's whole being to God, relaxing into the luminous silence beyond thoughts, words, and emotions. In an interview with the *National Catholic Reporter* in 2007, Father Keating described what he had learned from contemplative practice:

> There are remarkable similarities in content and method among the different traditions...It is the practice of furthering interior silence that makes all the difference.[64]

Christian spirituality in the 20th and 21st centuries, like so many other aspects of postmodern culture, has become incredibly diverse. However, the following three figures—two American Catholic monks, and a Cypriot Greek Orthodox healer—offer insight not only into the breadth of contemporary Christian mysticism but also the ongoing vitality of the Christian spirituality of light.

Thomas Merton: Shining Like the Sun

Like St. Augustine 15 centuries before him, Thomas Merton (1915–1968) was born into a non-Christian family and lived a rowdy secular and agnostic life before coming to Christ. As a graduate student at Columbia University, he was increasingly drawn to Catholicism and mysticism, reading William Blake, Aldous Huxley, and Augustine's *Confession*.

Slowly abandoning his secular ways, Merton embraced the Catholic faith and eventually began to explore a vocation in monastic life. In 1941, he was accepted as a novice Trappist (Cistercian) monk at the Abbey of Gethsemani in Kentucky. Merton thought that becoming a monk meant turning his back on a promising literary career, but his abbott, recognizing Merton's talent, instructed the young monk to write about his conversion—leading to *The Seven Storey Mountain*, a memoir that became a surprise bestseller in 1948. Over time, Merton grew into a world-renowned writer, poet, and contemplative. He also embraced interfaith and ecumenical dialogue, as well as corresponding with mystics throughout the world.

Merton longed to enter into a "deep experimental union" with a God who is seen within. After decades of contemplation, though, he knew that such ecstatic union by definition could not come from the mechanical operations of his ego. These significant realizations he chronicled in his soul-searching book, *Conjectures of a Guilty Bystander.*

> We must realize to the very depths of our being that this is a pure gift of God which no desire, no effort and no heroism of ours can do anything to deserve or obtain. There is nothing we can do directly either to procure it or to preserve it or to increase it. Our own activity is for the most part an obstacle to the infusion of this peaceful and pacifying light.[65]

According to Merton, as we develop spiritually, we are infused with a mysterious illumination that is truer and more natural than any argument or any impression of the physical senses:

> We enter a region which we had never even expected, and yet it is this new world which seems familiar and obvious. The old world of our senses is now the one that seems to us strange, remote unbelievable—

until the intense light of contemplation leaves us and we fall back to our own level.

Although this light is absolutely above our nature, it now seems to us "normal" and "natural" to see, as we now see, without seeing, to possess clarity in darkness, to have pure certitude without any shred of discursive evidence, to be filled with an experience that transcends experience and to enter with serene confidence into the depth that leave us utterly inarticulate.[66]

His deep commitment to contemplative practice and inter-religious understanding helped rebirth an interest in an authentic spiritual life in the modern era.

One of the most remarkable events in Merton's life occurred in the spring of 1958, after he had been a monk for over fifteen years. Leaving the monastery to run a business errand, Merton came to an ordinary street corner in Louisville, Kentucky, where he suddenly experienced an epiphany of love and light.

In Louisville, at the corner of Fourth and Walnut, in the center of the shopping district, I was suddenly overwhelmed with the realization that I loved all those people, that they were mine and I theirs, that we could not be alien to one another even though we were total strangers. It was like waking from a dream of separateness, of spurious self-isolation in a special world, the world of renunciation and supposed holiness... This sense of liberation from an illusory difference was such a relief and such a joy to me that I almost laughed out loud...As if the sorrows and stupidities of the human condition could overwhelm me, now I realize what we all are. And if only everybody could realize this! But it cannot be explained. There is no way of telling people that they are all walking around shining like the sun...At the center of our being is a point...or spark which belongs entirely to God...It is so to speak his name written in us...like a pure diamond, blazing with the invisible light of heaven. It is in everybody....[67]

Thus Merton describes his dramatic apprehension of a luminous radiance "shining like the sun, a pure diamond blazing with the invisible light of heaven." Not only did Merton find it in himself, but in that graced moment he also saw it in everyone. And his spontaneous response was to "fall in love" with "all those people."

Brother Wayne Teasdale (1945–2004), Catholic-Interfaith Mystic

Brother Wayne Robert Teasdale (1945–2004) stood in the forefront of the global movement to further interfaith understanding, mutual respect, and practical cooperation. Teasdale was raised in Connecticut in a Catholic family.

While in college, he visited St. Joseph's Abbey, a Cistercian monastery located near Spencer, Massachusetts. There, Teasdale came under the spiritual direction of the abbot Thomas Keating. Later, he was influenced by Father Bede Griffiths, and spent two years studying and meditating at Bede Griffith's Shantivanam Ashram in rural Tamil Nadu, in southern India. Griffiths was a proponent of Hindu-Catholic dialogue, and his Wisdom Christianity became the subject of Teasdale's doctoral dissertation at Fordham University.

Joining the Benedictine order as a monk, Teasdale taught at several colleges in the Chicago area, including the Catholic Theological Union in Chicago, where he lived for many years. Teasdale was also a major organizer of an international *Synthesis Dialogues.* The participants explored the values and relevance of mystical experience. In his major book, *The Mystic Heart: Discovering a Universal Spirituality in the World's Religions,* Br. Wayne wrote about how the deepening of spiritual perspectives can profoundly enable humanity to respond compassionately to the crises of the world.

Serving for many years on the board of the Parliament of World's Religions, he was a key figure in bringing together nearly 8,000 people in Chicago Illinois, during the summer of 1993, for an inclusive gathering by representatives of most of the planet's religious and spiritual traditions.[68]

Reverend Bob Thompson, a close friend and longtime associate writes:

> Wayne Teasdale developed the term "inter-spiritual." He said that "the dramatic shift in global human consciousness is preparing for us to live in a universal civilization in which human beings recognize their spiritual interdependence. We can be rooted in our own tradition, he said, without being stuck in it. Being rooted in a tradition is what keeps our feet on the ground. But we can also branch out. We branch out because more light is available than can be seen through the prism of our parochialisms. In this way we can cultivate a new and larger spiritual community; one that is rooted in our own tradition but not limited to it. We can move from a parochial understanding of religion to a universal understanding of inter-spirituality.[69]

Wayne Teasdale wrote fondly about how children, wanting to represent the cosmos with its numberless stars, will punch holes in a box. In this metaphorical child's eye view of the universe, next they "darken the room, put a flashlight inside the box, and turn it on. Light emanates gloriously from all the holes." He reflects:

> I think this is a wonderful symbol of the reality of divine and human identity. Human identity is similar to the little apertures of light coming through, and God is the light. All is really light, but the many holes of

light obscure the source. In the same way God is this infinite light that shines in the depth of our being as its origin...That light is our ultimate and permanent identity, and so death is simply a return to a more total awareness.[70]

Daskalos (1912–1995), the Cypriot Researcher of Esoteric Truth

The Eastern Orthodox mystic Stylianos Atteshlis (1912–1995) was born of Greek ancestry in Strovolos on the eastern Mediterranean island of Cyprus, where he lived most of his 83 years. He was educated in Cyprus and abroad, and spent several years in Africa. For many years, he earned his livelihood working in the Cyprus government printing office. While still a boy, it soon became apparent that, in addition to being a friendly and bright child, he was spiritually gifted, purportedly able to consciously travel to worlds of higher dimensions.

Atteshlis became widely known by the name Daskalos, a Greek word meaning "teacher," for his spiritual vocation as a loved and respected mentor and mystic-healer spanned the seven decades of his adult life.

As a mystic deeply rooted in esoteric Byzantine Christian teachings, Daskalos's personal studies and inner experiences affirmed that, at the deepest esoteric levels, the Divine Presence of which all the religious/spiritual traditions speak is grounded in Oneness. Sincere seekers of all backgrounds participated in Daskolos's spiritual companionship and meditation groups. His capacity as a physical and spiritual healer extended globally in his later years.

Daskalos's *Esoteric Teachings Book* linked the significance of meditation practice with spiritual growth. "If teachings, as theory, attempt to lay out the terrain of Truth, mark the guideposts, and suggest a path, then exercises and meditations are vehicles to carry consciousness to higher ground." He humbly emphasized the contributions of the great Teachers of many spiritual paths over the millennia. He spoke of the primacy of light and love at the heart of spirituality.

> Love, Light and Life belong to the primary Nature of Absolute Beingness. The Love of God is universal, ceaseless, impersonal and unconditional. It is the Love of God, expressed as Grace, which lies at the core of Creation. The Light is pure, luminous Self-consciousness which lives in the center of every Being. Everlasting Life is the eternal motion, generation and regeneration of expression....

> The light from its source is pure and luminous. Filtered down through ideas, universes, and layers of the Selfhood, it remains the same light, only diffused. It is as if numerous lampshades had been placed over a bright bulb. Exercises and meditations, coupled with sound theoretical under footings, can do much to clean these shades, help us

draw nearer to the source of the Light, and allow the Light from above to reflect more fully within our personalities."[71]

Daskalos's teaching not only centered on the direct experience of this inner light, but also affirmed that this Light was the spiritual essence of true Christian gnosis. Through a series of three initiations, the novitiate gradually reaches higher and higher levels of numinous presence. Daskalos reaffirms the teaching of John 1:9: "The true light, which enlightens everyone, was coming into the world."

> Each human being has inside him the light that enlightens every human being descending upon the Earth. Whether he knows it or not, he has his master and guide inside him. The daily life of every human being is an exercise leading him toward the three initiations.[72]

Making this point even more emphatically, he once remarked during an informal teaching session, how critical firsthand inner experience really is.

> "I hear people say," Daskalos went on, "that God is light, or that God is superlight, and they have experienced neither light nor superlight. But unless you have the experience you don't know. I repeat what Father Yohannan said in a previous lesson, 'Thoughts and beliefs are too weak as wings to help us attain great heights of knowledge,'" Daskalos concluded and sipped the last drop from his cup of coffee.[73]

Not only did Daskalos reaffirm the central core of mystical gnosis that this "mode of knowing" supersedes intellectual apprehension, but also that it includes all lower forms of comprehension and understanding. Daskalos drew salient comparisons with other mystical traditions and their methodologies, which he had studied. For example, he spoke of "sacred discs" in the physical body, referring to the *chakras;* and the higher bodies, which he termed psychic and noetic bodies through which the soul or conscious spirit work.

In the last years of his life, seekers of the truth from all over the world came to Stoa in Strovolos to hear his lectures and/or seek healing. Daskolos died peacefully in Cyprus, his native land, in 1995.

Sharing the Inheritance

The following beautiful story in many ways encapsulates the nearly two thousand years of contemplative practice in the Christian tradition. It crosses over continents and embraces every generation of those who have been touched by this inner radiance.

> Once a monk reflected, "I am a monk myself, and the one question I really wanted to ask was, "What is a monk?" When, I finally myself, I

received for an answer a most peculiar question from my inner voice: "Do you mean in the daytime or at night?" Now what could that mean?

When I didn't answer, the voice picked it up again, "A monk, like everyone else, is a creature of contraction and expansion. During the day he is contracted—behind his cloister walls, dressed in a habit like all the others, doing the routine things you expect a monk to do. At night he expands. The walls cannot contain him. He moves through the world and he touches the stars." "Ah," I thought, "poetry." To bring him down to earth I began to ask, "Well, during the day, in his REAL body...."

"Wait," the voice responded, "that's the difference between us and you. You people regularly assume that the contracted state is the real body. It is real, in a sense. But in this world we tend to start from the other end, the expanded state. The daytime state we refer to as the 'body of fear.' And whereas you tend to judge a monk by his decorum during the day, we tend to measure a monk by the number of persons he touches at night and the number of stars."[74]

"I am the light of the world," proclaimed Jesus (John 8:12); yet he also declared to his disciples, "You are the light of the world" (Matthew 5:14). This seemingly paradoxical set of affirmations actually holds the key to the heart of mystical Christianity. Christ, in oneness with God the Father (John 10:30), manifests the divine light in his own life. And yet those who embrace his wisdom teachings—who abide in him, as he abides in them (John 15:4), share in that same divine light—a light that mystics, from the apostles and the Desert Fathers and Mothers, to Hildegard of Bingen to Francis of Assisi, to St. Teresa of Avila, to George Fox, to Thomas Merton and Daskalos, have all recognized within themselves. Every generation since Christ has, with God's grace, had those who responded to St. Paul's call in his letter to the Colossian—to "share in the inheritance of the saints in the light" (Colossians 1:12).

Guidelines at the Heart of the Teachings

1. Seen on a mystical/esoteric level, Christ's message is an invitation for all people to acknowledge their own divinity. *We are created in the image and likeness of God.*

2. Christ's teachings alter the normal patterns of power and control in the human ego, to create the space for the light of God to shine within. *Become like a little child: Allow the light to shine within you.*

3. Foundational truths emerge: Love is light, and light is love. *Love God with all your heart, mind, soul, and strength; and love your neighbor as yourself.*

4. Christ's instructions to "judge not" and to "love your enemies" are invitations to embrace a non-dual consciousness, where binary categories such as good/evil, spirit/matter, male/female, and light/darkness are transcended. *Enter the Heart of Christ, and embrace the love of God for all sentient beings.*

5. Hildegard of Bingen saw that the light is a "living light." *The radiance of the mystical experience is an encounter with the life-giving energy of eternity.*

6. Every human being is "shining like the sun"—only we just don't see it. *Contemplation/meditation is learning a new, higher way of seeing: to see as the mystics see.*

7. Christian contemplatives today engage in deep and rewarding interfaith and inter-spiritual exploration. The closer we come to the center, the less separation there is between the paths. *All faiths are facets of One Truth.*

A Contemplative Practice

Commune With God. *Commune with God's Light every day for God is light, life and love.*

Each religious and spiritual tradition has emphasized the vital importance of meditation as a means to connect with God. The power of sitting in silence every day is the bedrock upon which the edifice of spirituality is built. Jesus's powerful words should be enshrined in our hearts, "Take heed that the light within you be not darkness." Make it our sacred duty to spend time connecting to this eternal Light every day. Even if we can only devote 15 minutes a day, we should make it a habit. Gradually over time we can increase it.

- Begin by committing at least 15 minutes every day to meditation.
- Gradually increase the length of your daily practice.
- Extend by going on periods of retreat.
- Finally, remain continuously in the "Light" at all times, even with eyes open.

Depiction of lights of six chakras in Hindu cosmology. *Chakra* in Sanskrit literally means "wheel," "disk" or "center." Chakra is a center of activity that receives, assimilates, and expresses life energy from the etheric body and transmits it to the physical body. There are six of these wheels stacked in a column of energy that spans from the base of the spine to the top of the head (Guda, Indri, Nabhi, Hriday, Kanth, Ajna). Each chakra is a cosmic lotus with a certain number of petals which contain the different consonants of the Sanskrit alphabet. Each chakra also possesses a specific color, element, has a presiding deity, and nourishes specific organs. Each controls specific functions of the body and includes visionary experiences of light (courtesy of Inner Traditions Publication rights, from the book *Chakras* by Harish Johari published by Inner Traditions).

CHAPTER THREE

Hinduism:
The Light That Illumines the Self

Atman is self-luminous, distinct from the five Coverings. It is changeless,
pure and ever blissful.

—Adi Shankara

The guru of all gurus, it is the self, it is the light that illumines the world
from within.

—Vasistha

The great 19th century sage/saint Sri Ramakrishna tells a story of one man who was about to cross the sea. A holy man named Bibhishana wrote Rama's name on a leaf, tied it in a corner of the traveler's garment, and said to him: "Don't be afraid. Have faith and walk on the water. But look here—the moment you lose faith, you will be drowned." The man set out on his journey, and began to walk across the surface of the ocean. Suddenly, he had an intense desire to see what was tied in his cloth. He opened it and found only a leaf with the name Rama written on it. "What is this?" he thought. "Just the name of Rama." As soon as doubt entered his mind, he sank under the water.[1]

For Sri Ramakrishna, the great sage of Calcutta, faith is not merely a matter of belief—it is the will of the spirit in action. To lose faith in the *Self* is to lose all. To know this Self is to know all. The essence of India's great mystical writings (such as the Vedas and the Upanishads) was knowledge of this eternal Self. For this reason the great Vedic sages perennially asked the question "What is that by knowing which everything else becomes known?" and in the same breath answered their own question, "It is the Self." This "Self" is none other than the eternal, unborn, ever-living consciousness that is the essence of Truth no matter what name we may choose to call it.

Over the millennia, the Indian subcontinent has witnessed the birth of many of the world's great religions. The term Hinduism broadly applies to an extraordinarily varied system of religious and spiritual beliefs and practices that has its roots in the five-thousand-year-old Indo-European Vedic culture. Unlike other traditions, the religion did not have a single founder or historical beginning. It is thus not easy to define the historic "mother" of these traditions, for Hinduism encompasses not only a religion, but also the broader culture and way(s) of life of roughly one of every six persons in today's world. And of the roughly billion people who ascribe to the many varieties of Hindu religious expression, over 90% live in the subcontinent of India.

Overview

The Indo-European migration from Central Asia into Northern India, and the subsequent development of their religious/spiritual life, found its first expression within the Vedas and the Upanishads. As the wellsprings for India's greatest spiritual philosophies, the Upanishads provide the earliest reservoir for what the writer Aldous Huxley coined the world's "perennial philosophy." Both the Vedic and Upanishadic scriptures were rooted and grew from the core realization of an absolute luminous Brahman (supreme reality) manifesting as primordial Light and Sound (*Jyoti* and *Sruti*). The Self or *atman* was none other than this self-same luminous consciousness animating all creation.

The esoteric teachings found in the *Yoga Sutras of Patanjali* (250–400 CE) later became the basic underpinnings of the practice and philosophy of yoga (which encompasses spiritual as well as physical exercises and practices). Patanjali's aphoristic classic not only provided the philosophic rationale, but also a highly refined practical approach to the accomplishment of the inner ascension leading to *samadhi* (the unity of the Self with Brahman). The system of yoga that he advocated was further developed and compartmentalized in the illuminating dialogue between Arjuna and Lord Krishna in the great classic, the *Bhagavad Gita (Song of God)*, written some time between the fifth and second century BCE.

Patanjali's Yoga Sutras provides the philosophic basis for much of what later became incorporated into the yogic tradition, which has continued to be codified and developed through to the modern era. Throughout its long history, the core as well as the fruit of yogic practice was a vision of the Self, world, and consciousness as seamless, procreative eternal Light (*Jyoti prajanaman*).

The rise of early Kashmiri Shaivism (300–400 CE) and the early Alvars and Nath traditions (600–700 CE) set the stage for the great philosophic thinkers and yogic sages of the early and late medieval period (700–1100 CE). From approximately the late 1270s through the early 1700s emerged the *Bhakti* movement, which reoriented Indian spirituality toward a heartfelt devotional and egalitarian ethos.

Great luminaries of the 19th and 20th centuries include Sri Ramakrishna (1857–1886), Sri Aurobindo (1872–1950), Sri Ramana Maharshi (1879–1950), and Paramahansa Yogananda (1893–1952). While each in their own way refined and added important insights into the fundamental practice and approaches of Hindu spirituality, their common goal and theological core remained essentially nondualist: affirming a single universal consciousness beyond all manifestations of duality.

Early Beginnings: Vedas and Upanishads

The luminous Brahman dwells in the cave of the heart and is known to move there. It is the great support of all; for in It is centered everything that moves, breathes and blinks.[2] (Mundaka Upanishad, 2.ii)

Long before the common era, the Sanskrit-speaking Indo-Aryans migrated south from Central Asia through Afghanistan to northern India, settling in the fertile lands of the Punjab. This process took place over many centuries. The only source of information about this migration is found in the religious texts known collectively as the Vedas (knowledge). In contrast with the highly developed civilization that had developed earlier in the Indus Valley whose spirituality was oriented around the Mother Goddess cults, the Indo-Aryan male deities and the hymns that celebrated them took place in a cosmos convulsed by intense conflict.

The second millennium BCE of the Vedic period was a period of great transition. But in its later stages, a spiritual genius began to emerge that inspired the collection of 1,028 texts and poems that became known as the Rig Veda. Known as the *shruti* ("that which is heard"), the Rig Veda was said to be revealed to the great *rishis,* the seers and poets of antiquity. The rishis developed the ability to receive inspired words, and in experiencing inner voices, developed techniques of concentration that enabled them to penetrate the subconscious mind. The texts were transmitted orally from generation to generation with considerable accuracy. The Indo-Aryans regarded sound as sacred, and when people listened to the recitations, they felt connected to the divine power.

However, the rishis were only a tiny minority within the Indo-Aryan community. On the brink of the Axial Age (a period of significant religious/spiritual transformation, the Indo-Aryans began to explore the religious life of the individual with longstanding implications. "The Aryans developed the idea of Brahman, the supreme reality..., a power that was higher, deeper, and more basic than the gods, a force that held all the disparate elements of the universe together, and stopped them all from fragmenting."[3] Indian visionaries, in drawing upon the yet deeper wisdom found in the Upanishads, helped usher in the Axial Age in India, beginning around the ninth century BCE. This time of profound religious and cultural transformation greatly influenced the subsequent rise of both the Hindu and Buddhist traditions.

No one knows specifically when the Upanishads were composed or by whom. Traditional Indian scholars generally date them about 1300 BCE, while modern scholars believe them to be compiled around 800 BCE. The word *Upanishad* suggests "sitting down near to." The gurus (teachers) would impart their mystically inclined teachings to a small group of eager students who sat at their feet to imbibe esoteric knowledge, not just conceptually, but also often experientially.

Perhaps for the first time, human beings were systematically becoming aware of the deeper layers of human consciousness. After the Vedic period, the Upanishads were the wellsprings of India's great spiritual philosophies. Inherent in this understanding is the recognition, born of direct personal experience, that a spark of Godhead resides in every living creature, and that this recognition is fundamental to humans manifesting their full potentiality.

Historian of religions Mircea Eliade (1907–1986) discerned elemental timeless patterns of spiritual life in Indian culture. He encapsulated his understanding of Indian spirituality as an inner mystic Light:

> Pure being, the ultimate reality, can be known particularly through an experience of pure Light; the process of the cosmic revelation ultimately consists of a series of luminous manifestations, and cosmic reabsorption repeats the manifestation of these different colored lights... Those who have reached the highest stage of spirituality have realized or at least approached the condition of a liberated one or Buddha—are also capable of giving out the light.[4]

It was this same eternal light that was not only the basis of all realization, but also the fundamental underlying reality of the manifested universe. The great sages summarized the essence of their exhaustive researches in a profound statement: *Aham Brahma Asmi* or "I am that."

In his text *Lila*, A. K. Coomaraswamy (1877–1947) traced the meaning of the Sanskrit word *lila* (e.g., cosmic play) to the root *lelay*, meaning to flame, sparkle, or shine. The cosmic lila embodied the shimmering, sparkling, spontaneous, and liberated play of the Absolute. The great Indian saint and poet Kabir (ca. 1440–ca. 1518) described lila as the cosmic dance of the absolute. Paradoxically, lila was not only the supreme manifestation of the luminous absolute, but also a prison house that kept seekers from leaving (to attain liberation). So long as the individual soul identified itself with the passing conditioned reality, it remained entangled in the web of *maya* or illusion. Only by reconnecting itself to the pure light of consciousness, which Coomaraswamy spoke of as the sacred sound *Shabda*, could the soul free itself.[5]

The Vedas (1500–1000 BCE) and Upanishads (700–400 BCE): India's Scriptural Light

The ancient Vedas contain the plea, "May I reach that Light on reaching which one attains freedom from fear" (Rig Veda 2.27) Eliade notes that the Upanishads, which are replete with quotes about inner Light, "insist" upon the theme that "being manifests itself by pure Light, and that man receives knowledge and being through experience of this supernatural Light."[6] Indian spiritual literature consistently holds the idea that this Light is essentially creative and generative, e.g., "Light is procreation" (*Jyoti prajanaman*, also referred to as *Nada* or *Udgit* in Sanskrit.)

In the Brihadaranyaka Upanishad 4.3.7, the atman is identified as "the person here who is the knower among the senses, the light within the heart *Antar Jyoti*," also translated as Inner Light. But this Self or atman is in fact part of the Supreme light of lights. The same text (2.2.4) also affirms "In the highest golden sheath/Is Brahman, without stain without parts/Brilliant is It, the light of lights—/That which knowers of the Self (atman) do know."[7] The Chandogya Upanishad says, "The light that shines beyond this heaven, beyond all, in the highest worlds beyond which there are none higher, is truly the same light that shines within the person."

The Shvetashvatara Upanishad (2.11) reports that "In deep meditation aspirants may see forms like snow or smoke. They may feel a strong wind blowing or a wave of heat. They may see within them more and more light: fireflies, lightning, sun, or moon. These are signs that one is far on the path to Brahman." The Nada Bindu Upanishad affirms "That which is beyond these (viz.), Para-Brahman which is beyond (the above Matras), the pure, the all-pervading, beyond Kalas, the ever resplendent and the source of all Jyoti (Light) should be known."[8]

The Upanishads contain lists of the specific forms in which the Light will appear to one along the way. The Shvetasvatara Upanishad notes the "preliminary forms of Brahman" that reveal themselves during the course of spiritual development as "mist, smoke, sun, fire, wind, phosphorescent insects, lightning, crystal, and moon."[247] The Mandala Brahmana Upanishad lists "the form of a star, a diamond mirror, the orb of the full moon, the sun at midday, a circle of fire, a crystal, a dark circle, a point (*bindu*), a finger (*kela*), a star (*nakstra*), the sun, a lamp, the eye, the radiance of the sun and the nine jewels."[9]

Within the context of the Brihadaranyaka Upanishad, Yajnavalkya, the personal philosopher of the legendary King Janaka, was a leading exponent of the new Upanishadic spirituality. He became convinced that at the core of the human person there was an immortal spark that was of the same essence as the immortal Brahman. He taught that through the physical eyes and ears, "You cannot see the Seer [the Atman] who does the seeing. You can't hear the Hearer who does the hearing...."[10]

One day a line of questioning King Janaka posed to his mentor sparked a particularly deep inquiry. It started with the significance of the ritual fire ceremony and moved on to "what is the light of man?" The king then moved to a layered line of questioning as it developed to include the light emanating from the sun, moon, and hearth, and then from within, asking:

> J: Yajnavalkya, what is the light of man?
>
> Y: The sun is our light, for by that light we sit, work, go out, and come back.
>
> J: When the sun sets, what is the light of man?
>
> Y: The moon is our light, for by that light we sit, work, go out, and come back.
>
> J: When the sun sets, Yajnavalkya, and the moon sets, what is the light of man?
>
> Y: Fire is our light, for by that we sit, work, go out, and come back.
>
> J: When the sun sets, Yajnavalkya, and the moon sets, and the fire goes out, what is the light of man?
>
> Y: Then speech is our light, for by that we sit, work, go out, and come back. Even though we cannot see our own hand in the dark, we can hear what is said and move toward the person speaking.
>
> J: When the sun sets, Yajnavalkya, and the moon sets, and the fire goes out and no one speaks, what is the light of man?
>
> Y: The Self indeed is the light of man, your majesty, for by that we sit, work, go out and come back.

The king replies, "Who is that self?" Yajnavalkya responds eloquently:

> The Self, pure awareness, shines as the light within the heart, only seeming to think, seeming to move, the Self neither sleeps nor wakes nor dreams...the human being has two states of consciousness: one in this world, the other in the next. But there is a third state between them, not unlike the world, in which we are aware of both worlds, with their

sorrows and joys...in this intermediate state he makes and dissolves impressions by the light of Self.[11]

It is said of these states of consciousness that in the dreaming state, when one is sleeping, the shining Self, who never dreams, which is ever awake, watches by his own light the dreams woven out of past deeds and present desires. In the dreaming state, when one is sleeping, the shining Self keeps the body alive with the vital forces of prana.[12]

Vedas: Inner Sound and Unstruck Melody

The Vedas also contain a rich concept of the nature of Inner Sound. The great scholar and mystic Sant Kirpal Singh opens his study *Naam or Word* with the following quote from the Vedas:

> *Prajapatir vai idam-agre asit*
> *Tasya vak dvitiya asit*
> *Vak vai Paramam Brahma*

"In the beginning was *Prajapati* (the Creator), With Him was the *Vak* (the Word), And the Vak (the Word) was verily the Supreme Brahma."[13]

In the article, "The Vedic Conception of Sound in Four Features," Jahnava Nitai Das outlines the rich teaching of the Vedic texts on the nature of Sound.[14] He quotes the Srimad Bhagavatam (3.26.33), which defines Sound by noting that, "Persons who are learned and who have true knowledge define sound as that which conveys the idea of an object, indicates the presence of a speaker and constitutes the subtle form of ether." The speaker in the higher, inner, nonmaterial forms of Sound is understood to be Absolute Brahman communicating with the individual soul (*jiva*). Sound is understood to have an ultimately nonmaterial source, and to be present in four major metaphysical forms, which correspond to the four great realms of existence or planes of consciousness:

> Para represents the transcendental consciousness. Pashyanti represents the intellectual consciousness. Madhyama represents the mental consciousness. And Vaikhari represents the physical consciousness. These states of consciousness correspond with the four states known technically as jagrat, svapna, susupti, and turiya—or the wakeful state, the dreaming state, the dreamless state, and the transcendental state.[15]

Das notes that, "one's experience of sound depends upon the refinement of one's consciousness" and "it takes a realized consciousness to experience the full range of sound, the full range of existence." Indian sages understood knowledge to have two forms: *varnamuk* or outer word or sound, and *dhunamuk* or the inner word or sound. These forms were also categorized as *apara vidya* or outer knowledge and *para vidya* or inner knowledge. Only the latter could grant spiritual salvation and was in fact the only true knowledge, all else being transient, impermanent, and without lasting value. This knowledge was gained through direct revelation and contact with the inner sound or Shabd, which was hidden within the self.

In the Rig Veda, the higher forms of Shabd (Shabda) are described as *guha*, meaning hidden within the self, as opposed to externally manifested speech (*laukika bhasha*).

The "Science of Sound" present in the Vedas is also explained in the Pancharatrik text known as Lakshmi-tantra as follows:

> Seated in the area...with effulgence equal to the rising of millions of suns, fires and moons. Like a wheel from the adhara becoming the sounds known as santa, pashyati, madhyama. Reaching the position of vaikhari, there situated in eight places, viz., the throat etc. Being the mother of all sounds I bestow enjoyments like a cow.[16]

The Upanishads contain similarly rich teachings on inner sound. In the Hamsa Naad Upanishad we find "Meditation on Naad or the Sound Principle is the royal road to salvation." The Nada Bindu Upanishad (31–36) provides specific meditation instructions and a detailed phenomenology of the Inner Sound:

31. The Yogin being in the Siddhasana (posture) and practicing the Vaishnavi-Mudra, should always hear the internal sound through the right ear.

32. The sound which he thus practices makes him deaf to all external sounds. Having overcome all obstacles, he enters the Turiya state within fifteen days.

33. In the beginning of his practice, he hears many loud sounds. They gradually increase in pitch and are heard more and more subtly.

34. At first, the sounds are like those proceeding from the ocean, clouds, kettle-drum and cataracts; in the middle (stage) those proceeding from Mardala (a musical instrument), bell and horn.

35. At the last stage, those proceeding from tinkling bells, flute, Vina (a musical instrument) and bees. Thus he hears many such sounds more and more subtle.

36. When he comes to that stage when the sound of the great kettle-drum is being heard, he should try to distinguish [the above] sounds more and more subtly.[17]

Introduction to Yoga: The Technology of Light

The Theophany of Krishna:
Yoga in the Bhagavad Gita (500–400 BCE)

Etymologically, yoga means a yoking and union, and connotes a binding to that which is Real. The practice of yoga as an inner, experiential means for seeking union within the Absolute predates the written history of the Indian subcontinent. The first cited usage of the term occurs in the Taittiriya Upanishad and, over the centuries, dozens of distinct schools and lineages proliferated with various teachings and inner technologies for approaching the divine.

The Bhagavad Gita (one of the most revered of Hindu sacred writings, which includes important teachings about yoga) steadfastly reaffirms the earlier Vedas' language of visionary and pure light (*Jyoti prajanaman*), especially the Lord Krishna's blazing appearance to Arjuna in the midst of this great philosophical treatise. Patanjali's aphoristic classic, the Yoga Sutras (250–400 CE), not only builds the entire philosophical system upon this inner Jyoti, but also develops it into a contemplative mystical science.

Perhaps the Hindu tradition's most renowned scripture, the Bhagavad Gita (literally, "song of the blessed One"), comprises the esoteric core of the Indian epic *Mahabharata*. Compiled several centuries before the common era by Vyasa, the Gita recounts events on the battlefield prior to the onset of the *Kurukshetra* war, pitting two sets of five half-brothers against each other to determine who would ascend to the throne of their dying father, the king.

The story commences with the young prince Arjuna brooding just before sunrise at the prospect of soon battling with his siblings. Seeking solace, he turns to his wise charioteer Krishna for counsel, in effect asking, "What should I do?" In response, Krishna speaks of universal duty and harmony, or *dharma*. He teaches Arjuna about the eternal atman, a spark or soul that, unlike the body, is eternal or immortal. Arjuna's problems, he states, come from mistaking the unreal for the real.

This confusion leaves Arjuna stupefied, unable to act in the world he would do better to transcend. Krishna instructs him that through inaction the universal dharmic order would come to a state of imbalance, and instead urges him to do his duty to his utmost, completely unattached to the fruits of his actions and keeping his mind always focused on the Divine

To deepen his teachings, Krishna discourses on various yogas, or modes for reuniting the Self with the Lord and returning to the Real. Among the most important are *karma* (service through action), *bhakti* (loving devotion), *jnana* (wise discrimination, cognate with gnosis), and *dhyana* (meditative absorption).

In chapter 6 of the Gita, Krishna imparts meditation instructions to Arjuna so that he might conquer the mind and attain oneness with the Lord:

He should fix for himself
a firm seat in a pure place,
neither too high nor too low.
Covered in cloth, deerskin or grass,
he should focus his mind and restrain his senses;
sitting on that seat, he should practice
discipline or the purification of the self.
He should keep his body, head,
and neck aligned, immobile, steady;
he should gaze at the tip of his nose
and not let his glance wander.[19]

The self tranquil, his fear dispelled,
firm in his vow of celibacy, his mind restrained,
let him sit with discipline,
his thought fixed on me, intent on me.[20]

Krishna counsels moderation in daily living, and responds to a doubtful Arjuna that training the mind, while difficult, is not impossible with "regular practice and detachment." Here Krishna employs the simile of Light, telling Arjuna:

like a lamp sheltered
from the wind is the simile recalled
for a man of discipline, restrained in thought
and practicing self–discipline."
When his thought ceases,
checked by the exercise of discipline,
he is content within the self,
seeing the self through himself.[21]

Here *light* describes the essential nature of mind, but in the presence of the fierce wind of undisciplined thoughts (*vrittis,* or whirls in Patanjali), this light flickers and dims. Conversely, then, we see that when the mind is stilled, there flows forth a great Light, which is the true nature of reality.

Later in their exchange (chapter 11), Arjuna, grateful for the spiritual discourse and instruction, says that he wishes for more. He cries out, "If you think

I can see it,/ Reveal to me/ your immutable self,/ Krishna, Lord of discipline."[22] Krishna responds, calling upon Arjuna to "Behold a million divine forms, with an infinite variety of color and shape...; behold the entire cosmos turning within my body." However, as Krishna points out, "But you cannot see me/with your own eye/I will give you a divine eye to see/ the majesty of my discipline (majestic power)."

Krishna then grants Arjuna a spiritual vision of his divine form.

If the light of a thousand suns
were to rise in the sky at once,
it would be like the light of
that great spirit.
Arjuna saw all the universe
in its many ways and parts,
standing as one in the body
of the god of gods.[23]

Arjuna reports on his vision:

I see you blazing
through the fiery rays
of your crown, mace and discus,
hard to behold
in the burning light
of fire and sun
that surrounds
your measureless presence.[24]

Arjuna describes the burning light that surrounds Krishna's majestic presence as measureless. While Arjuna's higher self longs for the unity and reality of the vision, his egoic self is not ready to embrace this divine unity and so recoils away.[25]

Ultimately, the Gita echoes the perennial wisdom: stripped of illusion, the true form of the Lord, who is the essence of all, is the resplendent Light of a thousand suns. And this Light, having taken on the human voice of Krishna, calls us to a life of wisdom and service through loving and detached surrender. Facing this Light, of course, requires the courage, dedication, focus, and surrender of a warrior like Arjuna.

Patanjali's Yoga Sutras: Light When the Mind Is Still (250–400 CE)

The authorship of the Yoga Sutras is traditionally attributed to Patanjali, of whose life very little is known. Scholars estimate that he lived and compiled the sutras around 250 BCE. The Yoga Sutras has a condensed tone and structure starkly different from the Gita's conversational feel. The 196 aphorisms read and function philosophically, reminiscent of Western classics like Euclid's *Elements* or Wittgenstein's *Tractatus*.

Just as Euclid commences by postulating the first principle, "a straight line segment can be drawn joining any two points," Patanjali opens with a terse and profound four-word summary of the yogic path, *"yoga shcitta-vritti-nirodhah"* (I.2). This translates as, "Yoga is the restriction of the fluctuations of consciousness." This is the heart of his whole system: Still and restrict the *prakriti,* which comprises all physical and mental activity, and you will achieve superconscious identity with the overself, known as *purusha.*

The foremost block to entering this deep stillness is the mercurial nature of the mind. Patanjali calls these seemingly inevitable perturbations *vrittis,* psychic whirls or vortices that turn without beginning or end. Vrittis are the habituated, reactive, and conditioned mental thought loops acquired through countless lifetimes of mental activity. They are the "tape loops" that have become ingrained neural pathways in our brains, spoken of by neuroscientists such as Dr. Rudolph Tanzi. Methods for achieving freedom from these ingrained, habituated thought forms or "whirling mental flow" are detailed in the second section of the sutras, the *Sadhana Pada.*

Here Patanjali discusses *kriya yoga* (action yoga, called karma yoga in the Gita and elsewhere) and *ashtanga yoga* (eightfold or eight limbed yoga). The eight enumerated limbs of the yogic tree are: *yamas* (social precepts), *niyamas* (personal precepts), *asana* (physical pose), *pranayama* (breath control), *pratyahara* (sensory withdrawal), *dharana* (concentration, often at the point mid eyebrows), *dhyana* (absorption), and *samadhi* (enlightenment).

The yogic recipe for spiritual development is universal, similar to the wisdom of other traditions: Live an ethical life, sound of mind and body, and through deep concentration withdraw your attention (sensory awareness) from the perceptual and cognitive flow of the world, or five outer senses and intellect. Then through intense concentration on the dawning light of consciousness enter the luminous worlds of spirit accessible from within the temple of the human body.

Patanjali teaches that those who achieve this withdrawal enter a state that is "sorrowless and illuminating" (I.36). Indeed, "through performance of the members of yoga (e.g. the eight arms of the Ashtanga path) and with the dwindling of impurity, there comes about a radiance of gnosis." (II.28). In this condition, "transcending the external and internal sphere…the covering of the inner light disappears" (II.51–2).

This is a common theme in mysticism. Light is the essential nature of the Self, but it is "covered" by the incessant thinking of the mind. These coverings, known as "veils" in Sufism and *koshas* in Vedanta, are like blankets thrown on a lamp. They obscure the light, which shines ceaselessly; indeed, the light reappears as soon as the coverings are removed. Five different types of koshas have been identified, each in turn with five subtle coverings of their own—making a total of 25 coverings called *prakrittis.* These include: the sense of ego (*ahankar*), intellect (*buddhi*), the three modes of activity (*gunas*), mind (*chit*), and five senses (indriyas). These are further divided between the five gross elements (*bhutas*), five subtle elements (*tanmantras*), five cognitive elements (*jnanedriyas*), and five instruments of action (*karmendriyas*). All of these must be removed, or more precisely, transcended, in the aspirant's upward journey. In practical terms the mind, intellect, and outer five senses must all be firmly under the control of the aspirant in order to redirect his attention inward toward its Source.

Thus Patanjali affirms as foundational to the yogic tradition the perennial truth that obscured beneath the spiraling commotion of the mind lies a field of sanctifying divine luminosity. As the yogic canon developed over the next two millennia, literature emerged with a much more detailed treatment of this theme.

Hatha Yoga: Lighting the Adamantine Body (200–1700 CE)

A recent *Yoga Journal* poll indicated that upward of 15 million Americans practice some form of hatha yoga, with 16% (over 2 million people) indicating that they did so to pursue a path of spiritual enlightenment.[26] As the most familiar type of yoga practiced in the west, hatha yoga stresses diligent work with the body's posture and breath as a spiritual and physical discipline. In Sanskrit, *ha* means "sun" and *tha* means "moon," and the combined word *hatha* means "forceful." Thus, hatha yoga is the focused practice of affecting transcendent energetic union in the microcosm of the yogi. It is the spiritual marriage between the solar/masculine and lunar/feminine energies within the self.

Understanding the character of this union, however, requires a more holistic view of the human body than the mechanistic conception of the body, common in the West. In the hatha yoga tradition, scholar Georg Feuerstein tells us, the "masters aspired to create a transubstantiated body, which they called 'adamantine' (*vajra*) or 'divine' (*daiva*)—a body not made of flesh, but of immortal substance, of Light."[27]

The *Yoga Bija* states that "the fire of yoga (tapas) gradually bakes the body." Yogis enact this bodily roasting through breath restraint (*pranayama*), intentional posture (*asana*), locking, constricting, and releasing of breath or muscles (*bandhas*), and various purification rituals involving inner and outer cleansing with water and medicinal substances such as turmeric. These disciplines aim to bring the normally dispersed, unbalanced, and sapped subtle energies of the body into dynamic, centralized alignment. This alignment, in turn, focuses and concentrates the attention or "Self" upon the nondual reality of light within the subtle body.

In hatha yoga, the subtle or esoteric body is conceived essentially as a system facilitating the flow of subtle energy, somewhat similar to the role of the circulatory system in the physical body. The further consciousness retreats from the Source, the more it is dulled by its contact with matter. As the soul becomes more and more cut off from its essential nature as Light, it begins to experience ever-greater levels of lethargy and disillusionment. Speaking metaphorically, such a lethargic soul is like a spiritual amputee devoid of life and love.

Central to Indian esoteric physiology are the six *chakras* (literally, "rotating disks") that serve as spinning powerhouses of light, pulling subtle energy into the physical body from the higher planes. These occur at the: brow (*ajna*), throat (*vishuddha*), heart (*anahata*), solar plexus (*manipura*), generative region (*svadhisthana*), and root (*muladhara*). The chest, throat, and region between the eyebrows are identified as regions of common knots or locks (*granthi*), which prevent the free flowing of spiritual energy.

The chakras receive energy from the divine and transmit it through the body through a series of *nadis* (literally, "tube, pipe") that function as the veins and capillaries to the subtle body. Three nadis are particularly important: The *ida* functions primarily on the left in a lunar/feminine/cooling capacity; the *pingala* functions primarily on the right as a solar/masculine/heating influence; and the *sushumna* runs through the spine as the balance and transcendence of the polarity.

The ida and pingala encircle the spine in a helical fashion. The spine, therefore, is energetically polarized. The dynamic Shakti energy coils at the base of the spine, and the static energy of Shiva resides at the ajna chakra. It is here at the eye chakra where the rivulet streams of the ida and the pingala nadis converge that energies from the higher inner planes can be contacted.

A foundational hatha yoga text, the *Hatha Yoga Pradipika* (1500 CE), describes the importance of balancing these subtle energy channels. The term *pradipika* comes from the Sanskrit verb "to flame forth," as the goal of the yogic disciplines is to facilitate the emergence of inner radiant fire within the consciousness of the seeker. It poses this question: If "the breath does not pass through the middle channel (sushumna), owing to the impurities of the nadis, how can success be attained?" (II.4) In other words, the nadis fail to conduct the flow of divine energy into the physical body when impeded by the gross and subtle impurities of greed, lust, anger, violence, and ego. As a result of these imbalances, the body experiences various degrees of ill health or disease.

Latent at the base of the spine is a powerful spiritual energy known as the *kundalini* (literally, "coiled"). This energy is often depicted as a snake or serpent, suggesting an archetypal resonance with the Western medical symbol of the staff of Asclepius. The *Pradipika* notes, "When the sleeping kundalini awakens by favor of a guru, then all the lotuses (in the six chakras or centers) and all the knots are pierced through" (iii.2). When this occurs, and a subtle energy balance and ordering has been achieved among the nadis (subtle nerves) and the granthi have been dissolved, then the yogi has fully prepared the body to be a vessel for the light. To facilitate this balancing, the *Pradipika* offers these instructions.

> Fix the gaze on the light (seen on the tip of the nose) and raise the eyebrows a little, with the mind contemplating as before (in the Śambhavî Mudrâ, that is, inwardly thinking of Brahma, but apparently looking outside). (iv.38)

> With steady calm mind and half closed eyes, fixed on the tip of the nose, stopping the Idâ and the Pingalâ without blinking, he who can see the light which is the all, the seed, the entire brilliant, great Tatwama, approaches Him, who is the great object. What is the use of more talk? (iv.40)

> The seat of Śiva is between the eyebrows, and the mind becomes absorbed there. This condition (in which the mind is thus absorbed) is known as Tûrya, and death has no access there. (iv.47)

The *Shiva Samhita* (c. 1500 CE) is one of the most philosophical of the hatha yoga treatises. It postulates Absolute reality as Brahman and the Atman as its individualized form. Human beings experience the atman as the self, and as a self-luminous entity or light. This same eternal Light (Jyoti) not only manifests as the conscious Self, but also as the transcendent truth behind the many veils of darkness and duality. "The entire universe along with the Lord is pervaded on all sides by the One—devoid of the duality—Complete Atman which is existence, knowledge, consciousness and bliss" (1.53).[28] The Atman is none other than the Light of awareness and consciousness itself. "The Self–illuminating is one of which there is no illuminator. Since Atman is of the nature of light, it is self luminous" (1.54). He who attains this existence revels in light. "The great yogi

beholds the flame as pure as the purest mountain. He himself becomes the pro-
tector of that flame merely by virtue of the power of his practice" (5.69). All the
tantras (a collection of Hindu sacred writings) discuss this same great light. By
contemplating it, the yogi is "sure to attain supreme perfection" (5.130). Related
to this is the practice of nada yoga that destroys the darkness of the world and
dissolves the consciousness in the highest state. This yoga manifests not only
the experience of light, but also of sacred sounds like a ringing bell and roaring
thunder. "In this way, as the practice progresses, the sound resembling that of
a bell etc, (is produced) which destroys the darkness in the form of the world.
Later the sound resembling roaring clouds is manifested" (5.43). Further on, the
treatise explicitly describes the internal practice of the Jyoti meditation using
what is termed the third or inner eye. "When (a yogi) meditates upon the cavity
of the skull (in the middle of his forehead) called *rudraksa* (the third eye of Siva)
he then perceives a flame brilliant like a mass of lightning" (5.62).[29]

Gheranda Samhita, the latest of the yogic manuals (1700 CE) reflects the
same grounding and practice of the inner music. "In the resonance (of the
unstruck sound) is a light and in the light is the mind. In it the mind attains
absorption" (iiv.77).[30]

Other Yogas

Although the *Yoga Sutras*, the *Gheranda Samhita,* and *Pradipika* were the
most prominent and well known yogic texts, other yogas developed over the
course of centuries. Practitioners of Agni or fire yoga experienced the same
internal light and inner music within the chakras. "There were many experiences
of sensing light energy in the centers, and radiating out, becoming flaming con-
suming fire...I could hear soft crackling sounds."[31]

Laya yoga, a Shaivic (associated with the god Shiva) system of yoga based on
focusing the mind in specific ways on the chakras, is a practice which can induce
kundalini energy to rise. Laya means "dissolution" and refers to the melting of
all the impressions that have accumulated throughout one's lifetime(s), thereby
liberating one's mind from all obstacles and limitations and freeing one from the
holds of karma. This also causes the seeds of habitual inclinations (*samskaras*)
to be dissolved and turned into primal energy. Laya yoga is usually called the
yoga of absorption, or absorbing the lower nature by the higher spiritual forces.

The *Vasistha Maha Ramayana* or *Yoga Vasistha*, one of the earliest Sanskrit
Vedantic writings, contains a dialogue between Vasistha, the great sage, and his
student Rama, hero of the epic Ramayana. Vasishtha instructs Rama to "behold
the self-luminous self which pervades everything"[32] and notes that the Light is

"the guru of all gurus, it is the self, it is the light that illumines the world from within."[33]

The *Yoga Vasistha* teaches that the "inner light itself is regarded as self-knowledge by the holy ones: and the experience of it is an integral part of self-knowledge and non-different from it. He who has self-knowledge is for ever immersed in the experience of it."[34] It invites the aspirant Rama to "abandon the false and fanciful notion of the ego-sense within your own heart. When this ego-sense is dispelled the supreme light of self-knowledge will surely shine in your heart."[35]

While most of the yogic texts begin with various different asanas and purifications, their fundamental premise remains identical. The primordial *atman,* or the Self, is the underlying reality. The atman is not other than Brahman and is the sole existence and reality. Only ignorance creates the seeming duality within the manifest cosmos. The great yogis and yogiswaras proclaimed in one voice OM, TAT, SAT: "Brahman is the absolute reality, knowledge and bliss, that you are."

Most classical yoga texts also emphasize the necessity of a competent guru in assisting those who want to deepen their yoga practice. Serious students should seek such a teacher to help them access the path of experiencing inner light and sound. Paradoxically, it is not the student who finds the guru, but the guru who finds the disciple. A Hindu proverb maintains, "The guru appears when the disciple is ready." Those interested in the deepest aspects of what yoga has to offer will in the fullness of time be led to an experienced master, to support the student in the ultimate goal of awakening to the source of divine love and self-understanding.

Sri Shankara:
Apostle of Radical Nondualism (788–821 CE)

According to Hindu legend, Hiranyagarbha first taught yoga or the Divine way, but his successors Gaudapada and Patanjali developed it into a regular science. As Sant Kirpal Singh notes, "all true yoga begins with dualistic assumption but ends up in a non-dualistic one."[36] Over time the essential teachings of Patanjali and others became mired in confusion and controversy and their simple essence was lost. Around the turn of the ninth century CE, a great spiritual adept named Shankara (788–821 CE) arose who reestablished the essence of the Advaita Vedanta or the philosophy of nondualism and forever changed the landscape of Indian spirituality.

Born of Brahman parents at Kaladi, a small village in western Malabar in southern India, by the age of ten Shankara was already a gifted prodigy endowed with amazing powers of reasoning, logic, and insight. After a period of intense inner search—and having found his teachers did not practice the lofty truths they preached—he sought permission to renounce all family connections and seek a life of complete renunciation. He persuaded his mother to let him take the monastic vow, promising that he would return to her before she died, and set out in quest of a realized teacher.

As legend has it, he met the great sage Gaudapada, a famous philosopher and seer, who had attained knowledge of the Reality. "Shankara asked the old man for initiation, but Gaudapada refused. He had made a vow to remain absorbed in union with Brahman. However, he sent the boy to his foremost disciple, Govindapada, who initiated and instructed him in meditation and whole process of yoga. Within a very short time, Shankara achieved mystical union.[37]

The next 20 years he spent teaching and reviving the ancient science of yoga and the true essence of Advaitism. By the time he passed on at the young age of 32, he had founded 10 monastic orders and many monasteries throughout India. This was the first time monasticism had been organized in India and Shankara's system still exists today and played a critical role in the final realization of the great 19th century sage of Dakshineshwar, Sri Ramakrishna.

Shankara reinterpreted the great scriptures in the light of nondualistic truth, showing they all spoke of one ultimate reality and that in the end the limitation of the dualistic approach would become apparent.[38] He regarded the so-called waking life of the individual as nothing but a dream—like any other dream, devoid of substance and reality. He argued that, as with any other dream, its unreality comes to our attention only when we awaken. The daily life of an individual is one in which the individual travels from limited relative consciousness (*jagrat*) to dream (*swapan*) and from dream to dreamless sleep (*sushupti*). These states are all relative in character and are impermanent. When an individual begins to ascend from these relative states through the practice of yoga to the states of pure consciousness, and then to cosmic consciousness and finally to super cosmic consciousness, the truth of their unreality becomes apparent. Shankara speaks of the one reality or power as "self-luminous and light" itself.

Oh Lord, dweller within;
You are the light
In the heart's lotus.
Om is our very self,
Om, the holiest word,
Seed and source of the scriptures.
Logic cannot discover

You, Lord but the yogis know you in meditation.
In you are all God's faces,
His forms and aspects,
In you also we find the guru.
In every heart you are
And if but once, only,
A man will open
His mind to receive you
Truly that man
Is free forever.[39]

The Self remains at the foundation of the ever-changing panorama of life. It is the ever unborn, eternally awake, the dreamless, and self-illumined essence. The Self is, by its very nature, a pure cognition distinct from the noncognition of the sleep state. Shankara sums up the essence of this philosophy in the following verse: "Brahman—the absolute existence, knowledge and bliss—is real. The universe is not real. Brahman and Atman (man's inner Self) are one."[40] In attempting to explain the nature of this Self or atman, Shankara insists that the Self is the knower of all states of consciousness—waking, dreaming, and dreamless sleep. His assertion that the atman is consciousness and is itself light, and not a reflector of light, forms the whole basis of nondualism.

> That reality sees everything by its own light. No one sees it. It gives intelligence to the mind and the intellect, but no one gives it light. That Reality pervades the universe, but no one penetrates it. It alone shines. The universe shines with its reflected light.[41]

Continuing, he elucidates the nature of this luminosity and its location in the universe: "Here, within this body, in the pure mind, in the secret chamber of intelligence, in the infinite universe within the heart, the Atman shines in its captivating splendor, like a noonday sun. By its light the universe is revealed."[42] This self-luminous light is both the material and subtle cause of the universe and of *maya*, the primal cause of illusion and ignorance. For Shankara, the Light of the Self is identical to the Light of the Brahman, which is its source and origin as well. It is ignorance or maya that has caused the self to identify with its own causes when it itself is its own cause and the source of all knowledge, consciousness, and bliss. Therefore to realize the Self is to realize the eternal unchanging nature of the Light that we are.

3000-2000 BCE

- Aryans enter northern India from central Asia, 2000-1000
- Rig Vedas ca. 1500 to ca.1000

1000-700 BCE

- Brahmanas 1000-700
- Aranyakas 800-700

300-1 BCE

- Emperor Ashoka, c. 304-232

100-400 CE

- Early Tantrism 300-400
- Yoga sutras Patanjali systematizes practice of yoga, c. 250-400

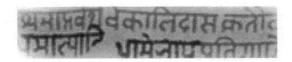

900-1200 CE

- Abhinavagupta ca. 970 - 1025
- Goraknath 11th century
- Ramanju 1017-1137
- Gita Govinda written 1180
- Madhava 1238-1369
- Nam Dev 1270 - 1350

1200-1500 CE

- Ramananda 1300-1400
- Lalleshwari 1320-1392
- Ravi Das 1450-1520
- Mirabai 1498-1547

700-500 BCE	500- 300 BCE
• *Upanishads (aka) Vedanta ca. 700-400* • *Mahavira ca. 527, founder of Jain religion* • *Ramayana and Mahabharata 500-400, Main texts of Hinduism* • *Bhagavad Gita, compiled by Vyasa, ca. 500-400*	• *Siddhartha Gautama 566-486, founder of Buddhism* • *Alexander the Great reaches northern India 400-300* 

400-600 CE	600-900 CE
• *Bhakti movement begins in South India, Alvars and Nyanmars 600-700*	• *Adi Shankara 788– 821 Main proponent of School of Non-dualism* • *Gaudapada 7th century* • *Bhagavata Purana written 900* • *Yoga Vasistha 5th - 14th century* • *Vasugupta, 860–925*

1500-1700 CE	1700-1900 CE
• *Tulsi Das 1532-1623* • *Dada Sahib 1544 - 1603* • *Hatha Yoga Pradipika 15th century* • *Shiva Samhita 15th century* • *Akbar the Great, 1542-1605,* • *Gheranda Samhita Late 17th century* • *Tulsi Sahib, 1763-1848*	• *Ram Mohan Roy* • *Sri Ramakrishna Paramahansa, 1834-1886, teaches "all religions are one"* • *Swami Vivekananda, 1863-1902*

1900-1950 CE	1950-2010 CE
. Mohandas K. Gandhi (Mahatma), 1869–1948 · Sri Aurobindo 1872 –1950 · Sri Ramana Maharshi, 1879 – 1950 · Paramahansa Yogananda, 1893–1952	. Dharmic Principles: the Swadhaya Movement, 1950s on · Hinduism increasingly spreads in West, 1950s on

Kashmir Shaivism: Shiva's "Magic"
(800–1200 CE)

The Non-dual (Advaita) Shaivism of Kashmir teaches that the Lord Shiva wishes to manifest the external world for the sole reason of (re)creating the possibility of finding himself and recognizing His own nature. Kashmir Shaivism sees the universe as a joyous game in which Lord Shiva projects his energy (*Shakti*) outward into an external world. In what is sometimes known as Shiva's "magic trick," the *jiva* (individual soul) must, in the words of scholar Paul-Eduardo Muller-Ortega, "play Shiva's game to its most serious and most hilarious conclusion."[43] This conclusion is the unmasking of the reality that it has been Shiva hiding himself from himself, and while hiding simultaneously standing in radically nondual relation to his creation, energy, and the individual soul.

The One Being of Shiva is understood as Pure Conscious Light, (*Prakasha*) and the universe is seen as a reflection or mirroring of this light. The counter-intuitive "trick" is that the object, light, mirror, and reflection are all absolutely identical, for there is no object outside of God consciousness. Particularly in the teachings on *Spanda,* the original deliberation of Godhead upon itself produces an emanation, a self-reflecting divine vibration of Light and Sound that undergoes multiple stages of involution and self-limitation before arriving at the material realm.

The ancient *Vijnana Bhairava Tantra,* first popularized by Paul Reps in his book *Zen Flesh, Zen Bones,* includes practices for contacting this Divine Light such as "Attention between Eyebrows, let mind be before thought. Let form fill with breath essence to the top of the head and there shower as light" and "Waking, sleeping, dreaming, Know you as light." It also includes practices on contacting the Inner Sound such as "stopping ears by pressing and...enter the sound" and "bathe in the center of sound, as in the continuous sound of a waterfall. Or, by putting the fingers in the ears, hear the sound of sounds."[44]

Later teachers of Kashmir Shaivism continue to emphasize these themes. For example, Vasugupta (860–925 CE), in the *Shiva Sutra,* says, "The enlightened adept is always awake; for him the second one [i.e., the world of duality] is a ray-of-light." The medieval Kashmiri woman Saint Lela (aka Lalleshwari, Laldyada, Lal Ded [1320–1392 CE]) wrote, "Concentrating on the om-sound, I made my body like blazing coal. Leaving behind the six crossroads, I traveled the path of Truth. And then I, Lallâ, reached the Abode of Light."[45] Muller-Ortega summarizes the Kashmir Shaiva experiences of Light:

> The primordial light is known by a great variety of terms in the non-dual Kashmir Shaiva tradition...The variety of words for light

employed by the Shaiva tradition may be thought to derive from the continuous attempt to describe the essentially indescribable contents of yogic experience which include great varieties of powerful and subtle phenomena of light.[46]

The Kashmiri sage Abhinavagupta (970–1025 CE) in his *Paratrishika-laghuvritti* outlines more specially the supreme light as the basis of all consciousness. When the moment of primal awakening arises and the heart is free from all defilements, it merges in the shining light that is the supreme Shiva. These teachings give a small taste of the internal experiences of the initiates of the secretive sects and sub-sects that comprise the Kashmir Shaivite tradition.

> Heart is called the place where there is repose in the pure light and pure consciousness...When the Heart is free of stains and a light occurs which illuminates the Supreme plane, by immersion in this shining light, one obtains identity with the Supreme Shiva, that is, with consciousness.[47]

The gleaming light of the heart activated by the practice of the mantra severs the knots of the heart and true knowledge of the Self is attained. Once released, however, this light can in no way be held back: It is unconcealable and unbounded. It begins to spread out from the inner reality of the Heart and invades the entire structure of finiteness. When this happens, it transforms the inertness of finitude into the vibrancy of life.[48]

The Early Bhakti Movement and the Light of Devotion (1200–1600 CE)

Namdev (ca. 1270–ca. 1350 CE) is one of the earliest Indian saints whose writings are available to us. Like most of the ancient Indian saints, very little survives which is indisputably his work. Over the centuries, his writings (and his life) have become shrouded in stories and legends to the point where it is difficult to separate fact from fantasy. According to a poem attributed to Namdev, he was born on October 26, 1270, in Maharashtra.[49]

There is a well-known story about Namdev's devotion to Lord Krishna that encapsulates his legendary purity and simplicity. Dama Seth, his father, in the course of his worship used to offer milk to Krishna. One day as he was going out on business, he asked his five-year-old son to make the offering in his absence. Namdev, following his father's instruction, offered the milk to the idol of the god, expecting the idol to drink the milk. When it did not touch the milk, he was deeply hurt. He felt there must have been some failing on his part that caused the deity to refuse the milk. He shed copious tears in repentance and resolved not to leave the place until the god drank the milk. It is said that the idol, moved by his devotion, drank the offered milk.

Another story—of Namdev's first meeting with his teacher—reveals a significant milestone in his early development, his conversion to a more egalitarian caste-free spirituality. It was in the temple of Nagnath that Namdev first met his master Visoba Khechar. Upon entering the temple, he found an old man suffering from leprosy lying with his feet placed on the image of Shiva. Namdev, shocked at this sacrilege, scolded the man and sternly asked him to take his feet off the idol. The leper, too weak to do it himself, asked Namdev to place his feet where God was not. Realizing the profundity of the remark Namdev, bowed at his feet and asked for initiation. The old man asked the youth to carry him outside. When Namdev placed him down on a clean spot, he found to his amazement that the leper had transformed into a handsome young man with a magnetic personality, who began showering his love upon Namdev.[50, 51]

Very little is known of Visoba Khechar except that he advocated a path free from exterior forms of worship and believed that a guru was necessary to help a seeker to achieve enlightenment. Like most of the early Bhakti saints, he refrained from the use of external observance and ritual, maintaining that God resides within the human temple made by God himself. The following quotation reveals his profound understanding of the nature of the ultimate reality as Light and radiant music—two of the cornerstones of Namdev's own spirituality.

> Although you may go on pilgrimages to all the holy places you would not be rid of the darkness of ignorance. Meditate on the supreme Lord... Serve your Master, who will impart to you the secret of the path of true knowledge. Then you will see the Lord within and your delusions will vanish. Within your body is the abode of the Lord, where brilliant light shines, and "Soham" resounds constantly day and night. There you will meet the supreme Lord.[52]

Namdev's poetry abounds with references to this bright light that shines in the heart of every human. Many of his poems speak of the radiant light and thunderous drum that he encountered on the inner planes. Namdev speaks with authority of the inner reality of sound and light.

Repeatedly, Namdev sings of the eternal Word, the *Shabd*, which resounds throughout creation. It is this vibrant sound that is the sole conqueror of desire, death, and delusion.

This inner sound is the wordless Word, an unspoken language and unwritten law. Here Namdev sings of the stage where he merges with this inner radiant sound, which he termed the "Lord's Name." This is the final stage of the inner journey referred to here as the region of *Sahaj* or effortless union. As Namdev makes abundantly clear, this radiant sound is indistinguishable from the absolute Lord. "The Lord's Name is his form, and his form is his Name, His Name is not apart from his form, The formless one has taken the form of the Name."This true Name stands apart from all other names of God, which are outer symbols of the true inner reality. The former are lifeless and inert, the latter life personified. He guided seekers to connect with precisely this reality.

In one of the more robust revelatory transmissions of any saint, but particularly in the early Bhakti tradition, Namdev's explicit reference to the inner melody, unstruck music, and divine light as the *summum bonum* of mystical spirituality serves as one of the loveliest statements of divine truth found in any language or tradition.

Like many great masters of the Indian tradition, Namdev ends this poem placing his success fully in the hands of his guru. His final attainment of the state of Sahaj arises unreservedly through the blessings of his spiritual guide. The single and unwavering need for an authentic spiritual master to bestow upon the disciple the gift of the Word (Shabd) remains to this day a powerful living tradition within India.

Dadu Dayal (1544–1603): Universal Bhakti

Dadu Dayal (1544–1603) welcomed all to the banquet hall of spirituality regardless of social class or birth status. He was by most accounts a follower of Kabir Sahib, and subscribed to the essential tenets of Kabir's *nirguna* (formless) approach to spiritual-ity. This was not merely the path of worshiping God beyond form (nirguna) but the path of connecting to the transcendent inner Light and Sound (Shabd) that was responsible for the entire creation. Dadu makes this clear in the following verse taken from Jan Gopal's *Dadu Janama Lila,* the earliest and most reliable text on the life of Dadu Dayal.

If you stay firm in the nirguna devotion,
The Unknown will help you.
And there will be no room for the corruption of a personal deity.[53]

Dadu was tireless in proclaiming this absolute reality beyond form, which he called the real "Name of God." This Name of God was the true *Ram* and the real *Hari*, which he speaks about again and again in the *Janama Lila*. The following verse gives ample testimony to this reality:

A divine voice sounded and resounded,
as if having no end:

Beyond Beginning and End,
There is the Unparalleled Reality
Without form,
Existing in itself, faultless:
No one knows its secret,
Indestructible, without beginning or end,
Untouched by suffering.
See and serve him in your heart, Dadu.[54]

Having received the gift of initiation from Hari who appeared in the guise of an old man, Dadu spent seven years doing many kinds of works. By some accounts, this old man was none other than Kabir himself. Later Dadu performed many external forms of worship until at last Hari appeared to him and guided him to follow the true path and turn his attention away from all eternal pursuits. At some later point, Dadu became an itinerant sage singing the praises of the Creator. Like Kabir and others in the nirguna school, he made clear reference to the divine light that was both the cause of creation and the inner method of return as well.[55]

He saw the splendour of the Divine Light,
While Ram-within dwelt in his heart.
Later, a voice spoke from heaven:
'May the whole world know the blessed Dadu.'[56]

According to the *Janama Lila*, Dadu continued his inner worship of the transcendent Brahma, the true formless Hari, but realized his search was not complete. In the opening stanza in chapter 2, Dadu sought the Supreme Brahma or *Par Brahma,* a specific reference to God beyond form that is accessed only with the help of the true saints. It is here that he witnessed the light of the eternal Name.

He left for Sambhar, full of love,
But was suffering from virah, (deep separation from God)
He was yearning for the Supreme Brahma
And the hidden light within him shone brighter.
He meditated deeply on the Name,
With detached soul and composed body.
Beholding the light, glimmering or bright
He realized his life was very successful.[57]

His meeting with Kabir while in *samadhi* proved to be both transformative and enlightening:

Boundless knowledge of Divine Reality
Dawned after he met the blessed Kabir in Samadhi,
And they discussed his doubts
About the divine experience.
He continually sang Kabir's poems and verses
And became his equal in word and deed.
After his meeting with Kabir,
He became an authority on the Divine Reality.[58]

Dadu's meeting with the Mughal Emperor Akbar, who in his era was an outstanding proponent of interfaith understanding among Hindus and Muslims, is important not only because of its historical context, but also because Dadu explains the mysteries of the Divine Reality clearly and succinctly to the emperor. Dadu outlined the path to Hari in two simple stanzas:

The soul, filled with passionate yearning,
stands expectant at the door of vision.
The surrendered heart is always present before the divine,
Watchful and alert, Dadu.
First destroy the physical desires,
Which tie you to worldly passions,
Give up all hopes in the three worlds,
And surely Brahma will reveal His Light.[59]

Dadu Dayal has continued to exert a large influence over the resurgent Bhakti movement, even up to the present era.

Sant Garib Das (1717–1774): Culmination of the Light of Bhakti

Indian spirituality continued to be influenced not only by the great gurus, but also by the followers of Kabir and Dadu Dayal. The Nirguna Bhakti School and its adherents continued to have a profound influence throughout northern India leading into the modern era. What seems to have begun as a reformist movement within orthodox Hinduism in the 13th and 14th centuries with Ramanand, Namdeva, and Kabir eventually became a vibrant spiritual tradition. Some of the most notable distinctions we have already mentioned include: 1) discarding of all caste distinctions and abolishing untouchability; 2) rejection of idol worship and idolatry; 3) giving up of all superstition, and discouraging pilgrimage and fasting; and 4) insistence on worship of one God as absolutely formless and nameless, and distinctly different from the avatars of Rama and Krishna. The Nirguna Bhakti school considered the guru or satguru as perfect as God himself and the source of all inspiration. Most important, they advocated the worship of the "Word of God" or Shabda, which was the extension of his essence and manifested as light and music. It was this school of Nirguna Bhatki to which Sant Garib Das (1717–1774) belonged and advocated.

The Nirguna Sant tradition to which Garib Das belonged can be traced to the writings of Namdev and Kabir. They are all mentioned in the writings of Garib Das.[60] By most accounts, Garib Das was born in 1717 into a Jat family in the village of Chhurani in the Rohtak district near Delhi. Though not a direct disciple of Kabir, he is said to have received initiation by Kabir in a dream and his writings bear a remarkable similarity to his self-disclosed guru. Many authorities consider Garib Das to be the greatest and the last of the "Bhakta poets who had as great a mastery of the popular poetic voice and language and style as that of Ghulam Farid had, but whose knowledge of Indian languages was greater than that of any other Indian poet of medieval India."[61]

Unlike many of the earlier Bhakta poets who left very little written works, Garib Das is said to have written over 17,000 padas or poems. Garib Das and his followers were unabashed in their insistence on the practice of the Word or anahad sabad or Shabda, which manifested as the supreme ineffable light. Here Garib Das explains the simple path (Sehaj) to God:

> If you wish to see the light within,
> sing the anahad sabad in pure mind,
> He who conquers the lower self is Brahmajnani,
> He enjoys bliss through self control.
> He who reaches the highest consciousness,
> After controlling all the doors of self,
> Reaches the brahmadvar; he sees the light of God.[62]

In another passage, Garib Das makes an explicit connection between the anahad sabad and the light and "unstruck music." This light is both the material and efficient cause of all that exists and inner cognition of it the very essence of spirituality.

> The moonlight is the Light of God.
> The blazing Light of God is spread everywhere;
> His light is the Light of the world,
> There is no end to His Light.
> His light shines in all its splendor,
> His eyes are shining with joy
> Kabir stands near His throne,

And waves the chauri over His head.[63]

The tradition of following a guru, or living spiritual teacher, had been embedded in almost all the authoritative texts from the classical Upanishads to the *Shiva Samhita*. Yet few teachers have spoken more eloquently of the importance of such an authentic teacher than Garib Das, who echoes the great Kabir. Here is a passage in which he warns of the danger of following a false teacher:

> The disciple whose Guru is blind, is bound to remain
>   utterly blind,
> When the blind leads the blind, both are annihilated.
> Blind is the Guru and blind the disciple,
> And blind the faith of both.
> They remain deaf to truth
> and never hear the Divine Music.[64]

Unwary seekers often do not fully understand the importance of the precaution against following a false guru. Garib Das, as well as many later Hindu masters, cautioned against following a false or imperfect teacher. Spiritual guides have a deep responsibility to the well-being of their students. Not only is the disciple's faith shattered if the bond of trust is broken, but also their spiritual receptivity may never fully recover. This is a reoccurring theme in the Bhakta and Nirguna schools of mysticism. As the disciple surrenders fully, one merges his/her consciousness into the consciousness of the teacher. Since the teacher is already immersed in the Divine Light, the student also merges in that same Divine Light. The "little light" merges into the "ocean of Light," as a drop of water is immerced into the sea.

Garib Das elucidates this fundamental principle of mysticism—light alone can know the Light and love alone can know its Source. "I have met a Satguru, who is an embodiment of the Supreme Spirit. His Light has been revealed to me in every pore of my heart ever since he has given me the Divine Name which I repeat continuously without effort (*ajapa japa*). The True Guru has intoxicated me with Divine Love. He has given me the cup of divine love to drink and awakened my consciousness."[65]

The Light Rekindled (1800–2000 CE)

The nineteenth century marked the advent of one of the most fertile periods of growth in the history of Hindu spirituality. Some of its greatest visionaries and mystics, not only illumined the Indian subcontinent, but also brought its timeless wisdom and vision to the West. Among those most well-known of this era—Sri

Ramakrishna, Swami Vivekenanda, Sri Aurobindo, and Paramahansa Yogananda —drew upon the yogic and Bhakti traditions, while seeking to infuse Hinduism's rich heritage with a renewed vision of spirituality for their times. Drawing upon the cumulative experiences of great Indian saints and sages over the millennia, they taught that the realization of inner Light and Sound was the *summum bonum* of mystic attainment.

Sri Ramakrishna (1834–1886): The Light of the Eternal Godhead

Sri Ramakrishna (1834–1886), born Gadadhar Chattopadhyay in a small village in rural Bengal, as a youth explored a variety of religious and occasionally mystical experiences. He became the priest of Dakshineshwar temple near Calcutta at the age of 19, where he resided much of the remainder of his life. Considered one of the most moving and original of all modern Hindu saints, Ramakrishna became known for his belief that all paths lead ultimately to the same goal. Proclaiming the intrinsic oneness at the heart of all religious and mystical paths, he abhorred the foolish misunderstandings that led people to disrespect, injure, or kill one another in the name of religion. From his perspective, everyone had the capacity to move toward God, and "all will realize God if they have sincerity and longing of heart."

Ramakrishna had rich mystic experiences of inner Light from an early age, saying, "When I was ten or eleven years old…I first experienced samadhi. There are certain characteristics of God-vision. One sees light, feels joy, and experiences the upsurge of a great current in one's chest, like the bursting of a rocket."[66] Throughout life, he notes, "I saw the visions described in the scriptures. Sometimes I saw the universe filled with sparks of fire. Sometimes I saw all the quarters glittering with light, as if the world were a lake of mercury. Sometimes I saw the world as if made of liquid silver. Sometimes again, I saw all the quarters illumined as if with the light of Roman candles."[67]

This Light was so strong as to be visible to receptive onlookers. One of his disciples recounts an event during which, "In the twinkling of an eye Sri Ramakrishna went into deep samadhi. An amazing transformation took place in the Master before the very eyes of the devotees. His face shone with a heavenly light."[68]

Ramakrishna often invoked Divine Reality in the form of Mother. He is best known for a comprehensive teaching, based on his own inner experiences of the mercy and divine power of the Mother. He emphasized the healing and balancing wisdom of the sacred feminine, equally relevant in his time and in our present-day world. He remarked, "I would see God in meditation, in the state of samadhi, and would see the same God when my mind came back to the outer world." Seeing God everywhere and in everyone was his greatest realization:

> After God-realization, which is the conscious union of the manifest with the Unmanifest, the same Reality is experienced as all dimensions of being and also as the dimensionless Ground or Source of Being—the open space of unconditional awareness. Every conscious being we gaze upon is perceived to be God. Inanimate structures as well as God...But the most complete Divine Manifestation, surprising as it may seem, is this human reality.[69]

Acknowledging the Divine manifested within each human being led Ramakrishna to see the vast potential hidden in the heart of every human being.

One of Ramakrishna's young disciples, a monk named Vivekananda, brought Hinduism to the attention of the West when he journeyed to America and captivated audiences as a speaker at the first Parliament of the World's Religions, held in Chicago in 1893. As one contemporary scholar of the world's religions has succinctly assessed the significance of Vivekenanda's contributions to Ramakrishna's mission and the world:

> Vivekananda (1863–1902) carried the message of Hinduism to the world beyond India, and excited so much interest in the West that Hinduism received global attention. He also reintroduced Indians to the profound ties of their great traditions. He taught detachment from material perspectives, in favor of evolved spiritual understanding.[70]

Sri Aurobindo (1872–1950):
The Light of Consciousness Alone Is Real

During his lifetime, Sri Aurobindo (1872–1950) became renowned as a Hindu mystic philosopher, recognized globally for his pioneering inquiries into the nature of human consciousness. Born Aurobindo Ghose in Calcutta, Bengal, on August 15, 1872, he lived in England from the age 7–21. Educated at Cambridge University he excelled as a student of classics. Upon returning to his native land, he soon enthusiastically became an advocate of Indian aspirations for independence. He moved in 1910 to the French colony of Pondicherry on the southeast coast of India. There, he began to write and meditate, as his interests gradually shifted from politics, philosophy, and poetry to yoga and mysticism.

Having earlier come into contact with the evolutionary thought of Henri Bergson (1859–1941), Aurobindo now sought to reconcile and synthesize this intellectual approach of natural philosophy with the deep insights of traditional Indian Upanishadic thought. In the process, he developed his own synthesis—a vision and philosophy of human progress linked together with spirituality, which he termed "Integral Yoga." He established an ashram in Pondicherry, seeking to develop a community in which the central goal of human integration could be both studied and practiced in daily living.

Aurobindo held that one could live in the modern world as a free and evolved human being with a new expanding consciousness. Among his many writings, *The Life Divine* was perhaps his magnum opus. This voluminous tome explored the great streams of Indian metaphysical (philosophical) thought, striving to reconcile the truths within its many strands. From this arose a synthesis of the concepts of physical and spiritual evolution. In sometimes arcane language, Aurobindo strove to explain that by shedding ignorance, humanity begins to come more fully in touch with the Spirit or Divine, and can then progress to higher levels of spiritual consciousness. His book's four chapters seek to provide a roadmap, from spiritual awakening to the ascent to sacramental consciousness, laying the foundation of a collective Divine Life on Earth.

Aurobindo made metaphysical references to "the seven colors of the light of the divine consciousness, the seven rays of the Infinite."[71] He opined that "as the crust of the outer nature cracks, as the walls of inner separation break down, the inner light gets through, the inner fire burns in the heart, the substance of nature and the stuff of consciousness refine to a greater level of subtlety and purity."[72] Our outer personality often stands as a bar to the perception of the inner light. But once this divine light enters the human consciousness, the soul begins to experience the innate yearning and aspiration for a higher life of spirit. The sage attests that humankind has the innate capacity "to live in the light and force of a higher, larger and more integral consciousness...." Enlightened persons need to move and act in the light of truth, which sees intuitively and spontaneously that which is required to be done, and the way to do it.[73]

Aurobindo's close collaborator in his spiritual work was Mirra Alfassa (1878–1973), who became known as the Mother. She and Aurobindo developed a strong mutual respect and worked very effectively together as spiritual equals. Aurobindo strongly believed that Integral Yoga offered "a means by which human beings can, at this critical stage of history, assist the evolutionary process and be drawn upward to a higher stage of spiritual capacity."[74] When Sri Aurobindo died in 1950, the Mother continued their spiritual work, directing the Ashram and guiding their disciples to work toward the goal of developing human unity.

Paramahansa Yogananda (1893–1952): The Bliss-Filled Yogi

Paramahansa Yogananda (1893–1952), born Mukunda Lal Ghose, wa
Indian guru who introduced many in the West to the teachings of medita
and kriya yoga through his widely read book, *Autobiography of a Yogi*. Sinc
publication in 1946, millions of readers (including the coauthors of this bo
have been both inspired and informed by Yogananda's life odyssey, beginn
with the search for truth that led him throughout India to the feet of his guru, ₹
Yukteshwar Giri (1855–1936).

Born into a devout Bengali family in the state of Uttar Pradesh, Yogananda
developed an extraordinary spiritual awareness at an early age, and began seeking out sages and saints, hoping to find an illumined teacher to guide him in his
quest. In 1910, at the age of 17, this yearning was fulfilled when he met his guru,
Swami Yukteshwar. Describing his first meeting with Yukteshwar, as a rekindling
of a relationship that had gone back for many lifetimes, he later wrote: "We
entered a oneness of silence; words seemed the rankest superfluities. Eloquence
flowed in soundless chant from heart of master to disciple." He recollected that
after a touch on his chest from his guru, awareness left his physical body and he
found himself in a "luminescent sea." His awareness continued to expand outward in this sea until it engulfed "the entire cosmos, gently luminous, like a city
seen afar at night, glimmering within the infinitude of my being."[75]

> The divine dispersion of rays poured from an Eternal Source,
> blazing into galleries, transfigured with ineffable auras....Irradiating
> splendor issued from my nucleus to every point of the universal struc-
> ture. Blissful amrita, nectar of immortality pulsated through me with a
> quicksilver fluidity. The creative voice of God I heard resounding as Aum
> the vibration of the Cosmic Motor.[76]

Yogananda echoes the perennial wisdom of the great Vedic sages in elucidat-
ing the deep connection between the experience of light and the innate bliss contained within it. The ineffable voice of God resounds within us as our highest Self.
That Self is bliss (*Ananda*) and that is who we really are. The experience of bliss is
not conditioned, transitory, or superficial but intrinsic, universal, and unlimited.

Yogananda's insistence upon personal experience as the true ground of all
religions was not new to the Upanishadic traditions. Only direct revelation, not
blind belief, he maintained, could bind the soul back to its Creator. "Intuition is
the soul's power of knowing God."[77] In 1920, Yogananda journeyed to the United
States where he widely shared the essence of the teachings of India's ancient
spiritual practices, its philosophies of yoga, and its traditions of meditation.

Consciousness Is Light

Despite the many streams and rivulets that have branched off from the great river of Vedic and Upanishadic wisdom, its essential spirit remains unchanging at its deepest core. The great Vedic scholars and sages summarized this seeming contradiction in this aphorism, "Truth is One, though sages call it variously." That truth, at its deepest level, affirms all faiths as facets of the same timeless, textured tapestry of light. Whether this light arose from the intense sadhana of the Nath yogis in the caves of the Himalayas or by an ecstatic priest on dusty streets of Bengal, the Peerless Light is the same Uncreated, Unborn, Self-luminous Reality behind all existence. The following story beautifully recounts the dynamic inter-play between Light and *transformation.* As this light enters into us, we are puri-fied, transformed, and resurrected without effort on our part. It is the miracle of transfiguration in the Light.

It is said of the early Bhakti saint Chaitanya Mahaprabhu, who lived in Bengal, that he was so enamored of God that he would be in continuous remem-brance of Him. Of course, every master has his own way of remembering God. For Chaitanya, he used to repeat the Name of God in the words, "Hari bole," which simply means "Say God's Name." However, because saints are one with the Nameless, any words they may utter are charged with that inner intoxication and bliss.

One day he went to a place where many washermen were washing clothes. A man speaks out of the abundance of his heart. Since Chaitanya's soul was over-flowing with the love and light of God, whatever words he uttered were charged with that radiation.

As he stood by one of the washermen, he said to him, "Hari bole!"—"Say God's Name!" The washerman thought that perhaps he was a mendicant and wanted money. So he kept quiet, and refused to utter the words. He said, "I won't utter the name you say." Again infused by the same inward illumination, Chaitanya Mahaprabhu told him, "You will have to, you must." Inwardly, the wash-erman thought, "Now he won't leave me alone; let me utter the name and finish it off, otherwise he will not go away."

So the washerman repeated the words, "Hari bole." As soon as he uttered the words (the very words were charged), he became intoxicated and stopped work-ing. He began to chant ecstatically, "Hari bole, Hari bole, Hari bole!"

When he began to do that, the other washermen took notice and asked, "What has become of our fellow brother? What is he doing?" They approached him and asked, "What is the matter?" He replied back joyously, "Hari bole!" Upon hearing those words filled with the saint's impulse, they too became intoxicated with the love of God. In a short while, all the washermen and washerwomen in the entire place left their work and started to dance in ecstasy. Through the gift of the saint's attention, each entered that state of bliss and continued chanting the holy name of God, "Hari bole, Hari bole, Hari bole."

As we have seen in almost every tradition, a competent saint or master can give through his touch, word, glance, or even a thought, a direct spiritual experience of the innate bliss, knowledge, and Light within (*satchitananda*). The light and love that pours out from the presence of a God-intoxicated master has the power to transform. But our capacity to receive this gift depends on our level of receptivity and purity. A master can only convey as much as our receptacle can receive. Until we are filled with that same intensity, real inward illumination is usually not possible.

Reverence for this ever-present illumination biding deep within the human breast has brought forth countless saints and sages. The Jyoti and Sruti (Light and Sound), the primal Self (atman), is the unborn, ever blissful, the guru of gurus, ever luminous, perennially abiding as Truth in the midst of duality.

Guidelines at the Heart of the Teachings

1. In the beginning was *Prajapati* (the Absolute), within Him was the *Vak* (the Word), and the Vak (the Word) brought forth all creation. *We are born from the Light and to the Light we must return.*

2. Light and Sound are the twin manifestations of the Word. *All creation is a manifestation of Light. The all is in the one and the one is in the All.*

3. He who knows the Self knows everything. *Self-knowledge precedes God knowledge.*

4. The entire play (*lila*) of creation is the shimmering, sparkling, spontaneous play of the consciousness with consciousness. *Experience the cosmic dance of union of the soul with the Lord.*

5. Realize the Self is the maker of its own reality. *As you think so you become.*

6. The human anatomy is a reflection of the divine anatomy of the spirit. *As within so without. There are universes upon universes and planes within planes as endless as the sands upon the beach.*

7. The essential requirements for inner ascension are the control of the five senses, contentment, truthfulness, nonviolence, and

the capacity to still the mind at will. *An ethical life is a step-ping-stone to spirituality.*

8. When the seeker enters into the inner worlds, he will begin to experience various manifestations of light and sound. They may include "the form of a star, a diamond, the orb of the full moon, the sun at midday, a circle of fire, a crystal, a star (*nakstra*), an eye, or sudden bursts of blue, red, or purple colors." *The body is the true temple wherein the Light of God resides.*

9. It is through the unconditional love, grace, and guidance of a competent teacher that one achieves success on the spiritual path. *Guru precedes God.*

10. Realize that only sustained, disciplined effort can establish the concentration needed to ascend within. *Effort and grace are the two wings upon which the seeker soars into the beyond.*

11. The experience of bliss (ananda) is not conditioned, transitory, or superficial but intrinsic, universal, and unlimited. *We are "little packages" of dancing bliss and happiness.*

12. Recognize it is only through an intense, unconditional love for all, that samadhi (unity) can be achieved. *Love and all things will be added to you.*

A Contemplative Practice

Remember God Continuously. *By remembering God we are transformed into God.*

If there is one single practice besides meditation that can catapult us forward in our spiritual life it is the continuous invocation and remembrance of God. Every saint, scripture and tradition has emphasized this point. It is the axis around which our spiritual evolution revolves. Every day, every hour, and every moment cultivate the inner remembrance of God. This can be done by selecting any name of God with which you resonate (Ishvara, Krishna or Ram).

- Begin by repeating God's name during moments when one's mind is free.
- Slowly increase this inner invocation throughout your entire day.
- Extend this remembrance to even challenging intellectual tasks.
- Finally, never forget God even for a nano-second.

Tenzig Rigdol (born Katmandu 1982). Depiction of Avalokitasvara entitled *Pin Drop Silence.* Tenzing Rigdol's figure of Avalokitesvara stands in a radiant *mandorla,* burning with the *light of his enlightenment* or nonexistence, while his eleven heads comment on realms of knowledge and simultaneous realization. His primary hands are held in *anjali mudra,* the gesture of veneration. Thus the figure makes direct reference to Shadakshari Lokesvara, who is understood to be an incarnation of Avalokitesvara (courtesy of Metropolitan Museum of Art).

CHAPTER FOUR

Luminous Mind:
Buddhism and the Heart of Clear Light

Luminous, monks, is the mind. And it is freed from incoming defilements...
for the well-instructed disciple of the noble ones
there is development of the mind.

—Gautama Buddha, Pabhassara Sutta, Anguttara Nikaya 1.49–52

Mind is not mind. The nature of mind is clear light.

—Astasahasrika Prajnaparamita

The Life of Buddha: Searching for the Wealth Within

There is a story of a Buddhist temple north of Sukotai, Thailand, where an enormous clay Buddha stood guard, humble and present, for over 500 years. One day while caring for the statue, a monk noticed a chink in the clay and peered inside. He was taken aback. Beneath the clay was pure shining gold! After carefully scrubbing and polishing the statue, what remained was one of the largest, most precious, and most beautiful relics in all of Southeast Asia. To this day, the golden statue draws and inspires legions of devoted pilgrims. The monks suspect that it had been covered up for protection during a time of political vulnerability—an apt metaphor for one's own innate tenderness and wisdom. In the same way, the Buddha teaches that beneath the clay-like dullness of our mental activity, everyone has an awakened radiant nature, ready to shine forth with radiant clarity when skillfully polished.

Siddhārtha Gautama, the man who inspired the statue, was born roughly in 600 BCE, 170 miles north of Varanasi in what is today Nepal. Later generations would come to know him as Shakyamuni Buddha, "Awakened Sage of the Shakya Clan." Siddhārtha means "he who achieves his aim." Millennia later, hundreds of millions still revere him for his achievement—his fearless victory over the mind.

At his birth celebrations, the infant Siddhārtha was observed by the hermit oracle Asita, who announced that the baby was destined to become either a great spiritual teacher or a benevolent universal political leader. According to the oracle, the choice would be determined by whether or not Siddhārtha would be exposed to such signs of human misery as sickness, old age, and death. Siddhārtha's father, Suddhodana, longed for his son to choose royal greatness, so he arranged for him to enjoy a life of luxury, and assiduously shielded him from all suffering. At a young age, however, the Buddha had a taste of his true calling. Slipping away from the gaiety of a springtime plough festival, the young boy stole away to repose in shade beneath a fragrant rose-apple tree. There he spontaneously sat cross-legged and closed his eyes, slipping easily into a state of deep calm and concentration.

At 16, he married Yasodhara, with whom he had a son, Rahula. They lived in splendor, rotating seasonally among multiple palaces. However, despite the luxury and the efforts of his father to protect him from the harsh truths of life, on a trip around the kingdom Siddhartha saw an elderly man. He was astonished. When informed by his charioteer Channa that all people would eventually grow old, he became despondent. Subsequent trips revealed the ubiquitous presence of disease, decay, and dis-appointment.

From a worldly perspective, the young Siddhārtha had everything: He was brilliant, athletic, rich, powerful, and healthy. And yet, he grew ever more miserable. Eventually, his sadness overwhelmed him. Feeling he had no other choice, one night he kissed his bride and child, and set out silently. In future generations, this fateful turn from worldly life in search of enlightenment would become known as "The Great Departure," and monks would symbolically emulate it in their ordination ceremonies. Legend holds that the gods silenced the hooves of his horse, and he vowed not to return until he had solved the problem of suffering.

Upon leaving, he studied under a series of famous ascetic teachers, eventually attaining mastery of their respective schools, and invitations to teach alongside them. He declined, feeling that although he had achieved deep states of bliss, peace, and insight, he had not penetrated to ultimate truth. So he set out on his own, practicing strict asceticism before eventually breaking down and realizing that his mortification ultimately left him no closer to attainment. Then, upon remembering the deep calm he felt sitting beneath the rose-apple tree, he sought to forge a "middle way" between the extremes of self-indulgence and self-denial.

Shortly after, at the age of 35, he sat down beneath a Banyan tree and resolved not to arise until he was enlightened. In a parallel to Christ's temptations in the desert, he was met by Mara, the archetypal inner voice of temptation. Mara sought to stop him, first with offers of worldly power and sensual pleasures, and then by attacking him with great armies. But Siddhārtha stood firm, calling on all of the earth to bear witness to his right and duty to seek total enlightenment.

> Vision arose, insight arose, discernment arose, knowledge arose, (and) illumination arose within. (SN 56.11)

The Buddha had attained his goal, and was henceforth known as the Victorious One. The awakened illumination he experienced was a natural feature of the "undefiled mind." Later, teaching to his assemblage, the Buddha pronounces in the Pabhassara Sutta:

> Luminous, monks, is the mind. And it is freed from incoming defilements. The well-instructed disciple of the noble ones discerns that as it actually is present, which is why I tell you that—for the well-instructed disciple of the noble ones—there is development of the mind. (AN 1.49–52)

The Luminous Mind in Buddhism

According to the dharma (the teaching and practice of Buddhism), when the mind is free of fetters, defilements, attachments, and aversions, it flames forth with intrinsic radiance. The Buddha and early Buddhist Theravadin literature regularly reference the "brightly shining heartmind" (Pāli, pabhassara citta) as an intrinsic quality of awareness. This theme is developed in Theravadin Abhidharma where it becomes the Bhavanga (Pāli, "ground of becoming"). In Tibetan Buddhism, we see this theme developed in the concept of the clear light (Tibetan Ösel, literally, "radiant light"), the pristine awareness and intrinsic clarity of the unfettered mind.

Elsewhere in the *Anguttara Nikaya* (AN 3.100), the Buddha likens spiritual practice to a blacksmith working over a piece of gold. The smith aims to strike a careful balance between blowing on the piece and sprinkling water on it, just as we should balance between equanimity and concentration when meditating. In this way, analogous to the workable metal, the monk develops a mind that is "pliant, malleable, luminous, and not brittle." Similarly, in the *Upakkilesa Sutta*, the Buddha teaches that there are hindrances in the mind, "obscured by which some contemplatives and brahmans don't glow, don't shine, don't dazzle" (AN 4.50).

In the *Sangiti Sutta*, light serves as a *nimitta* (Sanskrit, "sign") of progress, a theme further developed in the Theravadin tradition:

> A monk attends to the perception of light, he fixes his mind to the perception of day, by night as by day, by day as by night. In this way, with a mind clear and unclouded, he develops a state of mind that is full of brightness. (DN 33)

Light is not only a sign of meditative progress; it is also intrinsic to existence itself, and to Buddhist cosmology. In the *Kevatta Sutta* (DN 11) the Buddha recounts the story of one of his own monks asking divine beings about the foundation of reality. The monk "attained to such a state of concentration that the way leading to the gods appeared in his centered mind." He first approaches the attendants of the demigods and asks them if they know the answer to his foundational questions. They lament that they do not, and send him to the gods themselves.

These gods, known as Four Great Kings, admit the same lack of knowledge, and suggest he seek the audience of gods "who are higher and more sublime than we." Through depth of concentration, the monk presses onward and is sent successively higher by the gods, progressing past the realms of Sakka, Yama, Suyama, Santusita, Nimmanarati, Sunimmita, and Paranimmita Vasavatti. All reply in kind, saying that they do not know, and that he should ask the more sublime gods above them.

Finally, he appears in the court of Brahma himself. He asks where Brahma is, and the attendants of his court reply:

> Monk, we also don't know where Brahma is or in what way Brahma is. But when signs appear, light shines forth, and a radiance appears, Brahma will appear. For these are the portents of Brahma's appearance: light shines forth and a radiance appears. (DN 11)

Soon after Brahma appears, the monk asks him the same question about the foundation of reality. Brahma replies not with an answer, but with a bombastic statement of his power:

> I, monk, am Brahma, the Great Brahma, the Conqueror, the Unconquered, the All-Seeing, All-Powerful, the Sovereign Lord, the Maker, Creator, Chief, Appointer and Ruler, Father of All That Have Been and Shall Be. (DN 11)

Underwhelmed, the monk replies, "Friend, I didn't ask you if you were Brahma, the Great Brahma." Again, Brahma repeats his claims of greatness, and again the monk reminds him that this is not what he was asking. This repeats a total of three times before Brahma "taking the monk by the arm and leading him off to one side, said to him that while he did not want to admit so in his court where his devotees construed him as all-knowing, he himself did not know. He councils the monk, "Go right back to the Blessed One (the Buddha) and, on arrival, ask him this question." (DN 11)

Immediately, recounts the Buddha, "the monk disappeared from the Brahma world and appeared in front of me." The Buddha rephrases the monk's question as, "Where do water, earth, fire, and wind have no footing? Where are long and short, coarse and fine, fair and foul, name and form brought to an end?"

To this the Buddha replies:

> Consciousness without feature, without end, luminous all around: Here water, earth, fire, and wind have no footing. Here long and short, coarse and fine, fair and foul, name and form are all brought to an end. With the cessation of the activity of consciousness each is here brought to an end. (DN 11)

At the close of his first sermon (the Dhammacakkappavattana Sutta) on the four noble truths "when the Blessed One had set the Wheel of Dhamma in motion," the highest devas (angelic demigods) cried out that the awakener "cannot be stopped by priest or contemplative, deva, Mara, or God or anyone at all in the cosmos." And then the natural, intrinsic radiance of awakening shone forth:

> In that moment, that instant, the cry shot right up to the Brahma worlds. And this ten-thousand fold cosmos shivered and quivered and quaked, while a great, measureless radiance appeared in the cosmos, surpassing the effulgence of the devas. (SN 56.11)

Theravada Buddhism: Luminous Cords of Concentration

Theravada Buddhism (literally, "the Teaching of the Elders") regards itself as the most conservative of the major branches of Buddhism, and thus claims to hold close to the historical teachings of the Buddha. Theravadins trace their lineage back through 250 BCE to the time of the Third Buddhist Council, convened by the great Indian emperor and Ashoka who had become a pacifist.

For close to two thousand years, Theravada has flourished in Sri Lanka (where today about 70% of the population are nominally adherents) and most of continental Southeast Asia, including Cambodia, Laos, Burma, and Thailand. Worldwide there are perhaps 100 million Theravada adherents, although many folk practices shape the religious lives of the peasant laity. Theravada has enjoyed increasing popularity in the West, and is experiencing a revival in its motherland of India, where for centuries it had all but died out.

Within Theravada Buddhism, the Inner Light is a core mode of spiritual experience, yet not always referenced in the commentaries. We find in its textual tradition a clear record of experiences of inner illumination. These experiences have been interpreted in a variety of ways as both signs of spiritual progress and as the final or near final goal of enlightenment.

For many more advanced Theravadin teachers, however, the inner light is seen as a sign (Pāli, nimitta) of the fruition of concentration, and an entryway to the states of Jhāna (absorption). The Australian-born Thai forest monk Ajahn Brahm teaches that as concentration develops:

> ...the sixth stage is achieved when one lets go of the body, thought and the five senses (including awareness of the breath) so completely that only a beautiful mental sign, a nimitta, remains... this pure mental object is a real object in the landscape of the mind, and when it appears for the first time it is extremely strange. One simply has not experienced anything like it before. Nevertheless, the mental activity we call perception searches through a memory bank of life experiences for something even a little bit similar. For most meditators, this disembodied beauty, this mental joy, is perceived as a beautiful light. Some see a white light, some a golden star, some a blue pearl, and so on. But it is not a physical light. Their eyes are closed, and the sight consciousness has long been turned off. It is the mind consciousness freed for the first time from the world of the five senses.[1]

Brahm relates a series of contemplative signposts under which the nimitta of inner light will appear, instructing that it will only do so when: 1) the breath has been released as an object of concentration, 2) the five senses are completely withdrawn, and 3) the mind is completely free of any discursive movement. More recently, modern near-death research has also affirmed the necessity of the withdrawal of conscious awareness from the five senses, as well as intellectual activity ceasing before the arising of the inner light. This research strongly confirms that these basic stages of withdrawal of consciousness are universal and beyond specifics of religious or cultural conditioning.

As Brahm's teacher Ajahn Chah emphasized in his teaching, the need for the practitioner to develop the ability to "let go" is essential in focusing on the inner light. He pointed to a huge boulder on the monastery grounds and asked the fellow monk if he thought it was heavy. "Of course," the monk replied, "Don't you?" Ajahn Chah smiled and said, "Only if you try to lift it." Our grasping at an ultimately illusory separate sense of self, and our attempts to understand and control the world, are the ways we try to lift the metaphorical boulder. When we let go of such grasping, the boulder is no longer heavy—and we can access the inner light, which is found in meditation.

Brahm notes that this light:

> is strange but powerfully attractive..., it is a beautifully simple object.[2] If you do not experience it as enrapturing, this is because the main reason that the nimitta [of light] can appear dull is that the depth of contentment is too shallow. You are still wanting something. Remember—and this is important—jhānas are states of letting go. Incredibly deep states of contentment. So give away the hungry mind.[3]

U Ba Khin (1899–1971), a Burmese householder and high-ranking government employee who is perhaps best known in the West as the guru of S. N. Goenka, teaches that, with the "right attentiveness" and the "right exertion," the mind:

> becomes freed from hindrances, pure and tranquil, illumined within and without...powerful and bright. It experiences a light that is a mental reflex, with the light varying in degrees from that of a star to that of the sun. To be plain, this light which is reflected in the mind's eye in complete darkness is a manifestation of purity, tranquility, and serenity in the mind.[4]

U Ba Khin gives pointed attention to the universal, inter-religious and inter-spiritual character of this interior spiritual illumination:

> To go from light into the void and to come back to it is truly Brahmanic. It is our experience that under a proper guide this inner peace and purity of mind with light can be secured by one and all.[5]

U Ba Khin writes that, teaching the traditional meditation of *Anapana-sati* (mindfulness of incoming and outgoing breath), the student is encouraged to "focus his attention to a spot on the upper lip at the base of the nose," synchronizing awareness within and without the breath. In this process, according to U Ba Khin, signposts of success include:

> clouds or cotton wool...shapes of white as of smoke, cobwebs, flowers or discs, but when attention becomes more concentrated, they appear as flashes or points of light or as a tiny star or moon or sun. If these pointers appear in meditation (of course, with eyes closed), then it should be taken for granted that concentration is being established. What is essential, then, is for the student to try after each short spell of relaxation to get back to concentration with the pointer of "light" as quickly as possible.[6]

These signposts are reiterated almost identically throughout this book. Taken together, they attest not only to the fact that the inner light is a universal experience, but that specific sub-manifestations of the light can appear in a specific sequence across different cultures.

Turning the Light Around:
Zen, Tao, and Chinese Light Wisdom

The entire world is your divine light.—Zen Master Cho-sha (d. 828 CE)

Vast and far-reaching without boundary, secluded and pure, manifesting light, this spirit is without obstruction. Its brightness does not shine out but can be called empty and inherently radiant. Its brightness, inherently purifying, transcends causal conditions beyond subject and object. Subtle but preserved, illumined and vast, also it cannot be spoken of as being or nonbeing, or discussed with images and calculations. Right here the central pivot turns, the gateway opens. Facing everything, let go and attain stability. Stay with that just as that. Stay with this just as this.[7]

—Zen Master Hongzhi Zhengjue (1091–1157 CE)

Zen (*Chán* in Chinese, etymologically linked to the Sanskrit *dhyana* and Pāli *jhanna*, literally "meditation") is a branch of Mahayana Buddhism seeking direct realization of the nature of mind and reality. Historically, it represents a syncretism of Indian Buddhism (including Nargarjuna's Madhyamaka system) and contemplative aspects of Taoism present in China since the time of Lao Tzu. We have chosen to include Taoist contemplative practice in this section because of the deep interconnection between the traditions. Indeed, there was rich exchange and syncretism between Taoist and Buddhist monks and mountain hermits throughout Chinese history,[8] allowing us to speak of a broader Chinese contemplative tradition.

The Zen tradition ascribes its origins to a sermon in which the Buddha gathered before an assembly of "gods and men" and silently held up a single flower. After several disciples made attempts to interpret the Buddha's intent, the monk Mahākāśyapa replied with a simple broad smile. The Buddha acknowledged this response, saying:

I possess the true Dharma eye, the marvelous mind of Nirvana, the true form of the formless, the subtle dharma gate that does not rest on words or letters but is a special transmission outside of the scriptures. This I entrust to Mahākāśyapa.[9]

After incubating in India for almost a thousand years, Zen traveled to China via the Indian monk and former prince Bodhidharma (5th century CE).[10] Bodhidharma, called "The Blue-Eyed Barbarian" by his Chinese contemporaries, was heavily bearded, conversationally direct, and a spiritual warrior in temperament (he is said to have originated Shaolin kung fu). Most important, though, he was intensely dedicated to dharma practice, and a specific form of meditation he termed wall-examining (Chinese, *pi kuan*). After reaching China, he sat for nine years in a small cave facing the wall in open-eyed contemplation. Bodhidharma brought this ferocity to understanding his own mind, with an immediacy that recalled how Mahākāśyapa sought to receive the Buddha's transmission of the "true form of the formless."

Bodhidharma, when asked about the most essential practice for one determined to achieve nirvana, replied simply:

> the most essential method, which includes all other methods, is to
> behold the mind...If you can understand the mind, everything else is
> included.[11]

Interestingly, when Tibetan translators rendered Bodhidharma's text, they
rendered the original phrase "abides in wall-examining" as "abides in brightness," thus likening it to Ösel, the Clear Light, or radiance yoga.[12] In his cave,
Bodhidharma discovered that when he beheld his mind in naked purity, free from
all grasping, radiance blossomed forth.

> If, as in a dream, you see a light brighter than the sun, your remain-
> ing attachments will suddenly come to an end and the nature of reality
> will be revealed. Such an occurrence serves as the basis for enlighten-
> ment. But this is something you know. You cannot explain it to others.

> Or if, while you're walking, standing, sitting or lying in a quiet grove,
> you see a light...it's the light of your own nature.

> Or if, while you're walking, standing, sitting, or lying in the stillness
> of night, everything appears as though in daylight, don't be startled. It's
> your own mind about to reveal itself.

> Or if while you're dreaming at night, you see the moon and stars in
> all their clarity, it means the workings of your mind are about to end.[13]

Today, Bodhidharma is recognized as the first patriarch of Zen. He appointed
Hui-K'o as his successor. Zen flourished in China, and spread to Japan, Korea, and
Vietnam in subsequent centuries.

The Venerable Chinese Master Lin Chi (d. 866 CE) continued Bodhidharma's
teaching, noting that light is the natural foundation of consciousness, present
before the discrimination of the senses. Mind, he wrote, is "fundamentally one
pure radiance; divided it becomes the six harmoniously united spheres of sense.
Since the mind is nonexistent, wherever you are, you are emancipated."[14]

Following Lin Chi, Hongzhi Zhengjue (1091–1157) taught within the Caodong
school, which arose as one of the Five Houses of Chán during the Tang dynasty.
Hongzhi was a broad-minded and poetic writer, who examined the original, pure
radiance of emptiness, wistfully encouraging us to "roam and play in samadhi."
He taught a form of meditation known as "silent illumination" (Chinese, *mòzhào
chán*), which he described as a simple release into an open, silent, and expansive
freedom, after which:

> the original light appears, blazing through your skull...when you
> turn within and drop off everything completely, realization occurs. So we

are told simply to realize mutual response and explore mutual response, then turn around and enter the world.

With the depths clear, utterly silent, thoroughly illuminate the source, empty and spirited, vast and bright...you must take the backward step and directly reach the middle of the circle from where the light issues forth.[15]

The instruction to "turn around" and "take the backward step" is echoed in the Japanese master Dogen Zenji's (1200–1253) injunction *eko hensho*, which translates as "learn to withdraw, turning the light inwards, illuminating the self."[16] This theme that our mind is stuck in the material world. However, when it reverses its direction and looks inward with the "eye of the spirit," it will partake of the Divine effulgence or divine nectar (e.g. the inner light).[17]

Taoism: The Alchemy of Light

"Turning the Light" is also a key theme in Taoism. Many Taoists regard Light as a practical, even natural phenomenon, open to all who undergo mental and physical purifications and contemplative exercises. These practices were transmitted orally, and outlined during the Chinese Middle Ages in alchemical treatises. In parallel with Western alchemy, during the Tang Dynasty (618–907 CE), Chinese Taoist alchemy split into *neidan* (inner, esoteric, subtle) and *weidan* (outer, external, magical) traditions.

The true inner path focused on cultivating internal energy (*qi* or *chi*) along the subtle meridian system (Jing-Luo) to prolong earthly life and achieve subtle states of consciousness. In its most elevated forms, neidan involved working with the energies present in the body, as opposed to the use of external incantations, potions, and herbs.

Many of the neidan practices deal with basic meditative tasks such as stilling the mind or achieving emotional balance, as well as t'ai chi ch'uan and qigong subtle energy exercises. Often these practices culminate in the unity of Light. For example, in a text called *Turning the Light Around*, Master Yuan of the Cosmic Void teaches, "The method of congealing the spirit in the energy aperture is simply a matter of gathering in your seeing, reversing your listening, and turning around the Light to illumine the inward."[18] Another teaching, by Master Shui-ch'ing Tzu, instructs the practitioner to grasp the opening of the Gate and when cultivation is complete, the beam of golden light will penetrate your entire being.[19]

The Gate might refer to the esoteric third eye, and is an example of the veiled iconic symbolism found in alchemical texts. Taoist alchemical manuals from this period are replete with references to terms like "Cinnabar fields," and the "Seven

Stars of the Northern Dipper." The Taoist manual of esoteric physiology known as the Book of the Center clarifies the terminology of the Gate, however, saying:

> The Tao is me, it is the supreme lord of the central summit...The polestar which shines in my forehead, between my eyebrows, like the sun....It is my energy. I was born of that energy.[20]

The Taoist practice manual *The Secret of the Golden Flower* (which was a favorite of Carl Jung) provides lucidly clear instructions for how one can concretely seek this illumination. Students are schooled to seek the "transmutations of spiritual illumination" by undergoing "the whole work of turning the light around."[21] They are encouraged to seek the "one light within" with great care because the "light is easily stirred and hard to stabilize."[22] This Light is not to be mistaken for material light because "the light of the mind does not belong to inside or outside" and seekers are missing the mark if they "look to see it with [their] physical eye."[23]

In a section of *The Secret of the Golden Flower* entitled "The Secret of Freedom," the anonymous author provides a description of an actual concrete method employed for turning the light around:

> When you want to enter quietude, first tune and concentrate body and mind, so that they are free and peaceful. Let go of all objects, so that nothing whatsoever hangs on your mind, and the celestial mind takes its rightful place in this center. After that, lower your eyelids and gaze inwards...where light reaches, true positive energy comes forth in response.[24]

The text considers the common problems of drowsiness and distractedness in meditation, with recommendation to practice in the morning when rested and relatively free of distractions, to be steadfast and patient in cultivation, and to "understand that this device is not mechanical or forced. Just maintain a subtle looking and listening."[25]

With this method "you can seek experiential proof" for yourself and see that:

> In the midst of quiet the light of the eyes blazes up, filling one's presence with light. It is like opening the eyes in a cloud. There is no way to look for one's body. This is "the empty room producing light." Inside and outside are permeated with light, auspicious signs hover in stillness.[26]

As one's relationship to this discipline deepens, one finds that "with each level of progress in practice, the efflorescence of the light increases in magnitude. And the method of turning around becomes subtler."[27] The light acts as a current pulling the meditator toward heaven, and restoring the balance between yin and yang, leading to union with the absolute. Here the seeker discovers "if in accord with the celestial, the Way is naturally met."[28]

As further evidence of the universal Chinese contemplative light tradition, Taoist and Zen influence eventually spread beyond the confines of Taoism or Buddhism to influence Confucianism. For example, the Neo-Confucian scholar Chu Hsi (1130–1200 CE) deepened the traditional Confucian focus on self-cultivation of virtue to include contemplation. Borrowing from Zen and Taoist forerunners, he advises polishing and stilling the mind until its intrinsic luminosity shines forth, saying:

> Human nature is originally clear, but it is like a precious pearl immersed in impure water, where its luster cannot be seen. After being removed from the water, [the precious pearl] becomes lustrous of itself as before. If one would realize that human desires are what obscures [one's nature, one should be able] to find illumination.[29]

The light also appears, albeit scarcely, in the annals of koan practice (from the Chinese, *gong'aàn*, public record) for which Zen is perhaps best known. Koans are questions, stories, dialogues, or statements meant to frustrate and exhaust rational thinking, thus creating a crack through which awakening can be recognized. The Blue Cliff Record (Chinese, *Hekigan-roku*) is a collection of one hundred Chán Buddhist koans compiled in China during the 12th century Song dynasty. In koan 86, the Zen Master Ummon speaks to his assembly of the light, ending with this koan:

Everyone has his own light shining continuously now as of old...What is your bright light?[30]

Mahayana Buddhism: All Beings Have an Intrinsic Buddha Nature

That light pervaded all the triple thousand, great thousand world systems, world systems in the ten directions and world systems as many as the grains of sand in the Ganges River. In addition, divine flowers rained down and divine music resounded. Through the power of the Buddha, all sentient beings in the triple thousand, great thousand worlds too became possessed of the joy of the gods.

As soon as they are born, their bodies illuminate the triple realms and all ten directions' worlds. Limitless suffering is dispelled by this light, and sentient beings are sustained with all happiness.—Sutra of Golden Light, Chapter 5

In Mahayana Buddhism, everyone wakes up. All beings, it is said, have an intrinsic Buddha Nature, and this nature is the nature of Reality itself. The term *Mahayana* means "Great Vehicle," a transport ferrying everyone to realization, a vehicle kept afloat by the true hero of this worldview, the bodhisattva (Sanskrit, *bodhi*, wisdom; *sattva*, essence, being). A bodhisattva is an enlightened being[31] who undertakes a solemn vow to work tirelessly for the liberation of all beings, and not to rest until all have been saved. Modern scholarship believes Mahayana Buddhism originated in the very early Common Era, although the exact dates are unclear. At its inception, the Mahayana tradition was not a separate lineage, but rather a set of doctrines within existing Buddhist sanghas, espousing a more universal and devotional mood than traditional teachings.

Nargarjuna (c. 150–250 CE) was a principle early defender of Mahayana doctrine, and one of the great thinkers in the history of the world. He was so deeply revered that many Buddhists of later generations referred to him as the Second Buddha. A skilled dialectician and debater, Nargarjuna espoused the Socratic habit of primarily attending to the deconstruction of false views, The school of thought that developed around him was known as Madhyamaka, a middle way between what he saw as the twin pitfalls of essentialism and nihilism.

Later Madhyamikas (those that follow his Middle Way Buddhist philosophy) such as the Indian Chandrakirti (600 ca. 650 CE) wrote more clear descriptions of the dialectic of enlightenment. For example, Chandrakirti's Madhyamakavatara, itself a commentary on Nargarjuna, portrays the enlightenment process in descriptive, positive terms, rather than just focusing on what it is not. In Chandrakirti's vision, the ground of being radiates, as wisdom kindles the power of meditative equipoise:

> The ground of reality is called Luminous because here the wisdom fire that burns the tinder of phenomena glows with light and, in meditative equipoise, has the power to lay to rest all of the conceptual constructs related to the perception of dual appearance.[32]

Nargarjuna's Madhyamaka, along with the texts of the Yogacara school of Vasubandhu, Asanga, and Maitreya-nātha, represent a philosophical presentation of Mahayana Buddhism, and are complemented by more devotional and visionary literature exemplified by works such as the Saddharma Puṇḍarīka (Lotus) and Avatamsaka (Flower Garland) Sutras.

The Lotus Sutra, written roughly around the start of the Common Era, is the basic scripture of the Tien Tai and Nichiren sects of Buddhism, both of whom claim millions of adherents to this day. The text describes itself as a deeper continuation of the Pāli Sutras, mythically hidden from revelation until such time as humanity was ready to hear and absorb it. In the cosmology of the Lotus Sutra, an infinite array of Buddhas and bodhisattvas persist throughout all space, time, and dimensions, serving all beings toward the goal of liberation.

As the Buddha's discourse commences at the opening of the Lotus Sutra, the reader immediately encounters the motif of spiritual light. Bodhisattva Maitreya asks Bodhisattva Manjushri, "Why from the white tuft between the eyebrows

600 - 400 BCE	400 -300 BCE
• Siddhārtha Gautama c. 566 to 486 • Buddha enters nirvana 486 • First Buddhist Counsel 483	• Moggaliputta Tissa 342-322 • Second Buddhist Council 383 • Mahinda 282-222 • Reign of Ashoka 268-239

200 - 400 CE	400 - 600 CE
• Aryadeva 3rd or 4th century • Buddhaghosa 4th-5th century • Hui-yuan 334-416 • Vasubandhu 4th -5th centuries • Seng-chao 374-414	• Visuddhimagga c. 430 • Paramartha 499-569 • Bodhidharma 532 • Golden age of Chinese Buddhism 589-906 • Korean Buddhism enters Japan 538

300 - 100 BCE	100 - 200 CE
• First Buddhist missionary activity outside India 251 • Dutthagamani 2nd century • Fourth Buddhist Council 25 • Pali Tipitaka Cannon written c. 1st century -5th	• Kaniska late to early second century • Entry of Buddhism into China 65 • Ashvagosha second century • Rise of Mahayana Buddhism 100-150 • Lotus Sutra end of 2nd century • Nargarjuna c. 150–250

600 - 800 CE	800 - 1000 CE
• Beginnings of Chan (Zen) Buddhism • Vajrarana Buddhism in Tibet 7th century • Shantideva 7th-8th Centuries • Hsuan-tsang 600-664 • Chinese Buddhism enters Japan 658-666 • Classical Period of Korean Buddhism 668-945 • Candrakīrti 600-650 • Dharmakirti 600-660	• Tendai Buddhism Founded in Japan by Saicho 805 • Venerable Lin Chi d. 866 • Cho-sha d. 828 Zen Master • Shingon Buddhism founded by Kukai 806 • Padmasambhava c. 8th century • Genshin 942-1017 • Tai-mitsu Tendai Founded by Enrin 847

1000 - 1200 CE

- Naropa 956-1041
- Jetsun Milarepa ca. 1052 ca. 1135 CE or 1040-1123
- Classical period of South East Asian Buddhism 11th-15th Century
- Buddhism transmitted to China 1191
- Zen Master Hongzhi Zhengjue 1091-1157
- Honen 1133-1212
- Japanese Pure Land founded by Honen 1175
- Shariputta 12 century

1200 - 1400 CE

- Dogen Zenji 1200-1253
- Pure Land School in Japan, founded by Shinran 1224
- Ji Buddhism founded by Ippen 1275
- Tsong-sha-pa 1357 1419 Tibetan Master

1800 - 2000 CE

- Mahasi Sayadaw 1904 -1982
- Ajahn Brahm b. 1951
- World Fellowship of Buddhists formed in 1950
- Chögyal Namkhai Norbu, b. 1938
- Thich Nhat Hanh, b.1926-

1400 - 1600 CE	1600 - 1800 CE
• *Dge-'dum-grb-pa (Dalai Lama I) 1391-1475* • *Rennyo 1415-1499, head of Honganji school of Pure Land or Shinran school of Buddhism* • *Suzuki Shosan 1579-1655*	• *Bankei Yotaku Dalai Lama V 1622-1693* • *Hakuin Ekaku 1686-1769* • *Ryokan 1758-1831* • *Shwegyin Sayadaw 1822-1893* • *Beginning of American Buddhist Churches 1854-1883* • *Fifth Buddhist Council (Mandalay) 1871*

of our leader and teacher does this great light shine all around?"[33] Later, the text continues with an answer, highlighting that the light imparts a unique and important spiritual experience, "The supernatural powers of the Buddhas and their wisdom are rare indeed; by emitting one pure beam of light, the Buddhas illuminate countless lands. I and the others have seen this, have gained something never known before."

Similarly, both the Shurangama Sutra and the Lankavatara Sutra describe the Tathagatagarbha (roughly, the Generative Buddha Matrix or Womb) as "by nature brightly shining and pure," and "originally pure," though "enveloped in the garments of the skandhas, dhatus and ayatanas and soiled with the dirt of attachment, hatred, delusion and false imagining." This imagery imparts an important tension in Buddhist thought. Although some remain committed to anti-essentialist metaphysics of emptiness, they still often invoke Light as a spiritual attainment, linking it to Buddha nature, and the nature of Reality. It would seem that, for many Buddhist thinkers, the Light is itself the middle way, transcending the binaries of time and timelessness, form and formlessness, and existence and nonexistence.

The Huayen tradition, which flourished in China during the Tang dynasty (618–907 CE), continued to develop the intrinsic outcomes of Light in the Flower Garland Sutra. Here, spiritual Light flows from the third eye of the Buddhas, illuminating this and other dimensions, penetrating the awareness of the disciples, and ushering them into new worlds of spiritual knowledge. This Light, it is proclaimed, flows into their being through the top of their heads, illuminating and conferring all powers and the exalted station of Buddhahood.

> At that time, all Buddhas of the ten directions will emit from their glabellas (the location between the eyebrows) pure rays of light, which are called The Supernatural Power That Enhances The Universal Wisdom. These rays of light, together with countless accompanying lights, will universally illuminate all worlds of the ten directions, circulate them clockwise ten times, reveal the immense omnipotence of the Tathagatas, enlighten innumerable hundreds of thousands of billions of nayutas of Bodhisattvas, universally shake all Buddha-Worlds, eliminate all evil paths' sufferings, block out all demons' palaces, show all the places in which the Buddhas achieve Bodhi, and show the congregations, sublimities, and majesties of those Bodhimandas.

> In such a way, having filled the whole universe, permeated the whole Dharma-Realm, and illuminated all the worlds, these lights will come to this Bodhisattva Congregation, circulate it clockwise, and manifest myriad sublime things. Having done this, these lights will enter the great Bodhisattva's body through the summit of his head, and their

accompanying lights will enter into those accompanying Bodhisattvas' heads. At that time, this Bodhisattva will gain millions of Samadhis that he has never gained before, and then it is known that he Has Gained The Conferment, Has Entered the Buddhas' Realm, Has All The Ten Powers, and Is Counted As A Buddha.[34]

Traveling from China, Buddhism came to Japan in the eighth century, and has primarily taken four forms there: Nichiren, Pure Land, Zen, and Shingon. Pure Land Buddhism (also known as Amidist, for their devotion to Amitābha, the celestial Buddha of Infinite Light) is primarily a devotional form of Buddhism, popular among folk practitioners. But the central importance of Light as cathartic spiritual reality is not missing even in this tradition. The vehicle of Light is the omnipresent spiritual reality that both illuminates and confers the Buddha nature upon aspirants.

The light of Amitayus shines brilliantly, illuminating all the Buddha-lands of the ten quarters. There is no place where it is not perceived. I am not the only one who now praises his light. All the Buddhas, shravakas, pratyekabuddhas and bodhisattvas praise and glorify it in the same way. If sentient beings, having heard of the majestic virtue of his light, glorify it continually, day and night, with sincerity of heart, they will be able to attain birth in his land, as they wish. Then the multitudes of bodhisattvas and shravakas will praise their excellent virtue. Later, when they attain Buddhahood, all the Buddhas and bodhisattvas in the ten quarters will praise their light, just as I now praise the light of Amitayus.

The Buddha continued, "The majestic glory of the light of Amitayus could not be exhaustively described even if I praised it continuously, day and night, for the period of one kalpa."[35]

Shingon Buddhism teachings arose in Japan during the Heian period (794–1185 CE), and represent Japanese recasting of tantric themes. A Shingon monk named Kukai traveled to China in 804 for esoteric study. He settled in the city of Xi'an, and studied with the Chinese Esoteric Buddhist master Huiguo, a favorite student of the influential monk Amoghavajra (705–774 CE). He later returned to Japan as his lineage and Dharma successor, and established Tantric Buddhism in Japan. The word *Shingon* stems from the Japanese reading of the Kanji for the Chinese word *Zhēnyán*, literally "True Words," which in turn is the Chinese translation of the Sanskrit word *mantra*. To this day, Shingon Buddhism remains little studied and documented by outside scholars, existing primarily as a closely guarded chain of direct transmission.

One significant figure in this tradition of Self and self-denial is Myoe (1173–1232 CE), a Japanese monk with ties to both Shingon and Kegon (the "Flower

Garland" tradition, based on the Avatamsaka Sutra and related to the Chinese Huayan and the Korean Hwaeom traditions) Buddhism. Myoe popularized the use of the Mantra of Light (Japanese, *komyo shingon*), which in English translates roughly as "Praise be to the flawless, all-pervasive illumination of the great mudra. Turn over to me the jewel, lotus, and radiant light."[36] In his book *Shingon Refractions: Myoe and the Mantra of Light*, scholar Mark Unno recounts a passage in which Myoe discusses his own experiences of inner radiance, and that this invocation became an important Shingon Buddhist practice:

> In the summer of 1220, I was practicing samadhi of the Buddha's Radiance. On the twenty-ninth day of the seventh month of the same year, I received auspicious signs in the midst of meditation. That is, a sphere of white light appeared before me. Its shape was like that of a white jewel of approximately one foot in diameter. To the left there was a white light that grew from one foot in length to two feet and then three. To the right there was a light like a mass of fire. There was a voice that said, "This is the Mantra of Light."
>
> When I emerged from contemplation and thought about it, its profound meaning became apparent. The light, like a mass of flames, was the light to illuminate the evil paths of rebirth.[37]

This light "like a mass of fire" becomes not only the gateway to illumination but illumination itself without which the aspirant sinks back into the paths of death, rebirth, and suffering again. It is interesting to note that the description mirrors the depiction of lights both descending and ascending upon the aspirant in several traditions, especially the Sufi illuminists traditions.

Tibetan Buddhism:
The Clear Light of Dreaming, Dying, and Awakening

> *O, Child of Buddha Nature, listen! Pure Inner radiance, reality itself,*
> *is now arising before you. Recognize it!*
>
> —The Tibetan Book of the Dead

For Tibetan Buddhists, death is a cherished opportunity. It is a chance to dissolve the fetters of consciousness, to destroy the binding ties of the discriminating, lower mind. In death, one has the precious circumstances necessary to sever connections to the wheel of transmigration and to recognize one's true nature as essential radiant luminosity.

For over a millennium amid the snow-crested peaks and plateaus of the Himalayas, Tibetans approaching death would call on a qualified lama or yogi to administer the teachings and rituals of the *Bardo Thodol*, the Tibetan Book of the Dead.[38] This funerary text is the best-known Tibetan religious document in the West, and serves as ritual aid and spiritual guidebook for the transitions between life and death. Navigating the bardos (liminal or intermediate states) between lives is seen as a singularly potent opportunity for spiritual awakening.

These teachings on death and dying came to Tibet 1,300 years ago as a syncretic blend between classical Indian Buddhism and North Indian Tantra. They were transmitted by the great Padmasambhava, founder of the Nyingmapa (Ancient School) of Buddhism. Padmasambhava is seen in Tibet as an emanation of Amitabha, the Buddha of Infinite Light, and also known as Guru Rinpoche (Precious Spiritual Master). Tibetan legend states that when his work was completed, with 25 student adepts established in his lineage, he departed for a Buddha-field in the west in a body of pure light.

Modern lamas continue in unbroken lineage to administer the Bardo Todrol death rites to this day, arriving at the homes of the dying or recently deceased with the concentrated motivation to liberate the dying from cyclic existence. The lama opens the rite by taking refuge in the three gems—the Buddha, his teachings, and the community of followers—and dedicating the merits of his work not only to the dying person before him, but also to all sentient beings. He aims for the tone of his recitation to be melodious and even, hoping it to be soothing and inspiring to the dying person, who prepares to face a great spiritual challenge. (See chapter 8 for a fuller treatment of the process of dying.)

Invoking all Buddhas for support and to remind the dying that enlightenment is an eminently attainable birthright, the lama serves as a guide through the intermediate realms. He entreats the dying one to release his bonds of attachment, recognize projections of mind as such, and attain Buddhahood, in which one realizes "the essential nature of emptiness is radiance, and the essential nature of radiance is emptiness." Subsequent to the preliminary invocations, ideally at the start of physical death, the recitation begins by calling out:

O, Child of Buddha Nature, (call the name of the dying person), the time has now come for you to seek a path. As soon as your respiration ceases, the luminosity known as the "inner radiance of the first intermediate state," which your spiritual teacher formerly introduced to you, will arise....[39]

As physical death begins to set in, the lama transitions to explicit instruction, meant to be enacted immediately:

That which is called death has now arrived...concentrate your thinking as follows: 'I have arrived at the time of death...For the benefit of all sentient beings, who are as limitless as space, I must attain perfect Buddhahood...I must recognize the time of death as the arising of inner radiance, the Buddha-body of Reality, and, while in that state, I must attain the supreme accomplishment of the Great Seal.[40]

So begins the journey and, from the start, the consciousness of the dying person has the ability to merge into the luminous nature of mind, and thus end transmigration. Indeed, many adepts are said to do just this, causing transference of consciousness (Tibetan, *phowa*) to one of the intermediate god realms, or in the case of Dzogchen, to the Dharmakaya itself (Sanskrit, literally, "truth body"). Most beings, however, encounter some hesitation, confusion, or attachment, which prevents this.

Padmasambhava himself recognized the mental contingency of these events, stating, "Indeed, if you are intent on seeing beings of like nature in this intermediate state, then they will be perceived. If you are not so intent, they will not be perceived."[41] Moreover, liberation depends on being able to see the visions for what they are: mental projections. The lama thus calls out:

> Recognize them! For they have arisen from your own pure vision! O, Child of Buddha Nature, these buddha fields do not exist extraneously. They are the aspects of your own heart... they have arisen, atemporally, from the natural expressive power of your own awareness. Therefore recognize them as they are![42]

The recognition of the wrathful and peaceful deities as projections of the grasping mind allows one to dissolve indissolubly into these illusory appearances, and attain the Buddha Body. This process of recognizing the ultimate "emptiness of form" is a feature embraced by many contemplative traditions. In Hinduism, for example, sarguna bhakti (worshiping God with form) is later replaced by its higher form or nirguna bhakti (worshipping God without form). Beyond recognizing illusions, the dying are enjoined to recognize light as the source of pure and pristine cognition:

> At that moment, you should fearlessly recognize the white light, white and dazzling, radiant and clear, to be pristine cognition. Have confidence in it! Be drawn to it with longing devotion! Pray with devotion, thinking this is the light of the transcendent lord Vajrasattva's compassion. I take refuge in it.[43]

Eventually, if it becomes clear that the dying person will not achieve enlightenment while in the bardo realm, he is encouraged to hold clear and altruistic intentions when selecting a new body, so as to secure a birth amenable to spiritual progress and enlightenment in the next lifetime. Through it all, however, emptiness does not imply lack, as it might be construed in the West, but rather radiance and the intrinsic light of our own nature. Indeed, Padmasambhava clearly equates emptiness with radiance and radiance with emptiness as the twin aspects of the same inner reality:

If you do not know how to meditate, directly examine that which is producing your fear and terror. This essence is a stark emptiness, completely without any inherent existence in any respect whatsoever! This stark emptiness is the Buddha-body of reality. Yet, this emptiness is not a vacuous or nihilistic emptiness. The essential nature of this emptiness is an awesome, direct and radiant awareness...Indeed, emptiness and radiance are not separate: the essential nature of emptiness is radiance, and the essential nature of radiance is emptiness.[44]

This is a beautiful vision of the dying process, grounded in deep compassion and contemplative wisdom. Indeed, in a recent conversation with a Tibetan Geshe (the equivalent of PhD in Buddhist philosophy), Thupten Tendhar noted that, for Tibetans, the research on near-death experiences was nothing new. It was just a modern restatement of centuries-old wisdom.[45] Of course, the Tibetan spiritual canon does not just cover the dying process. It is extended to all consciousness.

Naropa and the Natural Light Beyond Sleeping and Dreaming

Subhuti: Even Nirvana, I say, is like a magical illusion, is like a dream—How much more so anything else! Gods: Even Nirvana, Holy Subhuti, you say is like an illusion, is like a dream? Subhuti: Even if perchance there could be anything more distinguished, of that too I would say it is like an illusion, like a dream.[46]

Like Prince Siddhartha 13 centuries before him, Mahasiddha Naropa (956–1041 CE) was born in the foothills of the Himalayas to an aristocratic family, and showed great spiritual promise and interest as a child. Like his counterpart, he soon after became unsatisfied by worldly life. Haunted by a piercing spiritual longing, he eventually renounced secular life in favor of a life wholly dedicated to the spirit. He took ordination at the local Kashmiri monastery, and graduated three years later from Nalanda, an enormous center of Buddhist learning with over five hundred faculty some from far-flung regions.

He rose in academic rank swiftly and, over the next eight years, his reputation grew immensely. Then one afternoon beneath the Banyan tree, an old lady renowned for her incredible ugliness approached Naropa. "Do you understand the words of the dharma?" she asked the great professor. "Yes, of course," he replied, politely although inwardly he was repulsed by her ugliness. She promptly cackled with laughter, noting his inability to see beyond her distressing exterior form. She then asked, "And do you understand the meaning of the dharma?" Again, Naropa replied in the affirmative. Upon hearing this, the old hag burst into tears, proclaiming forcefully that Naropa had no true taste of enlightenment. Indeed, if he had, he would have been unaffected by her seeming ugliness and recognized her intrinsic Buddha nature within.

Naropa was forced to admit that he had substituted a lack of true attainment with scriptural learning and complex dialectics. "How do I find true enlightenment?" he asked. "My brother is the great yogi Tilopa," she explained, "and he can guide you on the path of direct mystical experience." Upon hearing the very name of his future spiritual master, Naropa's heart is said to have swelled with intense devotion and longing.

Realizing the imperative need for a competent spiritual master, he set out to find his teacher. The legend of his life recounts 12 painful trials, all eventual sources of growth, which Naropa had to navigate before meeting Tilopa. Naropa came to realize that it was not until he had achieved sufficient inner purification that he could meet his future guru. Eventually, greatly humbled, he came to the feet of Tilopa, who accepted Naropa as his student. Tilopa guided Naropa to enlightenment, and eventually designated him as his successor, establishing the Kagyu lineage that persists today.

Tilopa was born to the Brahmin caste, but had, since receiving a vision from a Dakini, wandered India, assimilating the corpus of deep esoteric and tantric teachings present in northern India at the time. From Saryapa, he learned of inner heat (Sanskrit, *candali*, related to the more common kundalini; Tibetan, *tummo*). From Nagarjuna, he learned radiant light yoga (Sanskrit, *prabhasvara*; Tibetan, *Ösel*) and various teachings on working with the subtle body (Sanskrit, *maya deha*; Tibetan, *gyulu*). From Lawapa, he learned dream yoga (Tibetan, *gyi Nyeljor*) and from Sukhasiddhi, the teachings on projecting consciousness during life, death, and the bardo.

On the outer level, the practitioner of Ösel yoga visualizes an array of sacred mantras, mandalas, and deities that then dissolve into radiant light. On the inner level, it involves gathering the vital energies or winds (Tibetan, *lung*) into the central channel from the right and left channels, strongly homologous to the subtle anatomy described in Kundalini and hatha yoga texts. The XIVth Dalai Lama summarizes the goal of the practice: "To gather the energy-winds and the subtle minds that ride on them, basically by means of different types of absorbed concentration focused on these spots."[47]

The gathering together of the subtle energies to a point of concentration yields an inner vision of spiritual light. Secret tantras are principally oral, and revealed only during empowerments and initiations. In fact, many Tibetan monks will complete 18 years of formal education, with emphasis given to studying the Middle Way, ethics, Perfection of Wisdom, logic, and debate, before beginning the study of the tantras.

In these teachings on luminosity yoga, the tantras, including the Anuttarayoga (unexcelled or highest yoga) Tantra, are in concert with other Tibetan schools, including the Great Completion (Tibetan Dzogchen) and the indigenous Bön tradition. On this point, the XIVth Dalai Lama states: "[O]ld translation Dzogchen and new translation Anuttarayoga Tantra offer equivalent paths that can bring the practitioner to the same resultant state of Buddhahood."[48] Dzogchen, like most of the traditions outlined in this text, stresses that beneath gross and subtle mental activity is a nondual, nonconceptual field of radiance.

Naropa's teachings, and the Tibetan canon in particular, appear to be unique in their instruction to maintain a lucid awareness of this light during dreaming and deep sleep. Dream yoga in Tibet is distinct from Western Jungian influenced dream interpretation. In dream interpretation, one attends to the symbolic or archetypal meaning of dreams, or perhaps interacts with them imaginally, as in Fritz Perl's Gestalt dream work. In Tibet, by contrast, at the deepest level the symbols of the dream are all seen as illusions, fabrications of the mind that obscure a deeper reality.

The principal practice with dream yoga is to be disciplined and consistent in regarding all waking and dreaming states of consciousness as illusions. Dream yoga instructs the seeker to constantly remind himself, dreaming and waking, "These things that appear are appearances, but they are not truly existent."[49] In this way, one learns "by setting free the apprehender and the apprehended in the expanse of self awareness, [then] the immutable energy-mind of clear light is revealed." To achieve the clear light of sleep, Padmasambhava advises us to: "Fall asleep as before, with your awareness clear and vivid, and do not lose that sense until your consciousness dissolves into clear light."[50]

Thus, milam dream yoga is a third practice, distinct in important ways from both Western models of lucid dreaming and Jungian dream interpretation. In ordinary lucid dreams, people gain awareness that they are dreaming and can thus modify the contents of the dream at will. Lucid dreamers tend to retain a separate sense of self, and to focus on ego gratification, whereas practitioners of milam yoga seek to dissolve the self and all objects in the "inner light" that grounds both the self and the field of awareness.[51]

The daily cycle of waking, dreaming, and dreamless sleep, as well as the micro-cycle of consciousness that occurs in the gap between thoughts, mimics the greater personal and cosmic cycles of life, death, and rebirth. All of these stages are bardos, intermediate states in the Great Wheel. Beneath and beyond all the "way stations" of limited mind is pristine radiance, waiting ever patiently for clarity to dawn.

The Buddha Nature of Enlightened Compassion

All major schools of Buddhism—Theravada, Mahayana (including Zen), and Tibetan—have described the direct inner experience of light in various ways. It is seen as "radiance" (Ösel) or "clear light" in Tibetan Buddhism, "white light" or "luminous cords" in Theravada, and in Mahayana as the "luminous mind" and "inner radiance." In all cases, this experience is pivotal to the onset of enlightenment and the realization of ultimate reality. In Mahayana and Tibetan Buddhism, luminous or radiant inner light is not only a common feature, but also an essential teaching of the nature of emptiness. Indeed, "emptiness is radiance" and "radiance is the emptiness" express twin aspects of the same nondual reality. Some of the greatest adepts, including Chandrakirtri, Bodhidharma, Padmasambhava, and Naropa, all referred to the essential reality as "radiant luminosity" and light as the natural "foundation of consciousness." In the Theravadin tradition, though less well-documented than other schools, light nevertheless remains an essential experiential component of the inner contemplative path and intricately linked to the various levels of jhanas or degrees of concentration in many Theravadin schools. Most important, it is through this experience that the innate qualities of compassion and loving-kindness are revealed to be our own Buddha Nature. Light/radiance remains the core of every sentient being, as the great Zen master Ummon has said: "Everyone has his own light shining continuously now as of old....What is your bright light?"

The following Chinese traditional wisdom tale encapsulates the interplay between the role of the teacher as a vehicle for the radical transformation of the aspirant through the power of compassion and forgiveness. Put into a contemporary context, one could well imagine the following scenario:

A fierce warrior is said to have single-handedly attacked and killed at least a dozen innocent Buddhist monks. One day while in the process of looting a monastery, he came upon a sage who sat alone and undisturbed in the midst of the mayhem. The great sage sat quietly, simply radiating equanimity, compassion, and loving-kindness. As the warrior approached the sage with the intent of killing him, he raised his sword in front of the sage's face. When he was just about to slice off his head, all of a sudden he was stopped in his tracks by an unseen, unknown power.

Standing there, waving his sword in anger, he shouted, "Don't you know who I am? With the flick of my wrist I can cut off your head without a shred of remorse." The sage continued to radiate loving-kindness and forgiveness without a trace of fear or anger. Then he replied, "Don't you know who I am? I can sit here without blinking an eye while you cut my head off."

At that moment, the warrior felt a transmission of light enter his being. In an instant, he realized who the sage truly was and that he, the warrior, was the fearful one. In that moment, his heart opened and he entered into a luminous white radiance. Miraculously transformed, he bowed down in full prostration before the sage. With complete humility, he asked, "O great one, teach me what is heaven and what is hell."

The monk's whole being continued to radiate divine light. Then he replied, "I will teach you what is heaven and hell. Hell was when you came in here having killed many innocent monks without the slightest trace of remorse. Hell was when you felt no connection to the suffering of others and were filled with pride and ego. Heaven is when you dropped your sword and realized the true radiance of your own Buddha Nature. Heaven is when you suddenly began to feel the pain and sorrow that you have caused many others. Now, when you realize that all sentient beings are part of your own Buddha nature, this is heaven."

Guidelines at the Heart of the Teachings

1. Recognize the essential need for a wisdom teacher who is a living embodiment of radiant Light, whose personhood is infused with this light and sends it out in all directions. *Seek the Source of Wisdom from the fountain of Living Wisdom.*

2. *Realize that the Light of each person's intrinsic Buddha nature is this "radiant luminosity."*

3. *Recognize that all the qualities of compassion, wisdom, and forgiveness arise spontaneously from the experience of our intrinsic nature, our truest spiritual heritage.*

4. *Realize that the prerequisite for entering the "clear light" is concentration upon the subtle energy currents within the body through meditation.*

5. *Begin to examine the reasons for the very real temporal experience of fear, terror, and pain as inherently empty of any ultimate reality.*

6. Continue to meditate on this nondual Light/Radiance, until all conceptual frameworks that are rooted in delusion are gradually extinguished. *The only remedy to end suffering is to dwell in one's Inner Light.*

7. *Recognize that it is human desires that obscure the innate luminosity of one's Buddha nature.*

8. The more we can dwell and abide in this Light the more human suffering is diminished or even extinguished. *One ounce of practice is worth a ton of theory.*

A Contemplative Practice

All Beings Are Buddha. *Practice Compassion and Forgiveness to all.* Every tradition has recognized the primal need for the practice of compassion born out of unlimited forgiveness. As the story of the Buddhist monk so well illustrates it is through compassion that we can lift others and ourselves out of the pits of hatred, greed, and delusion. Compassion arises naturally from the heart of one who realizes the true ground of Being which is our own Buddha nature. When we realize our own perfect nature we can see the same Light shining in all no matter how distressing the disguise. It is this practice which is the crowning achievement of all spiritual endeavors.

- Begin by inwardly praying for the wellbeing, happiness, and peace of all sentient beings.

- Slowly reach out to whoever may be suffering or afflicted in one's own home, neighborhood and workplace.

- Extend this to forgiving all those who may have wronged us intentionally or unintentionally.

- Finally, continually embrace all sentient beings as one's very self.

The above image is of a postcard issued in the Russian Empire, early in the 20th century...The ethnographer Hoppál identifies the shaman woman to be of Altai Kizhi or Khakas origin. The ethnographic photo itself..., after which the postcards were issued, had been taken by ethnographer S. I. Borisov in 1908...Note that the standing woman is holding a shaman's drum, not a gong (Public Domain,1996).

CHAPTER FIVE

Shamanic Light:
From the Archaic Past to
Present Time

...When I looked up, I saw a white light. Inside this light I saw the
ancestors and the Sky God. They taught me things about healing and the
spiritual universe. It took place with no words.

—Bo, a Kalahari !Kung Bushman Shaman

At least 4% of the world's population can be described as indigenous people. "There is a distinctive type of spiritual specialist found among many indigenous peoples. They are called by many names, but the Siberian and Saami word "shaman" is used by scholars as a generic term for those who offer themselves as mystical intermediaries between the physical and the nonphysical world for specific purposes, such as healing."[1]

Shamanic origins go back to the mists of pre-history, and foreshadows aspects of developments found in unitive religious and spiritual thought throughout the ages. Illustratively, they see human beings by their very nature to be stewards, preservers and restorers of mother earth and its varied life forms.

Here we will provide a glimpse of light, external and Inner, within shamanic spirituality.

In 1994, the curator and anthropologist Jean-Michel Geneste brought four Ngarinyin aborigine elders from Australia to view the 17,000-year-old cave art at Lascaux in southern France. He was following up on a hunch that these fine Magdalenian animal paintings would have internal, spiritual meaning for the contemporary shamans. The elders confirmed their belief that indeed, this was a site of spiritual initiation. The ancient cave artists of Lascaux, they were certain, had practiced a version of the same shamanism that they, many millennia later, still practiced in their native Australia. It was their conviction that this was unsurprising, because the "old ways" stretched back much further even than these paintings.

Of course, the 17,000 years between that visit and the paintings they were viewing were as a blink of the eye in the long human story. Whereas 4,500 (or more) generations separate the earliest Homo sapiens from the present, a mere 200 generations separated the Ngarinyins from the original cave painters in Lascaux.

While Geneste focuses on recorded history over the last 4,000 years, the evidence suggests that spiritual illumination traverses our entire human history. As far back as we can see, inner light is both a core motif and a lived experience for our ancestors, as they envisioned how the cosmos functions and how they personally related to the divine.

Across cultures, indigenous creation descriptions reference the pre-differentiated universe as a dark and featureless expanse of water, stirring and then shimmering with immense creative Light at the time of creation. Variations of this vision are found in the Mayan Popol Vuh, the Babylonian Enûma Elish, and the Hebrew Genesis. Light is ubiquitous to our human stories about ourselves across recorded culture and history.

In shamanic cultures, however, Light is often a core experience, and one that is alive in indigenous cultures around the world to this very day.

The living traditions of shamanic illumination have been well-documented by the American scholar Bradford Keeney, who originally created a career for himself studying cybernetics under Gregory Bateson and applying it to research in family therapy. As his career matured, however, Keeney increasingly distanced himself from the Western psychotherapeutic tradition. Increasingly, he acted as a cultural anthropologist, seeking out traditional indigenous healers and ecstatic spirit guides.

He sought out and studied with traditional Balians (Balinese) and Brazilian faith healers, African Christian Shakers of St. Vincent, a Zulu high Sanusi, the Guarani forest shamans of Paraguay, a charismatic Black Louisiana church, a Dine (Navajo) medicine woman, a Lakota Yuwipi medicine man, and a Japanese healer in the Seiki Jutsu tradition.

He prayed, fasted, danced. and attended to symbols in his dreams, all the while deepening his access to shamanic consciousness. Broadly speaking, in his experiences, shamanism was much akin to the definition of Mircea Eliade, the pioneering Romanian scholar of shamanism, who wrote, "a first definition of this complex phenomenon, and perhaps the least hazardous, will be: shamanism = technique of ecstasy."[2]

Shamanism was communal at its core, with chosen members of a community undergoing deep trials and rigorous training. If successful, the shaman inherited a complex set of social functions that included healing and medicinal work, peacekeeping in the community, interpreting dreams, applying spiritual wisdom and guidance to pressing problems, initiating the next generation of shamans, and serving as a guide for the community to deeper connection with one another, with nature, and with the spirit world beyond.

Keeney's most moving encounter was with the !Kung Bushmen of the Kalahari desert. One night at home in the United States, he dreamed vividly of contacting a group of shamans he intuitively recognized as the oldest healers in the world. During the dream, he saw and felt deeply drawn toward their location in the desert of southern Africa. Upon waking, he read all he could of the Kalihari Bushmen and felt deepening kinship. Weeks later, he fortuitously received an overtly unrelated, yet synchronous, invitation to guest lecture on psychotherapy in South Africa. He quickly agreed, contingent on the willingness of the university to arrange to take him to meet with the Bushmen.

Months later, after an arduous trek into the remote desert, past the ends of all the roads, after hours driving on little more than lines in the sand, Keeney and his guides arrived at the Bushmen settlement. Three elders, whom Keeney immediately embraced, greeted them. They told Keeney that they had dreamed of him too, that they were expecting him, and welcoming him home. That evening, they invited him to participate in their sacred dance.

Keeney would participate in many dances over the next 12 years, and eventually come to be embraced by the Bushmen themselves as a great shaman, fully initiated into and partaking of their spiritual life. The dances and culture he was drawn into were deeply communal in nature, and involved ecstatic shaking, dancing, and trance states, all seeking contact with the "Big God" or "Sky God."

Their descriptions are in some ways reminiscent of descriptions of Kundalini in India or Tumo in Tibet. The Bushmen experience this energy, which is known as n/om. N/om is seen as the ever-vibrating presence of God's love and, once the Bushman is sufficiently resonant, he is drawn into the Light. The Bushman Bo recounts his first such experience:

> I felt a heat in my belly and at the bottom of my back that slowly came up my spine and right out of the top of my head. When I looked up, I saw a white light. Inside this light I saw the ancestors and the Big God. They taught me things about healing and the spiritual universe. It took place with no words.[3]

This Light weaves their world together, both socially and cosmically. Once their vision is spiritually refined, they see "threads" of spiritual Light connecting one another in deep sympathetic resonance, and also see threads and "ropes" of Light leading to the sky, where they can contact their ancestors and the Big God. Ascension on these ropes into the Light is seen as the pinnacle of spiritual experience:

> If the power inside me is strong enough, I will see a special light. Bushmen Doctors see different kinds of light. It may be a cloud of light in front of them, or a light hovering over the entire community of dancers. When you're very strong you will see lines or strings of light that go up to the sky. The lines may be the thickness of a blade of grass or as big as a rope (tau) or chain (ketanga). When they go up to the sky, they are white in color or shiny like silver metal.[4]

Keeney found this experience of inner illumination repeated across disparate indigenous cultures that were wholly disconnected geographically from one another, suggesting Light mysticism was a global phenomenon even before more overt cultural exchanges of the Axial age. The North Dakotan Lakota medicine man Gary Holy Bull recounted how "Spirit often presents itself as a light, whether it be bluish or white sparks or a mellow glow of warm light."[5] While in deep prayer, Ava Tapa Miri, a Guarani forest shaman in Paraguay, received a sacred song from the forest spirits while "a very bright light came to me and gave me the power to be a strong shaman."[6]

The Balinese shaman I Gusti Gede Raka Antara told Keeney that "when nature's energy flows through you, you will feel your body having many hearts. They will all beat their rhythms. These hearts can pump an energy that brings forth the sacred light. The most powerful light is blue."[7] Mother Samel of the syncretic African/Christian shaman Shakers of St. Vincent says that with fasting and prayer and ecstatic dance, "the Spiritual Light comes to you in many forms...."[8]

A century earlier Knud Rasmussen, a Danish explorer of northern Canada, found that among the Iglulik Inuit Eskimos when a young man or woman wishes to become initiated into the spiritual realms they go to the Illumined Master (*Angakok*) who "extracts the disciple's soul from his eyes" teaching the disciple to "draw the soul from the body" and gifting her with *angakoq* or *qaumaneq*, a "lightening" or "enlightenment" that "consists of a mysterious light which the shaman suddenly feels in his body, inside his head, within the brain, an inexplicable searchlight, a luminous fire."[9]

The Angakok spiritual adept told Rasmussen that this light was absolutely requisite, saying "every real shaman has to feel qaumaneq, a light within the body, inside his head or his brain, something that gleams like fire."[10]

Again traversing cultures, Eliade details how young aboriginal Australian seekers go for initiation to the master. The aboriginee adept is one for whom "Light shines from his eyes." During their initiatory death/rebirth, the young aspirants are "filled with a substance considered to be solidified light (and) when mystically resurrected, said to bathe in an interior supernatural Light." According to Eliade, despite over 10,000 miles separating them, these Australian medicine men share "the same identification between spiritual Light, gnosis, ascension, clairvoyance and supercognitional faculties found in the Eskimo shamans."[11]

A similar universalism is expressed by the modern Cherokee artist Sara Bates, who recounts a regular "experience of communing directly with an inner Light." She relates that "this is a common type of experience in my spiritual tradition" and notes an interesting conversation in which one of her colleagues said, "'Do you think you have to be Cherokee to have this type of experience?' He thought, of course, that I would say 'Yes,' but I said 'no, of course not.'"[12]

Interestingly, while this appendix deals with the oldest traditions, most of these quotes come from the last two generations, as shamanism is primarily an oral tradition. But this is no new venture for the shamans. The Bushmen, for instance, explicitly teach that they have always sought and contacted the Light, for countless generations. When asked, the Bushman spiritual doctor Bo told Keeney directly that "We sing the same songs, dance the same dance, and see the same God as we did since the beginning of man. This is how it was for the first Bushmen."[13]

Painting by Hieronymus Bosch, entitled *The Ascent of the Blessed.* Descriptions of near-death experiences (NDEs) date back to Plato's *Republic,* and though the gods have changed, the experiences have almost always been deeply spiritual and religious. In *The Ascent of the Blessed* Hieronymus Bosch (El Bosco) painted the pathways to death as a tunnel depicting souls drifting skyward carried by winged beings to an illumined rapture. His paintings captured the belief that heaven could set tortured souls at peace. Many people who claim to have experienced NDEs have depicted their experiences. These drawings and others have been published in P. M. H. Atwater's *The Big Book of Near-Death Experiences* (courtesy of Web Gallery of Art).

CHAPTER SIX

Ineffable Light: Visions of Light in Life, During Death, and in the Afterlife

....for you are all of light and children of day,
we are not of the night or the darkness.

—St. Paul (I Thessalonians 5:5)

A wonderful story told in the East illustrates the journey of the spirit in life and after death. A holy man once embarked upon a sea voyage. As other passengers boarded the ship, one by one they saw him and, as was the custom, asked him for a piece of advice. The sage would only say the same thing to each one of them. He seemed merely to be repeating a routine admonition, the kind of aphorism that holy men echo from time to time.

"Try to be aware of death until you know what death is."

Few of the travelers felt particularly attracted or interested in this advice.

After they embarked on their journey, a terrible storm blew up. With little chance of escaping this catastrophe, the passengers fell upon their knees and started praying to God for help. They screamed in terror, prayed wildly for a miracle, but soon lost hope entirely. Meanwhile the sage sat in silence, reflective and entirely unconcerned with what seemed their imminent death. His face showed no sign of fear or anxiety, but shone with an inexplicable inner radiance.

Eventually, the buffeting stopped and the sea and sky became calm again. Only then did the passengers notice how serene the sage had been throughout the entire episode. One of them, perplexed by his strange behavior, asked him, "Did you not know that during this frightful tempest there was nothing more than a solid plank between us and certain death?"

"Ah, yes indeed," replied the sage, still radiating the same sublime light as before. "I realized at sea it was always like this. I also reflected that on land, in the normal course of events, there is *even less* between us and death."

This wisdom tale highlights not only the fragility and impermanence of life, but how close death is to us at all times. The sage remained calm because he knew not only what death is, but also what lies beyond its gates. He was fearless and completely centered because he was already infused in the light that descends from the beyond. Like all great mystics, for him the mystery of death had been solved and no longer carried any sting.

Rumi, the great 13th century master and poet, not only regarded the moment of death with joy and exaltation, but also realized that what lies beyond death is infinitely more beatific than anyone has ever imagined.

> I died as a mineral and became
> a plant, I died as a plant and
> rose to animal,
> I died as animal and I became a man.
> Why should I fear? When was I less
> by dying? Yet, once more, I shall die
> as man, to soar—With angels
> blessed, but even from angelhood I
> must pass on; all except God doth
> perish.
> When I have sacrificed my angel soul,
> I shall became what no mind e'er
> conceived, Oh, let me not exist, for
> non-existence
> Proclaims in organ-tones, "To Him we shall return."[1]

For centuries, visionaries, saints, and prophets have spoken eloquently about their mystical encounters after leaving the body. With the advent of the study of near-death phenomena, their writings have become widely available, not only to the scientific community but also to the public at large. Visions of the Light have been a central feature of most sacred traditions, whether occurring as a result of an intense spiritual training or a traumatic event such as an accident or near-death experience. The process of leaving the body became known as the sacred art of dying (*Ars Moriendi*) and was practiced by mystics in many traditions. St. Paul referred to it cryptically when he said "I die daily" (I Corinthians 15:31). The Zen Master Bunan said, "While living, Be a dead man, / Be thoroughly dead—And behave as you like, / And all is well."[2] Tibetan Buddhists referred to this process as entering into the "radiance of the clear light of pure reality. Recognize it."[3] Likewise, Hindu masters spoke often and with great detail about the methods of dying. Gopal, one of the great bards of Hinduism, tells us, "Die before dying, die living." Krishna, in one of his most eloquent soliloquies, counsels Arjuna to follow the path, which will lead to what the Vedic seers call the Eternal.

> Let a man close up all [the
> body's] gates, Stem his mind
> within his heart,
> Fix his breath within his
> head, Engrossed in
> Yogic concentration.
> Let him utter [the word] Om, Brahman in
> one syllable, Keeping Me in mind;
> Then when his time is come to leave aside
> the body, He'll tread the highest Way.
> How easily am I won
> by him Who bears Me in
> mind unceasingly,
> Thinking nothing
> else at all—A Yogin
> integrated ever.[4]

Thanks to scientific research into meditation and the near-death experience, a significant body of anecdotal evidence corroborates the great mystics' and saints' testimonies. This evidence, gathered from over six hundred studies and thousands of Near-death Experiences (NDEs) and Out-of-Body Experiences (OBEs), has radically altered our understanding of God, death, and what lies beyond it.[5] A 1982 Gallup Poll taken in the United States estimated that about eight million people had undergone an NDE sometime during their lives. A decade later about 13 million out of 260 million Americans reported having an NDE at some point in their lives. This meant that approximately 5% of American adults have had an NDE, and extrapolating from these numbers, an average of about 774 people per day somewhere in the country undergo a near-death experience during that time-frame.[6] This does not include the many others who have OBEs or sudden visions of light (radical epiphanies) during meditation. The frequency and increasing visibility of all of these testimonies is having a cumulative influence in reshaping public perceptions of mysticism and spirituality itself.

Near-death Research and the
Experience of Divine Light and Music

The cumulative evidence now overwhelmingly supports the view that divine light and music[7] are an integral part of the visionary and auditory experience of of many of those who have had near-death experiences. More important, the evidence suggests that these experiences are not just culturally, religiously, or intellectually preconceived or imagined, but exist *a priori* as universal, eternal spiritual realities. The work of NDE researchers such as Pim Van Lommel with young children asserts that the experience of Light is not culturally...transmitted nor a projection of the subconscious.[8] In short, the experience of light and celestial music is the underlying fundamental unity of the inner spiritual worlds.

The implications of these findings are vast and potentially far-reaching. These conclusions suggest that we are in the process of a major paradigm shift, the likes of which has not occurred since the cultural transformations in 16th century Europe, prompted by the publication of the Gutenberg Bible. We are entering what some have called a golden age of spirituality in which all faiths are seen as facets of the same truth, and where apparent theological differences in religions are ultimately transmuted into an experiential unity.

In our day, the widespread knowledge of inner spiritual dimensions of reality has been made apparent by the research into NDEs—research that is now available for all to explore and digest. Following the research into near-death phenomena, entire new fields of knowledge have emerged. The study of NDEs prompted the concept of nonlocal or unified consciousness, which allows us to understand much better a wide range of special states of consciousness. These include "mystical and religious experiences, deathbed visions (end of life experiences), perimortem and postmortem experiences (nonlocal communication), heightened intuitive feelings (nonlocal information exchange), prognostic dreams, remote viewing (nonlocal perception), and the mind's influence on matter (nonlocal perturbation)."[9] Some of the emerging implications from these findings suggest that while there may be many paths to Truth, the spiritual reality behind them is *essentially one*. The great explorers of inner space have corroborated this truth through their own experiences of divine light and music despite significant differences in language, culture, and degree of evolution. The consensus of the greatest mystics of the world's traditions, regardless of time, culture, age, ethnicity, or prior spiritual training, corroborates evidence of a scientific nature, supporting their personal experiential findings.

Visions of Light in Life, Death and in the Afterlife

There is a single universal all-encompassing Light, which exhibits three attributes: love, life, and intelligence or wisdom. These three attributes repeatedly appear in NDEs. (We will address later in this chapter the visions of light in normal circumstances.) Specifically, such appearances of light generally occur in the seventh stage of more advanced near-death experiences.

Researchers have outlined the stages of NDEs as follows.

1. In the first stage, persons undergoing an NDE generally experience some form of strange or altered state of consciousness without pain or bodily sensation.

2. In the second stage, they experience feelings of deep peace and quiet and the loss of all physical pain.

3. In the third stage, they usually find themselves separated from their body. Here they can view their body from somewhere above it. Their sense of hearing and sight is greatly heightened, and they can often see through things and move through walls without limitations. These "new senses" operate beyond the limitation of the time-space continuum. Through this new extrasensory perception, they now begin to be aware of another reality.

4. In the fourth stage, they find themselves moving in a dimensionless space through a dark tunnel, sometimes accompanied by the sound of bells or rushing of water.

5. The fifth stage is reached when they sense a non-earthly environment and often a dazzling astral landscape with gorgeous colors.

6. In the sixth stage, people often meet deceased ancestors whom they clearly recognize.

7. The seventh stage is reached when they see some light at a point in the distance and are magnetically drawn to it, enveloped by it, and then embraced by it or met by some being of light which then guides them further.

Dante in his epic *The Divine Comedy* speaks of this last stage of the journey: "I have been in that Heaven that knows his light most, and have seen things, which whoever descends from there has neither power, nor knowledge, to relate."[10]

P. M. H. Atwater noted in her book that many children and adults have an element of light in their account. She also believes that a new generation of children are incarnating who will be more empathic and compassionate as a result of their Near Death Experiences.[11]

The Attributes of Love, Life, and Wisdom

The same inner light experienced by the great saints, sages, and mystics is, in both intensity and degree, witnessed by those who undergo NDEs. It is also, in many cases, identified as or with God, and as the source of love, and substance of Life. Many who experience NDEs see this same eternal "ringing radiance" as the source of perfect wisdom or super intelligence.

As the light enters into and embraces the inner spirit, the person often experiences a sense of deep, profound transformation. After the NDE, this trans-formational catalyst often results in significant lifestyle and character changes with far-reaching effects. Along with this powerful transformational catalyst comes a new acceptance of oneself and interest in the meaning of life. Life itself takes on a higher purpose, filled with ever-increasing amounts of joy and peace never known before. This element of lasting transformation distinguishes the experiences of inner light from other non-light meditative experiences, and is well-documented in the extensive work of Dutch cardiologist Pim Van Lommel.[12]

The vast field of near-death studies has accomplished a great deal in validating these phenomena as real and not hallucinations or drug-induced. Yet surprisingly, very little direct research has explored the meaning of the visionary experiences of light and sound, which figure prominently in many NDEs. In trying to understand these experiences coherently, we have chosen to view them through the eyes of a cross-section of those who have actually experienced them. For our purposes, these experiences can be generally classified into six broad themes or categories:

1. God's Light and Music is omni-present all-encompassing.
2. The Light is experienced as all-embracing unconditional love and wisdom.
3. Human life is an expression of the infinite continuum of Light, appearing and reappearing through countless lives and bodies (viewed as reincarnation or transmigration).
4. Spiritual evolution is the highest purpose of human life.
5. The process of evolution is a self-reflective process free of eternal judgment.
6. The Light is the central element in reshaping and changing people's lives.

In the following personal accounts, we have selected some of the most powerful and archetypical experiences that illustrate one or more of these six themes.

Near-death Experiences

The Buddha of Unchanging Light: Lingza Chokyi

To underscore the universal nature of this phenomenon, we begin with a classic account of the near-death experience from Tibet. *The Tibetan Book of the Dead,* long considered one of the most powerful texts dealing with death and dying, welcomes the dying person who is about to enter the Light with these words, "O son/daughter of an enlightened family....your Rigpa is inseparable luminosity and emptiness and dwells as a great expanse of light; beyond birth and death. It is, in fact, the Buddha of Unchanging Light."[13]

Central to understanding Tibetan wisdom concerning near-death experience is the concept of the *delok,* "one who has returned from death." Traditionally, deloks were people who left their bodies as a result of some illness and find themselves traveling in the *bardo* or afterlife realms. They would often travel through the hellish realms, and sometimes paradises and Buddha realms. When they returned, they would recount their experiences to others and admonish them to lead more truly spiritual lives. Often deloks had a very difficult time making people believe their stories. Nevertheless, the accounts of some of the better-known deloks were written down and sung all over Tibet. Contemporary Tibetan scholar Sogyal Rinpoche recounts one of the stories told to him of a well-known delok.

Lingza Chokyi was a delok who lived in Tibet in the 16th century. At the time of her experience, she left her body but did not realize she was "dead," something that occurs in a number of NDE testimonies.

She felt intense joy and happiness when her spiritual master started praying for her and "immeasurable happiness when finally she came before the master who was praying for her, and her mind and his became one."[14] Later, she heard someone she thought was her father calling her and she followed him. After a while, she arrived in the bardo realm.[15] Finally, she was sent back to earth, as it was not her time to die. With a new perspective on life, she spent the rest of her life telling people what she had learned.

This tradition of deloks continues in Tibet today. Deloks are from various social backgrounds. Having had an NDE, the delok returns, tells people what special messages she or he received and instructs them how to live more spiritual lives. Some deloks are even known to "die" on special Buddhist holidays for a number of hours and return, bringing with them special messages from the dead to the living.

The Light as Unconditional Love: Howard Storm

Howard Storm was an avowed atheist who was hostile to all religions and those who practiced them. "He considered all belief systems associated with religion to be fantasies for people to deceive themselves with." Locked as he was into a view of life devoid of spirituality or higher purpose, the concept of God meant nothing to him. All this was to change dramatically. On June 1, 1985, at the age of 38, Howard had a near-death experience caused by a perforation of his stomach. This led to one of the most remarkable afterlife experiences on record.

While many NDE survivors typically experience some transformational shift after returning to normal life, Howard's transformation entailed a 180-degree turn into a new and higher life of the spirit. Through an experience of divine love, he changed from an atheist to a staunch theist, and from a self-centered recluse to a compassionate humanitarian.

Shortly after he realized he had left his body, he heard a soft quiet voice speaking to him. He describes how this voice inside his head repeated a line from a nursery song he had heard in his childhood. The voice, which was his own, sang the song, "Jesus loves me, Yes, I know...." This inner voice kept repeating again and again until he screamed out inside "Jesus save me...."

> When I did that, I saw off in the darkness somewhere, the tiniest little star....Then I realized it was coming toward me. It was getting very bright, rapidly. When the light came near, its radiance spilled over me, and I just rose up—not with my effort—I just lifted up. Then I saw...—I saw all my wounds, all my tears, all my brokenness, melt away. And I became whole in this radiance....
>
> I knew that he knew everything about me and I was being unconditionally loved and accepted. He was a concentrated field of energy, radiant in splendor indescribable, except to say goodness and love....And we, I and this light, went up and out of there. We started going faster and faster, out of the darkness. Embraced by the light, feeling wonderful and crying, I saw off in the distance something that looked like the picture of a galaxy, except that it was larger and there were more stars than I had seen on Earth. There was a great center of brilliance. In the center there was an enormously bright concentration. Outside the center millions of spheres of light were flying about entering and leaving what was a great beingness at the center.[16]

In many ways Howard's life before his NDE is emblematic of millions of people who are actively hostile to spirituality, whose lives are focused solely on the material world and the temporary pleasures associated with it. In his case, he had no belief in anything that could not be physically seen, touched, or felt. After his NDE, he accepted the reality of the spiritual world—which, though not visible with the physical eyes, was more real and tangible than any physical reality he had ever known. Following his single experience with this great "being-ness of light" as he understood it, his life was never to be the same again. He understood in the depths of his soul, that the being of light that he encountered was an all-forgiving, all-knowing presence, which unconditionally loved and accepted him. He now knew he was loved in a way no words could possibly describe. The being of light knew, and fully accepted, everything he had ever done, said, or even thought.

As Howard continued on his inner journey, the being of light escorted him to a huge concentration of light where he saw a "great being-ness" at the center. As he approached this effulgent radiance, he met and spoke with many other luminous beings of light, all of whom unconditionally embraced him and loved him. As he gazed around, he saw countless other radiant beings filling the sky so densely as to appear as one. His entire conversation during this time, as is the norm with many NDEs, was conducted telepathically, without the aid of words or language as we know it.

He recounts how he was magically held in space yet motionless for what seemed like a very long time. While this was transpiring radiant beings surrounded and engulfed him with their transparent light bodies. Their selves were in such harmony with the Creator that they were really just one.

He was told that one of the reasons these beings longed to return

> ...to their source, was to become invigorated with this sense of harmony and oneness. Being apart for too long a time diminished them and made them feel separate. Their greatest pleasure was to go back to the source of all life.[17]

In this amazing chronicle, Storm experienced a tiny drop of the great ocean of unity consciousness known to mystics. In this new heavenly realm, he realized there is only one language and that is love. Love binds all souls together and they are in fact one light in myriad different forms. He realized that nothing separates him from anyone else: indeed, as the great Hindu sages declared, *Aham Brahm Asmi* or "all consciousness is one."

This peace literally goes beyond intellect and human capacity to judge or fathom. After Howard Storm's NDE, over time, he not only completely changed his lifestyle, beliefs, and character, but also went on to write and share his experiences with thousands of others.

God As "An Explosion of Light": Christian Andréason

The story of Christian Andréason follows many of the archetypical patterns of the NDE: he went through a dark tunnel, was ushered into various regions of light, met a luminous being of light who took him through a review of his past lives. The next steps in his journey, however, went well beyond the normal NDE, and included a face-to-face and soul-to-soul encounter with the most rapturous light, which he equates with the very essence of God. His experience of "God as Light" filled him with an ecstasy and peace that he had never even remotely experienced before. However, what makes Andréason's journey even more significant is his travel backward through time to the pre-eternal moment of creation. Here he narrates his journey at warp speed, outside the time-space continuum, to the primal moment when Creation first began. He then relives the first moment of Creation as a burst of ineffable light not unlike many of the scriptural testimonies given by mystics of various religious traditions. His detailed description often resembles certain aspects of the recent creation theories proposed by certain quantum theorists as an instantaneous burst of energy.[18]

Andréason's remarkable story begins after he has left his body, passed through a dark tunnel, and been escorted to heaven or what he perceives heaven to be. In nearly all NDE accounts, the participants' understanding of heaven involves a non-dogmatic intuitive knowing or divine disclosure. The full meaning of this divine Light and its effect on him are only fully revealed after a profound four-dimensional past lives review. His particular past life review is unique for its illuminating insight into the significance of past life reviews, not as "punishments," but as catalysts in the pilgrim soul's journey to understand itself and correct its errors. Andréason is mystically brought to a room where the walls and ceilings are made of pure crystal and are emanating light while four gigantic translucent screens project all the experiences of his past lives.

> The effect was amazing. Then as I looked up, I saw four translucent screens appear (and form a kind of gigantic box around me). It was through this method that I was shown my life review. (Or rather I should say my lives in review.)[19]

Andréason is given a "life review" by these beings of light, who show him his past, present, and even aspects of his future. Before the review ends, his entire conception of God is altered forever. He is shown the "Throne of Heaven" or what he believes to be a non-linear luminous Being of Light. He is then unshered into a great hall in the center of a luminous golden city where he perceives the "highest presence of God." This golden city made of "light" has been referred to in different traditions as one of many heavens located in a high realm. He describes his experience as he enters the threshold of this region:

> As I entered the room, I was washed with a brilliant white, golden and rose colored Light which filled me with indescribable happiness. I knew this light had created me, as it had everything else. The Light was God..., both Father and Mother Creator mixed together...
>
> I was lifted high up into the Great Light, and as this happened, I felt fully embraced by my Creator. I knew without a doubt that this omnipresent being found great delight in me and I clearly heard [the] thought that I was considered a perfect being of the Creator's Creation.[20]

Andréason's experiences reveal two of the most prominent features in near-death literature; that this Light is God and that God is Light, and that this all-loving Light created him, loves him, and, in its eyes, views him as already a "perfect being." God sees him, and indeed, sees all souls as eternally perfect. Not surprisingly, many mystics have corroborated his testimony in a variety of religious traditions. The soul, which is a part of God, is already perfect, immortal, fearless, and brimming over with divine wisdom and love.[21] The errors we have made are due to our minds. Through the agency of our own minds, we have made choices, which have led us away from this light. The further we move away from this light, (God) both literally and metaphorically, the more the soul experiences pain, suffering, separation, and continuous restlessness. As the soul comes to understand its identity as Light, it willingly and passionately seeks reunion with its source. The more each soul realizes its own unique essence as love, the more it sees all souls as unique and perfect expressions of love as well.

Christian Andréason then traveled to what he perceives as the primal beginning of Creation. Here he witnessed the primal "explosion" of Light and the center of God's being as a "singing, pulsing, Joy-filled ball of bright Golden Light." This experience of the beginning of Creation as a singular explosion of light does not happen in past or future time, but in the eternal now. Creation is not a past event but a continuous act of recreating itself moment by moment. Scientists may well find many parallels with recent research on the Big Bang Theory and the origin of creation with these and other similar accounts. It also coincides with the most recent string theory now advocated by Quantum physicists.

> I was then shown the time we call the beginning of Creation. There was a huge explosion, coming from a singing, pulsing, Joy-filled ball of bright Golden Light. I knew that I had been a part of this great Light, as have the rest of us. From this light exploding, I found myself happily and quite excitedly hurtling through space and time. I arrived safely in a perfect place of peace and amazing splendor. I knew immediately that

this place was geared toward the expansion and education of every Soul that came here....[22]

Andréason immediately understood he had been taken to a "realm" where he would continue his spiritual training and evolution. His realization that the evolution of the soul does does not stop at the time of death but continues forward came as a surprise to him. Each soul finds itself in the region most suitable to his own evolutionary journey. The divine plan carefully and precisely provides the specific "curriculum" most appropriate for the soul's continued progression.

Andréason echoes in passing the theme of God as Light and "singing" music, but his description goes beyond the usual testimonies in elaborating the birth of creation as an explosion of great light and one of singular joy and happiness. Even more important, he understands that he, and indeed all souls are a part of this great all-encompassing light.

Here is the tacit recognition of our collective divine origin as divine Light and the "Word of God" as actual inner sound or music. This inner sound is the creative life principle that brings all creation into being. Immediately afterward, he is taken to a special "realm" where he recognizes that his entire purpose since the moment he was created is to expand and educate his soul. Ultimately, his highest purpose is to return to the Source of his very being and the source of all-being, which is God. Andréason then reveals an almost scientific perspective on the nature of God and Creation. His testimony is particularly relevant in light of the recent discoveries in quantum and unified field theory in the new physics:[23]

> God is an essence of absolute Love, Light and beautiful sound. What I understood to be the Word of God, is actually the Sound or Music of God. God is a great Light-filled Being who sings all tones simultaneously and uses this method to bring all things into existence....He then extends his Light and helps that Creation to take form. All of us hold Light and Tones within....We are here to learn how to better use them by living life in a difficult environment for the spirit and Soul...the physical body.[24]

God as "pro-creative Sound" and radiant music is quite common in many NDE accounts, but Christian's testimony strikes a new note. He sees with the eyes and heart of a mystic when he tells us it is "God (who) uses His Sound to create all things and give them life" and "All of us hold light and Tones within." He comes to the powerful realization that each of us is here to perfect our soul and learn how to better use this Light and Sound. We are here to deepen our understanding of these eternal principles by living in this difficult environment we call the earth. As the physical realm entails constant toil and struggle, it provides the environmental catalyst whereby the vision and growth of the soul can be expedited. The great mystics of many traditions have noted that, on the higher spiritual regions, the soul's progress is much slower because of the blissful surroundings and intensity of love that the soul experiences. The impact of living in these difficult earthly surroundings is like fire applied to iron; fire purifies the metal of its foreign substances and makes it even stronger.

He comes to realize that as he strengthens his soul's connection to this "Great Light-filled being," he will more quickly realize his soul's immortal nature. The more he reconnects to his Source the more he will experience the qualities of compassion, love, truth, fearlessness, immortality, and peace. Andréason comes to the profound understanding that the soul's purpose here is to harmonize with this Light and bring abiding peace, joy, and happiness to all. Christian Andréason's past life, while amazing in its detailed reference to "scientific data and universal codes," echoes universal themes of the immortality of the soul, and realization of oneself as soul or spirit.

> Without ever having to turn my head, I saw my past, my present, my future and there was even a screen that displayed a tremendous amount of scientific data, numbers and universal codes. I saw the beginning of my known existences as a Soul and saw that I had existed spirituality long before this incarnation…I saw that it is a big Universe out there and God has it all organized perfectly. Each of us is sent where we can obtain the best growth according to our Divine Purpose.[25]

The Light of Perfect Wisdom: Tiffany Snow

Tiffany Snow's NDE account illustrates many of the core themes already brought forward in other NDE accounts, including God as Light and Music, the Light as the pro-creative power of the universe, and the Light as eternally loving and all-forgiving. Her testimony additionally introduces a new central theme of many NDE accounts, including "the Light as Perfect wisdom and knowledge" and the inner subtle dynamics of light bodies and spiritual travel.

Tiffany's account differs substantially from our previous accounts in two respects. She had no particular belief in the supernatural. Snow had no prior acquaintance with or knowledge of the mystical realities beyond death. As a direct result of her NDE, her inner spiritual eye was opened and she became a witness to the unseen world of the spirit on a daily basis. As time passed, she became an ordained minister through which she employed her gifts to help heal and guide others to a deeper and more enriching view of life. Tiffany was a successful songwriter and record producer in Nashville when lightning struck her and almost took her life. In looking back, she noted wisely, "The best thing that ever happened in my life was almost losing it."[26] Her account, remarkable in its detail, begins when she was "standing in the pouring rain with arms out-stretched, (when) the lightning struck, and I did an uncontrollable electrical dance as my muscles spasmed. I felt no pain, and all went black. I died." She does not recall a passage through a dark tunnel but, like many other accounts, she simply finds herself in a new world of light.

> Next I found myself standing on nothing, way up in the universe, and there were distant colorful planets all around me. I could see misty pinpoints of stars, and when I moved my arm back and forth it made the stars look wiggly, like a reflection on water....
>
> Meanwhile, we were speeding toward a great elliptical ball of spin-ning light, brilliantly white in the middle and yellowish on the outside edges. The closer we got to it, the more I felt overwhelming Love; it seemed so warm and comforting. I felt like a child being held....
>
> I wanted to go on. I felt like a magnet, irresistibly drawn. The desire to "blend" grew stronger the closer we got. I knew the light beyond was the very Presence of God, heaven itself. A flowing luminosity appeared in front of me. Coming together to form a head, shoulders, and body a voice called out from the golden sparkles massed in front of me. "What have you learned?" he asked.[27]

Tiffany's powerful testimony underscores a common reoccurring theme—that God is a Supreme all-embracing Light which communicates through a non-verbal universal language of love. However, two aspects of her testimony shed extraordinary new insight into the nature of the inner spiritual realties and are rarely found in most NDE accounts. Tiffany notices that she is traveling in what mystics call a "light body," which is a translucent, mirror image of her physical body. This light body has 360-degree vision and can see all things and through all things. As a soul enters into the new realms of light, the soul's horizons are vastly expanded. It intuitively understands life in these worlds is much richer and full-er, and communication is nearly instantaneous. It comes to realize that this new "light body" is exactly like its physical body, but made up of finer translucent par-ticles of light. Overall, it finds itself filled with a spiritual peace and ecstatic joy it has never known before. We have mentioned in previous chapters the various references to this mystical light body in the various religious traditions.[28]

St. Paul in the New Testament said:

> But God giveth it a body as it hath pleased him, and to every seed his own body...There are also celestial bodies and bodies terrestrial: but the glory of the celestial bodies is one and the glory of the terrestrial is another...There is a natural body, and there is a spiritual body...Behold I show you a mystery; we shall not all sleep, but we shall all be changed. (Corinthians 15:35–32)

Tiffany later comes to understand that this light, while far more bright and beautiful than any physical light, can also be intensely purifying. Her story contains a warning that is common among many contemplative traditions.

> But this brilliant, blinding light could not be dimmed. It was like a fire that totally consumed me, and it was more brilliant that any earthly light....
>
> I still remember being on my knees while this brilliant, blinding light broke and crushed my hard-heartedness; the prideful nature that predominated in me and through sinful living had actually made a home in me.[29]

Tiffany's experience of intense purification, while not common in most NDE literature, is actually quite routine to mystics who enter into the spiritual realms on a daily basis. Those who are fully conversant with this light know that it is not only all-loving and all-embracing, but also deeply purifying, transforming, and ultimately healing. As the luminosity of the soul increases, so does its capacity to experience greater and greater light.

One of the most interesting features of many NDEs is what is now known as a past life review. These experiences are typically "facilitated" by several beings of light that reveal to the soul its past, present, and, on rare occasions, even the future. These reviews take place in eternal time where there is no sense of past or future, neither is there any sense of judgment toward the souls. The purpose of the review is to show the soul the effect of its actions on others and on oneself while instructing each soul in the fundamental truth of the universe, that all consciousness is one. Brian Krebs describes his unusual life review.

> I felt a presence next to me, a man, and he asked if I was ready for my life review. I said yes. All of this not a verbal thing, but just a knowledge. Then I saw something like an HO scale train set below, a city. I went to this city and I went through my life. I went through every moment and every feeling. I was not afraid as I was still in the light. I talked with the man about my life. But I do not remember any specifics.
>
> I then went to twelve beings of greater knowledge. They were in front of me and stood in a row. They were not human. They had no feelings of anything like judgment or authority, but seemed strong in themselves. They seemed taller than I did and they wore silver white robes. They had white skin, large heads and large eyes. I do not remember them having a mouth. Above them was a spirit. It was like a star as we see one from earth, but in size it appeared the same size as the heads of the beings. The spirit went to my left and hovered above the first being. I remember it was like a video of knowledge springing from the being's hands, which were held in front of them.[30]

The knowledge conveyed to the soul is boundless, transformational, and indescribable in human language. Its primary aim is not to condemn or punish, but to reveal to the soul the inherent unity of all life. Every thought, word, and deed has an effect on others and oneself. Hindus have called it the law of karma or action and reaction; a Christian corollary to this can be found in Galatians 6:7 "you reap whatever you sow." It is, in common language, the law of cause and effect or Newton's first law of thermodynamics: every action has an equal and opposite reaction. In the process of revealing our past actions, the soul experiences within itself the pain or joy it inflicted on others. Thereby, it comes to see the naked reality that whatever one does to others is ultimately done to oneself.

In the next segment of this account, rare in NDE literature, the soul is given an even greater experience of the infinite nature of eternity and its true purpose here.

> Suddenly, an enormous explosion erupted beneath me, an explosion of light rolling out in the farthest limits of my vision. I was in the center of the Light. It blew away everything, including the fog. It reached the ends of the universe, which I could see, and doubled back on itself, in endless layers. I was watching eternity unfold.
>
> The light was brighter than hundreds of suns, but it did not hurt my eyes. I had never seen anything as luminous or as golden as this Light, and I immediately understood it was entirely composed of love, all directed at me. This wonderful, vibrant love was very personal, as you might describe secular love, but also sacred....
>
> This light gave me knowledge, though I heard no words....I was learning the answers to the eternal questions of life—so old we laugh them off as clichés. "Why are we here?" To learn. "What's the purpose of our life?" To love. I felt as if I was remembering things I had once known but somehow forgotten, and it seemed incredible that I had not figured out these things before now.[31]

One of the greatest realizations, which arise after returning from these encounters in the light, is the deep recognition of *who we are*. A profound sense of detachment toward one's own body arises spontaneously from the experience of this ineffable light. With it comes the knowledge of the nature of the true Self. The real self is not the body or the mind but the indwelling consciousness. She sees in the end, "Whatever constituted the self I knew as me was no longer there. My essence, my consciousness, my memories, my personality were outside, not in, that person of flesh."[32]

A Mandala of Souls: Mellen-Thomas Benedict

Mellen-Thomas Benedict's NDE stands as one of the most extraordinary accounts in recorded history, both for its comprehension of the nature of spiritual reality and his insight into the universal matrix of light. His story confirms many of the themes already discussed, including the experience of God as Light, the infinite loving nature of God, and the importance of realizing this light in one's own self. Since his NDE, Mellon-Thomas has been studying the mechanics of cellular communication and the relationship of Light to life called quantum biology. His research is providing dramatic new perspectives on how living cells respond to light stimulation resulting in, among other things, high-speed healing. Dr. Kenneth Ring, one of the pioneers of NDE research, remarked, "His story is one of the most remarkable I have encountered in my extensive research on near-death experiences."[33]

Mellen-Thomas was dying from terminal cancer, having been diagnosed over a year earlier. He described himself as someone with little spiritual inclination and an often cynical view of the world. Like our other case studies, he had no previous spiritual training and little interest in spirituality. Unlike our previous profiles, however, he had been increasingly despondent over the growing ecological and nuclear crisis engulfing the planet. At the time of his NDE, he was a self-employed stained-glass artist who had no medical insurance. But, following his diagnosis, he had begun a mindful journey toward healing. He experimented with many kinds of alternative healing modalities and began reading about spirituality as well. As he approached his end, he avoided taking drugs since he wanted to be as conscious as possible. After nearly 18 months of gradual deterioration, he knew he was reaching his end.

> I remember waking up one morning at home about 4:30 am, and I just knew this was it. This was the day I was going to die...I went back to sleep. The next thing I remember is the beginning of a typical near-death experience. Suddenly I was fully aware and I was standing up, but my body was in the bed. There was this darkness around me. Being out of my body was even more vivid than ordinary experience. It was so vivid that I could see every room in the house. I could see the top of the house, I could see around the house. I could see under the house. There was this light shining. I turned toward the light. The light was very similar to what many other people have described in their near-death experiences. It was so magnificent. It is tangible, you can feel it. It is alluring; you want to go to it, like you would want to go to your ideal mother's or father's arms. As I began to move to the light, I knew intuitively that if I went to the light, I would be dead....

The light kept changing into different figures...archetypal images and signs. I asked the light, "What is going on here? Please, light, clarify yourself for me. I really want to know the reality of the situation."[34]

Mellen-Thomas's experience up to this point reflects many common features of near-death experiences, including 360-degree vision of the soul, the loving nature of the Light, and the appearances of archetypal beings of light. What seems unique to his story are the multiple forms of beings and the explanation for the revelations of these varied forms. Here the Light takes on multiple forms, each an archetypal representative from the Source. This all-knowing light replies to Mellen-Thomas's questions in accordance with his capacity to receive.

I cannot really say the exact words, because it was sort of telepathy. As the light revealed itself to me, I became aware that what I was really seeing was our Higher Self matrix. The only thing I can tell you is that it turned into a matrix, a mandala of human souls, and what I saw was that what we call our Higher Self...is a matrix. It's also a conduit to the Source; each one of us comes directly, as a direct experience from the Source. We all have a Higher Self, or an oversoul part of our being. It revealed itself to me in its truest energy form. The only way I can really describe it is that the being of the Higher Self is more like a conduit. It did not look like that, but it is a direct connection to the Source that each and every one of us has. We are directly connected to the Source.[35]

Mellen-Thomas's experience attests that each soul is simultaneously connected to every other soul in a spherical "mandala of souls." All individual souls only seem to be separate. From the perspective of our ordinary senses, our bodies appear to be physically separate entities. From the spiritual perspective, however, these boundaries and limitations are an illusion that keeps us from seeing all consciousness is One. If anything separates us, it is the nature of our thinking and degree of understanding. Furthermore, since consciousness is indivisible, all souls are eternally one with their Source. We are part of a universal consciousness, connecting everything. As Mellen-Thomas later realized, the more powerful the experience of Light and Sound the greater the realization of this oneness.

His realization goes significantly beyond the stereotypical language of most near-death accounts, and sounds like the revelations of the mystics and saints profiled in previous chapters. In this section, he becomes one with this Higher Self matrix, and intuitively recognizes what great spiritual masters have been saying for thousands of years, "All Consciousness is One." In the words of the Vedic sages, "God is all consciousness, the soul is a part of God, and therefore soul is pure consciousness."

So the light was showing me the Higher Self Matrix. And it became very clear to me that all the Higher Selves are connected as one being, all humans are connected as one being, we are actually the same being, different aspects of the same being. It was not committed to one particular religion. So that is what was being fed back to me. And I saw this mandala of human souls. It was the most beautiful thing I have ever seen. I just went into it and, it was just overwhelming. It was like all the love you've ever wanted, and it was the kind of love that cures, heals, and regenerates.[36]

Mellen-Thomas later experienced an even greater degree of spiritual expansion, as his soul entered what he called the "stream of consciousness." The ineffable Light, knowing his desire for greater understanding, took him on a journey to what he perceived to be the pre-eternal beginnings of creation. Here he realized that there is no limit to his own consciousness. As his own consciousness expands, the universe expands with him. As he ascends, his soul becomes universalized as his individual self begins to merge in the Greater Self—and the Greater Self into what the mystics have called cosmic consciousness, and even greater super cosmic consciousness. Mellen-Thomas finally arrived at the moment where his perception expanded infinitely in all directions. Here he witnessed the primal act of creation going on endlessly as an eternal recreation of itself on a moment-to-moment basis.

When I say that I could see or perceive forever, I mean that I could experience all of creation generating itself. It was without beginning and without end. That's a mind-expanding thought, isn't it? Scientists perceive the Big Bang as a single event, which created the universe. I saw that the Big Bang is only one of an infinite number of Big Bangs creating universes endlessly and simultaneously. The only images that even come close in human terms would be those created by supercomputers using fractal geometry equations.[37]

His NDE ushered him into the consciousness of the mystics, where the secrets of the universe, causation, and creation are all simultaneously revealed. As such, his experience echoes that of mystics who traverse these worlds on a daily basis. Mellen-Thomas came to understand that everything is of God. "Every hair on your head, through every leaf on every tree, through every atom God is experiencing God's Self, the great 'I am.' I began to see that everything that is, is the Self, literally, your Self, my Self. Everything is the great Self." As he rode back on this infinite stream of light, he saw, "All energy this side of the Big Bang is light. Every sub-atom, atom, star, planet, even consciousness itself is made of light and it has a frequency and/or particle. Light is living Stuff." Not only is this light the living essence of which we are, but also it is the essence of everything. As a living vibration, the light is perceived in two ways in many NDEs—as light, and also as sound, music, or what Mellen-Thomas referred to as "sonic booms." Here he describes his understanding of this aspect of his experience:

> I could see all the energy that this solar system generates, and it is an incredible light show. I could hear the music of the spheres. Our solar system, as do all celestial bodies, generates a unique matrix of light, sound and vibratory energies.[38]

Mellen-Thomas returned to his physical body and felt that he was forever changed. All his questions about himself, his purpose, the universe, and creation itself "were answered on the other side." His testimony speaks of a man who has traveled light years in his own evolution: "We are literally God exploring God's Self in an infinite Dance of life. Your uniqueness enhances all of life."[39]

Becoming the Love You Already Are: Laurelynn Martin

Laurelynn Martin's NDE, while dramatic and insightful like the others we've considered, exemplifies the more personal quality of many such experiences. Her NDE confirms a single overriding reality: *We are here to become the love we already are.* By "giving love one receives and experiences the tremendous love of the universe." Ultimately, the primary realization of most near-death survivors is a deeper understanding of the importance of love.

Indeed, the spiritual Master Sant Kirpal Singh put it succinctly, "God is love,, the soul is love and the way back to God is also through love."

Laurelynn's near-death account begins after she left her body while on the operating table. She found herself free of pain and enjoying a state of inner freedom and happiness, while watching the surgeons perform the operation below. Gradually, she ascended to a higher realm.

> I had traveled to another realm of total and absolute peace. With no physical body my movement was unencumbered. Thought was the avenue for travel. I floated up through blackness where there was no fear, no pain, no misunderstandings, but instead a sense of well-being. I was enveloped by total bliss in an atmosphere of unconditional love and acceptance. The darkness was warm and soft, a blanket of velvety love, stretching endlessly. The freedom of total peace was intensified beyond any ecstatic feeling I've ever felt on Earth. In the distance, a horizon of glorious white, golden light beckoned me forward.
>
> As the brilliance increased and the encompassing rays stretched to meet me, I felt that time, as we know it, was nonexistent. Time and existence were a blending and a melding of the past, present and future into this one moment. A sense of all-knowing enveloped me. Every part of my being was satisfied with an unconditional love beyond description. All

questions were answered. An inner peace without striving or achieving was created and understood.[40]

Her initial experience confirms the character of the inner regions of the near-death experience. These regions are filled with joy, peace, and unconditional love. They overflow with divine acceptance and forgiveness, bursting with a light and peace that defy description or understanding. As she travels further, she meets her deceased brother-in-law who had passed away seven months earlier from cancer. Her essence moved to meet his. A profound new understanding arises from this meeting.

> I heard his smile, saw his laughter and felt his humor. It didn't make sense, but it made complete sense. We were separate but we were also one. It was as if I had come home and my brother-in-law was here to greet me. I instantly thought how glad I was to be with him, because now I could make up for the last time I had seen him before his death. I felt sad and a bit guilty for not taking the time out of my busy schedule to have a heart-to-heart talk with him when he had asked me to. I realized I was not being judged by him but by myself. I was in his position dying, wanting to say goodbye to those I loved, and then meeting people like myself not "getting it" not getting that all the achievement, money or recognition in the world cannot be taken with you when you die. The only thing you take with you is the love you give away.[41]

This recognition of universal unconditional love characterizes the highest mystical experiences, regardless of spiritual or religious tradition. Laurelynn's ultimate realization was that life was about "people, not pursuit." "I was putting pursuits first as a means to seek approval and love from people. Once I understood, I forgave myself for my actions and in the act of forgiving I received love in abundance." In our fast-paced, success-driven world, we have lost sight of the only real treasure: love. As soon as we move out of the "fast lane" and into the "vast lane," we come to see the naked emptiness of all ego-driven pursuits. As one teacher put it, "we don't need any more successful people in the world; we need more compassionate and forgiving people in the world."[42]

The Gift of Unconditional Love: Reverend Juliet Nightingale

The final account, taken from Juliet Nightingale's NDE posted on her website "Toward the Light," affirms the theme of love and compassion that arises from the deepest experiences of light and sound. Following her NDE until her death in 2009, Juliet served as a major spokesperson for the near-death movement as a member of the International Association for Near-Death Studies (IANDS). She chaired the membership committee on the IANDS board of directors, belonged to the Friends of IANDS Coastal Connecticut, and also hosted her own live Internet radio show, which often explored issues related to NDE phenomena.

Her account began with leaving the body, the usual transition into the beyond, and her first encounter with a being of light.

> I became aware of a "Being of Light" enveloping me. Everything was stunningly beautiful—so vibrant and luminous...and so full of life—yes, life!—in ways that one would never see or experience on the physical plane. I was totally and completely enveloped in divine Love. It was unconditional love...in the truest sense of the word. I was in constant communion with this Light and always aware of its loving presence with me at all times. Consequently, there was no sense of fear whatsoever... and I was never alone. This was a special opportunity to experience being at one with the ALL—never separate...and never at a loss.[43]

Like many other near-death survivors, Juliet seems unable to describe the experience of divine love, for such love lacks any parallel in ordinary human existence. Our language is inadequate for describing the sense of total peace, security, and acceptance pulsating in every cell of the body. Her story continues with a life review process, in which she found no judgment, but felt completely supported and indeed enveloped in light and peace. She also recounted her experience of being in a light body and then a grand "tour" of various locations and places in the inner worlds.

> At one point, I perceived myself as being on a guided tour, as it were—visiting and observing different places, beings and situations— some very pleasant...The best way I can describe this "tour" was like being in a circular enclosure of window—each pane revealing something different...but when I'd focus on one particular pane, I'd suddenly see the pane become full size....[44]

Juliet experienced deep compassion, as she saw souls suffering. Such universal compassion, arising spontaneously, is an attribute of this all-embracing divine love. For this newfound love seeks to heal others as it heals itself, forgive others as it forgives itself, and love others as it loves itself. Juliet's feelings of compassion formed the essence of the NDE transformation. "The prevailing feeling that I had whilst observing these souls was one of deep compassion and a yearning to comfort them. I wanted so much to see them relieved of their horrible suffering." However, she was comforted in knowing that all souls, "without exception, eventually return to the light...according to what was revealed to me."

The last piece of this amazing chronicle is the most revealing, for she was asked or instructed by this "being of light" to take on an active co-creative role in this divine work. No longer would she be a passive bystander, but she would become an active participant in the compassionate service of helping others.

After experiencing the "tour," adventures and times of play and creation, etc., things became more serious...and I was again in direct communion with the Being of Light. I was now being asked to "help" or "assist" in some way...in creating and determining the outcome of certain events, situations or even things affecting others! Me? Just little me? Oh my, I thought. That's a grave and serious responsibility. I felt so honored...and so humble...being asked to participate in such a feat....But what if I failed to do my part as needed? Then, I was assured that everything would work out exactly as it should—even if I couldn't complete things as desired. It seemed that the point in all this was the fact that we co-create with the Light...and we are also part of the Light. Furthermore, no matter what happens...the Light Source will always be in control... and be there to see things through...despite any shortcomings on our part as souls....[45]

Radical Epiphanies

While the experience of near-death survivors has been the subject of much research in recent decades, other sudden spontaneous visions of light or sound have garnered less attention. Yet, these unprepared-for revelations of light— what we call "radical epiphanies"—are no less powerful and transformative.

One of the most stunning examples of the third kind is detailed in the life of Jacques Lusseyran, a French resistance fighter in World War II who had become blind at the age of eight. His experience parallels those of many mystics as well as of near-death survivors. It brings further understanding to the central features of the NDE experience and underscores our fundamental premise: Light is the core substratum of reality in both its physical and nonphysical aspects. He describes the personal new way of "seeing" that he discovered shortly after going blind, and how this led directly to his experiencing the "inner radiance."

At some point, some instinct—I was almost about to say a hand laid on me—made me change course. I began to look more closely, not at things but at a world closer to myself, looking from an inner place to one further within, instead of clinging to the movement of sight toward the world outside.

Immediately, the substance of the universe drew tighter, redefined and peopled itself anew. I was aware of a radiance emanating from a place I knew nothing about, a place which might as well have been outside me as within. But radiance was there, or, to put it more precisely, light. It was a fact, for light was there. I felt indescribable relief and happiness so great it almost made me laugh. Confidence and gratitude came as if a prayer had been answered. I found light and joy at the same moment, and I can say without hesitation that from that time on light and joy have never been separated in my experience. I have had them or lost them together...I saw light and went on seeing it though I was blind.[46]

Lusseyran not only discovered this "radiance" brings with it deep happiness, but it is also a source of continuous and lasting peace, intuitive wisdom and gratitude. His experience of inner light, though physically blind for the rest of his life, continued to exert a profound transformational shift in terms of his empathy, acceptance of others and interest in the meaning of life.

Radical epiphanies include those who have had sudden in-depth encounters with this inner effulgent radiance without any signs of sickness or ill health. They were in every respect perfectly normal and healthy humans. The Religious Experience Research Unit (RERU) at Oxford University in England has amassed a large body of descriptions that fall into this category. Three specific experiences bear quoting here for their long-term transformative and spiritual perspective.

> Vauxhall station on a murky November Saturday evening is not the setting one would choose for a revelation of God. The third-class compartment was full. I cannot remember any particular thought processes which may have led up to the great moment...For a few seconds only (I suppose) the whole compartment was filled with light...I felt caught up into some tremendous sense of being within a loving, triumphant and shining purpose. I never felt more humble. I never felt more exalted. A most curious, but overwhelming, sense possessed me and filled me with ecstasy. I felt that all was well for mankind...All men were shining and glorious beings who in the end would enter incredible joy. Beauty, music, joy, love immeasurable and a glory unspeakable, all this they would inherit....[47] (RERU 385)

This radical epiphany mirrors with surprising detail both the typical NDE and mystical revelations from many traditions. Not only is the revelation often sudden and unpremeditated, but it also reveals the same unconditional love filling each person with overwhelming peace and joy. A similar example occurred to a young lady when discussing the mysteries of creation and the "life force." Someone asked, "But where is it? And what is it?"

> In between her question and the uncontrollable tears, which started to filter down my face, was a timeless moment. Something invisible, yet momentous was happening in the room, [which] all

of a sudden seemed to be filled with light, a whitish, yet warm, light. It seemed to be both in the room and within me.

Although "it" was obviously outside, it was also part of me; yet a part of me with no physical location. It was united completely with a region of my mind. The curious thing is that I *felt* the light. Although my eyes were open, the perception of the light was an interior perception. I continued to see everything in the room quite clearly, but all the objects were lit up by this interior light. As soon as I perceived this light I felt great joy and peace. I wanted to worship the force which was manifesting itself in such an inexpressible way.... (RERU 1519)

Like so many mystics, she described her sudden epiphany in a tone of reverential awe. As the light envelops and embraces the seeker, a radically different mode of perception accompanies this new awareness. An element of timelessness arises, in which "each object was perfect in itself and perfect in its relation to everything else in the room." Such a sense of timelessness is integral to the revelatory mystical experience. As the soul transcends the physical time/space continuum, it enters into nonlocal, boundary-less awareness which is supratemporal in nature. In this new dimensionless space everything is intensified, shining, and rooted in ineffable oneness.

A third witness from Oxford's collection of religious experiences reconfirms many of the important characteristics associated with the phenomena of transcending physical consciousness and entering into the light. This experience is remarkable for its duration. Unlike NDEs that are usually single events, this spontaneous epiphany occurred continuously for six mornings in a row.

During the early hours of the morning, and for six successive mornings altogether, I found myself awake and conscious of being suffused with a sort of warm light and a feeling of great expansion into it. And simultaneously I was aware of a strong current of "something," which filled me with power and changed my breathing from shallow to great deep, rhythmical and strong inhalations and exhalations. I felt immersed and integrated into a great sea of light and power, expansion and joy....

As never before I was conscious of the reality of power which transcended that of the physical world. Overwhelmed, astonished and not a little awed (but not in the least frightened) by it, and at the same time deeply thankful and comforted, I realized I should never feel "alone" again...I felt transmuted into a state of heavenly glory—a kind of intoxication; my body felt lighter and I was more conscious of all things, both animate and inanimate, on the earth and throughout all creation everywhere.[48]

Many NDEs and OBEs involve this profound sense of having found heaven and, with it, a spiritual equanimity in daily living. This all-embracing calm often heralds greater acceptance of one's life along with a higher calling. Central to all these experiences is the realization of an ever-living Light beyond time and space. The recipient perceives this new reality with a "hidden organ of perception" that both includes and most often transcends the five physical senses and opens one into a cosmic all-embracing unity.

In this state, the lines between subject and object, and seer and seen, begin to dissolve. One knows instantly, suddenly and emphatically, without the aid of the intellect or five senses. One becomes the receiver and that which is received. The Light is simultaneously within, beyond and moving through them like a radiant riv-er of knowledge and understanding. Integrating this visionary experience of Light becomes the single most important and transformative task in the person's life.

Our last selection dramatically portrays the revelatory power of Light as it descends into human consciousness. This Light is both all encompassing and transforming in its spiritual force. While standing in a village church during the singing of the *Te Deum,* an English mystic, W. L. Wilmhurst, recalls a memorable experience of light. It came to him rather quietly and gracefully, but then wells up into a conflagration of celestial brilliancy.

> I caught sight, in the aisle at my side, what resembled bluish smoke issuing from the chinks of the stone floor. Looking more intently, I saw it was not smoke, but something finer, more tenuous, soft, impalpable, self luminous haze of violet colour, unlike any physical vapour. Thinking I experienced some momentary optical defect or delusion I turned my gaze farther along the aisle, but there too the same delicate haze was present...I saw from all parts of my being simultaneously, not from my eyes only. Yet for all this intensified perceptive power there was as yet no loss of touch with physical surrounding, no suspension of my faculties of sense....
>
> Then I felt happiness and peace beyond words. The luminous blue haze had engulfed me and all around me became transformed into golden glory, into light untellable...But the most wonderful thing was that these shafts of waves of light were crowded to solidarity with the forms of living creatures...,a single coherent organism filling all space and place, yet composed of an infinitude of individual existences...."[49]

Unity Consciousness: The Final Frontier

The culminating spiritual gift that often accompanies the more profound and dramatic NDEs, radical epiphanies, and extended OBEs is the attainment of unity consciousness. This attainment evokes not only a deeper understanding of the recipient's own purpose in life, but also the realization that this awesome Light is woven into the fabric of both animate and inanimate life. Light not only flows from God, and through God, but also is of God. Creation and Creator are irrevocably linked in a grand matrix of light. Within this Light is a love that encompasses all opposites, transcends all suffering, and embraces all humanity. Such love is universal and unconditional for all life. It is adorned with the luminous qualities of mercy and compassion and signifies a willingness to serve a higher divine purpose.

Many of the most profound NDEs reflect this realization. Juliet Nightingale reflected on her own NDE, "How important it was that I be very loving and creative…and never damaging in any way…and that's the gift. I realized at that point, how totally connected with all life…through all the universes…I am. I felt one with the All—never separate, never apart. Still, there was no fear. Still, there was only love."[50]

Many great spiritual teachers echo this same chorus of compassion and mercy, arising out of the experience of unity consciousness. The Buddha preached it, Moses invoked it, and Jesus the Nazarene reaffirmed it. "Do unto others as you would have them do unto you" and similar guidance is the heart of the message of near-death experiences, radical epiphanies, and out of body experiences. One near-death survivor summarized the impact it had on her life:

> All I know is that it's made all the difference to my life. It's given me a purpose and a joy. A determination to help other people. I know I was sent back because I've got work to do for God. I now know that there are laws governing the universe. God does not break these laws, they are part of his own nature. But when we transgress these laws suffering and disease follow and the only way to reverse this is to learn to live in harmony with God's laws.[51]

The fundamental law of the universe encapsulated in these visionary experiences reveals that we are all one essence. Unity already exists. We have simply forgotten it. When we break this universal spiritual law, we unwittingly and unconsciously bring suffering upon others and ourselves as well. We do not realize the power of our thoughts and words, and that lack of realization keeps us from seeing the truth—both of divine love and of our own forgetting. However, this deep realization of truth is echoed in the words of one near-death survivor. "The first thing I saw when I awoke in the hospital was a flower, and I cried. Believe it or not, I had never really *seen* a flower until I came back from death. One big thing I learned when I died was that we are all part of one big living universe. If we think we can hurt another person or another living thing without hurting ourselves we are sadly mistaken."[52]

The little things in life, which we take for granted in our pursuit of money, fame, or power, appear with a luminous beauty when we learn how to truly see. NDEs, OBEs, and radical epiphanies—whether sudden or extended—carry the same consistent message: that an acute sense of the importance of kindness, compassion, and other such ethical and humane qualities is integral to visionary Light experience. We see admonitions to live our lives in alignment with these principles in the world's spiritual traditions as well. The ancient Jewish prophet Micah makes clear, as does every other mystic traveler who encounters the Inner Divine Light, what our simple duty is to one another. "What does the LORD require of you but to do justice, and to love kindness, and to walk humbly with your God?" (Micah 6:8).

One near-death survivor eloquently summarizes the ultimate life lesson immersed in the "radiant presence" of this supreme all-knowing Light:

> ...It was just my personal intelligence confronting that Universal Mind, which clothed itself in a glorious, living light that was more felt than seen since no eye could absorb its splendor...I was filled with God's knowledge, and in that precious aspect of his Beingness, I was one with him. But my journey of discovery was just beginning...We are aspects of one perfect whole, and as such are part of God, and of each other.[53]

Guidelines at the Heart of the Teachings

1. Realize there is a life beyond filled with a richer, fuller, more vibrant, and loving expression of life. *This place is a school to learn the tough lessons of unconditional love.*

2. The entire universe with all its regions upon regions has been created for one single purpose—our evolutionary journey. *We are all returning to the Source.*

3. Realize whatever trials, sufferings, and pain we are experiencing is the result of our own thoughts, words, and deeds. *As you think so you become.*

4. Understand whatever we do to others we are ultimately doing to ourselves. *All consciousness is One. Unity already exists.*

5. Realize each of us is here to align ourselves with the Ringing Radiance that is both God's expression and essence. *God is Love, Light, and Life.*

6. In order to reconnect with our Source, learn the ABCs of Life: *"A" light has to "B" light in order to "C" light.*

7. *All Truth, bliss, peace, wisdom, and glory are revealed through and in the Light.*

8. By consciously bringing ourselves into the Light, every moment becomes a precious gift, as it is an opportunity to bring light and love into the world.

9. A mantra for conscious mindful living: *Be Bliss Now and Be Love Now.*

As we have seen in the case of the aforementioned NDEs and radical epiphanies, one does not have to undergo a close encounter with death after a traumatic accident to experience the radiance of inner light. In reality, the gift of meditation, prayer and other contemplative practices is our birthright as human beings.

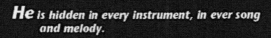

He *is hidden in every instrument, in ever song and melody.*

All creation reflects His glory.

There exists not a sparkling wave nor a fiery star that does not reflect His Light.

Darshan Singh

CHAPTER SEVEN

Meditation and the Experience of Inner Light and Sound

The Sound of the Word is the prime cause of all. It is also the be-all and end-all.... The Word and the Spirit are of the same origin and both spring from the essence of the Nameless One.

—Swami Ji

No words need to be spoken, but the silence speaks volumes of love from heart to heart. Nothing is said, but everything is heard.

—Rajinder Singh

Since the dawn of the world's ancient religions, the inner Light shines as a glistening thread knitting them together into a beautiful tapestry. The journey of discovery through the various periods of time uncovers a consistent and unifying experience within each of these religions—there is a divine Light and Sound latently within each person that can be experienced. The saints, Masters, mystics, and teachers whose voices echo to us through the ages attest to their own revelatory experiences of seeing this inner Light and hearing this celestial Sound. They also have revealed that this contact with this Light and Sound came through a process of going deeply within themselves, when sitting in silent prayer, or meditation.

A natural question a modern reader may ask is, "If this Light and Sound experience was available to those who lived in much earlier times, isn't it possible that we too could have such access? If so, then how?"

Fast forward the practices of the saints and Masters of the earliest world religions and we find that what they had done in millennia past can be replicated today.

The near-death experiences described in various ways throughout history, attest to regions of Light beyond the physical realm experienced in our daily lives. The same consistency of realms of Light experienced by those who have had near-death experiences or epiphanies, as described in detail in the previous chapter, further supports what the saints and mystics have described for thousands of years. But one need not have to experience the trauma which often invoke an NDE in order to tap into inner Light and Sound Current.

Through the ages there have been spiritual Teachers who have explained and taught the practice so people could have the inner experience for themselves. Meditating on the inner Light and Sound basically involves a simple practice(s), the efficacy of which is not limited by the various terms it may have been referred to in different cultures and languages. The terminology may have multiple names, but it is the practice that proves the results. Such practice involves sitting in silence, focusing one's attention within, and experiencing the inner Light and Sound which is already within each person.

Meditation on the inner Light and Sound is taught as a practical "inner science," which can be practiced universally by people of all backgrounds—be they theists, agnostics or atheists. Such an approach to meditation and contemplative practices thus provides opportunities to discover the inner Light that is described in the esoteric teachings of almost all traditions.

A fascinating wisdom tale of the tradition illuminates both the gift of enlightenment and the indispensable role of a competent master or mentor.

"An ancient Indian monarch, King Janak, had a great desire to attain spiritual enlightenment. He called to his court all the saints and sages of his kingdom and asked who among them could grant him enlightenment in the length of time it took to mount a horse. Of all those in the assembly, only one, a hunchback with eight physical deformities, named Ashtavakra, stepped forward. Those assembled jeered at him, for they saw only his outer form.

"Ashtavakra focused his attention on the king, and the king's soul immediately withdrew to higher realms. Ashtavakra verbally called out to Janak again and again, but there was no reply, for the king was lost in inner bliss.

"Later, the saint brought the king's attention back to the physical body and asked him, 'Have you obtained the enlightenment you sought?' King Janak replied, 'I have obtained it, O holy one, and it is far greater, more glorious and blissful than I had ever dreamed.'"[1]

This story insightfully illustrates two universal principles, not only of the mystical life in general, but also of the spiritual tradition of meditation on the inner Light and Sound. First, the celestial regions of Light, spoken of by mystics through the ages, cannot be comprehended by the intellect or mind alone. This level of spiritual experience entails direct inner personal experience—inner revelation beyond the grasp of feelings, emotions, or logical inferences. Only when the body and mind are still, will the inner door open. Second, this gift can be given by a Master who can lift human souls into the heavenly regions within.

Teachers of this practice maintain that true faith arises through "seeing." It is a matter of inversion, not conversion. For those whose inner eye and inner ear have been opened through a process called initiation into the Light and Sound, the quality of one's daily life can be uplifted in many ways.

Origins of some forms of meditation on the Light and Sound can be found within the practices of almost all mystical traditions extending far back in history. In this chapter we will focus on the experience of meditating on the inner Light and Sound and how anyone can learn the practice to try it for one's self.

As a Teacher dedicated to making this personal experience of Light and Sound through meditation available to people of diverse cultural backgrounds throughout the world, Sant Rajinder Singh Ji Maharaj (b. 1946) explains:

> Experiences of the Divine are not reserved for a select few. There is but one prerequisite for such experiences—a sincere desire to know God. Just as a bubbling spring provides water to all alike, so too God nourishes all who seek to drink from the eternal, divine spring. We do not even have to go to the spring itself; through the Power of the Divine, that spring can gush forth wherever we are, whenever we have a deep yearning to quench our spiritual thirst...It can find us on every continent and in every city and remote village. Regardless of our age, social status, culture, or outer appearance, the spring of divine love does not discriminate, but flows freely to all who seek its nourishing waters."[2]

Divine Light and the Sound Current

The Light and Sound can be likened to a current, the primal cause of all that lives and moves. From this divine current all creation sprang forth. This individual soul and the Light and Sound current were of the same essence and spring from the same divine Source.

The Sound or Word is the prime cause of all
It is also the be-all and end-all...

The Word and the spirit are of the same origin and both spring from the
    same essence of the Nameless One.

It is both the cause and the effect, and all were created by it.

The Word is the preceptor, as well as the disciple, and is resounding in
    the heart of all.[3]

—Swami Shiv Dayal Singh

The Light and Sound are both the means and the end of the seekers' journey. The current not only is the connecting link to the Creator but the Creator itself and the innermost essence of the disciple as well.

Masters affirm that God can never be reduced to a mere theological or academic discussion. The only way to reach the Creator is through direct experience within. The pathway towards the Divine is walked without feet, touched without hands, seen without physical eyes, and heard without physical ears. It is a universal path ingrained within the very fabric of one's being, transcendent of one's background and experienced within the depths of one's soul.

These Teachers maintained that since creation was born through Light and sustained through Light, the way back to the Source was/is also through this Light. It was this current from the ocean of all consciousness which could be contacted through the aid of a spiritual guide or Master. By linking the aspirant to this primal Light and Sound within each individual they could ride the current back to its Source.

The Cosmology of Light and Sound

Sant Rajinder Singh describes the inner journey of Light and Sound from his own direct experience by using scientific analogies and comparisons. He asserts the methodology of meditation can be practiced as an "inner science of spirituality." Brought up under the guidance of two spiritual Masters coupled with a strong academic background in the sciences, technology, and communications, in his writings and lectures he often refers to contemporary research and discoveries in these fields.

The human soul has the innate potential to experience heightened spiritual understanding that in many lives sadly goes unrealized. Addressing this situation, Sant Rajinder Singh writes poignantly of the spiritual journey of the soul. In the following excerpts he lyrically describes a portion of the mystic's travel through the inner realms:

> True knowledge comes from seeing for one's self. We may read what others have written or hear what others say, but we are never fully satisfied unless we have the experience for ourselves. The spiritual gifts given by a Master are immortality, love, and bliss. Within us lies the unlimited power of the soul. Tapping into it can enrich and transform our life.[4]

In this powerful rendering, he describes the immense joy and bliss the soul experiences, as during meditation it leaves the physical body behind and enters into the inner regions.

Passing beyond the intermediary region, we enter the astral realm. We are greeted by a myriad of brilliant lights of colors not even known to us in the physical realm. They sparkle with a light more dazzling than diamonds, rubies, or emeralds of this world. This music resounding in this realm is indescribable. The intensity of sound that fills our soul with uplifting bliss is beyond any sounds we know in the physical realm.... The astral is made of matter with more consciousness than the physical world realm, but there are still more ethereal regions awaiting us.[5]

Describing the next phase of the aspirant's inner journey, Sant Rajinder Singh continues:

This realm is made up of equal parts matter and consciousness. This makes it even more ethereal than the astral region. The lights of the causal realm are far brighter and more luminous. The music is far more enchanting. The causal realm is much vaster than the astral realm. It has incredible continents with unimaginable high mountains, cascading rivers and oceans of light, sights, and sounds inconceivable to our physical mind.[6]

He explains the nature of what takes place in this realm.

In each realm there are throngs of souls engaged in all sorts of pursuits. In the causal realm we can move without our physical or astral bodies and journey at the speed of thought. Whatever we think we can manifest. We can travel anywhere in this realm instantly. It is also a realm in which we can see our past lives, a realm in which all the records of our past lives are stored. Thus we can trace back the history of our karma and see how it has influenced our lives.[7]

As the soul moves forward, Sant Rajinder Singh explicates the importance of this region:

The physical, astral, and causal realms are under the control of the universal mind. The mind is what keeps us distracted in the lower realms, whether physical, astral or causal. It prevents us from knowing ourselves in our true state as the soul, and from knowing the Divine Creator, God....The supracausal realm is mostly consciousness with only a thin layer of illusion.[8]

He continues:

Here we find a pool of nectar, called the Mansarovar, in which the soul bathes and sheds its causal body. The soul is now covered only with a thin veil. This realm is beyond the mind and senses. There is absolutely no physical language that can give us an inkling of what the supracausal realm is like. We have only pale analogies. Since the physical, astral, and causal minds have been left behind in the lower worlds, the mind is of no help to us here. This realm is directly experienced by the soul with only a thin covering.[9]

Sant Rajinder Singh further explains that the supracausal realm is a realm of mostly consciousness and only a thin layer of illusion:

> The soul, stripped of its covering of the mind, realizes that its true essence is the same as God. We experience that as soul and we shine with a brilliant light.[10]

As the soul proceeds past the supracausal realm it enters the purely spiritual realm of Sach Khand. At this stage, the soul attains union with the Creator. Few mystics have been able to render in language the exquisite joy that the soul experiences, as it reunited with the divine Beloved. Nevertheless, the poet Rumi, in his *Masnavi*, gives us a rare glimpse of this state:

> Listen to the sound of the flute.
> Listen to its plaintive notes
> For ever since it was cut off from the reed bed
> It has been telling a tale of separation.
> I want a heart
> Torn by separation
> That I may unfold to such a one the pain of love.
> For every one who is separated far from his Source,
> Wishes back the time
> When we were one with it.
> The fire of love
> Is tangled in the reed notes
> As the fervor of love is in the wine.
> That sound is a friend
> To all separated lovers who
> Yearn to tear away the veil.
> The one who secretly hears this
> Is senseless.[11]

This particular passage can be mistaken for a mere poetic rendering of the state of intense separation. Rumi masterfully captures the lover's infinite longing that enraptures the heart of the lover. His body of writing testifies to his profound inner attainment, filled with clear and transparent portrayals of the inner realms.

After passing through the supracausal realm a rare soul begins its final ascent to the purely spiritual regions of Sach Khand or the true *(Sach)* realm *(Khand)*. On its way it is immersed in a mesmerizing stream of infinite cascading splendor and sonorous Sound which pulsate unendingly within its soul. In the following passage, Sant Rajinder Singh lyrically describes Sach Khand:

> Here, bliss and love surpass those experienced in all the realms below it. Sach Khand is the realm of all spirit with no matter or illusion. This is the luminous and infinite realm of the Divine. In Sach Khand, its true home, the soul fully merges into the Divine. The light of Sach Khand is beyond those of all the other realms. Millions of outer suns of the physical realm would not equal even one small portion of the Divine in Sach Khand....With all the intensity with which a worldly lover rushes into the arms of its beloved and consummates their love, so does the soul rush into the arms of the Divine in Sach Khand....Pure Light and Sound bathe us and the soul shines with the brilliance of sixteen outer suns.[12]

While recognizing that mere words are inadequate, Sant Rajinder Singh nonetheless conveys the feeling of awe in extolling the sheer ecstasy and the splendor of the soul's final merger. His description of the grandeur of the highest spiritual regions where the soul becomes universalized and begins its final merger in its Creator is rare in its explicit illumination. In this final region, the soul merges into God absolute which is beyond all form, name, or expression.

Masters have been able to give seekers their own illuminating experience of merger with the Creator and becoming one with the ineffable Light. Having experienced this, the human soul then realizes it is of the same essence as God.

While such advanced Mentors throughout the ages have traditionally been both detailed and often poetic in their narration of the inner journey, they also understood that any description was at best a pale analogy of the real experiences. Like all saints they understood that these descriptions—like the vast majority of mystical "ascension maps," diaries, poems or poetic revelations—were mere fragments of a much larger, unrecorded mystical landscape. Since the inner terrain is of such unimaginable vastness, any verbal descriptions were, at best, rough approximations of the full reality. The closest analogy given by Masters who have attained their union with God is that it is like a drop merged back in the ocean or a ray of light reunited with its source, the sun.

St. Teresa of Avila (1515-1582) refers to the same process of finding the inner Light through inversion. In her classic, *The Interior Castle,* she refers to the human form as a castle, entering which we find the resplendent Light of God:

"The problem we face is how to enter within the castle of the body. There are many souls who merely prowl around the castle, but never enter it. They do not know what treasures are inside the castle or how many beautiful rooms it has. You must have heard that the way within is to invert. But how to do it is the question. The door to enter the castle is that of prayer with attention. I do not call the action of moving the lips prayer. In this you do not know to whom you are praying and to whom you are making your petitions. The way within is not through verbal prayer, but through mental prayer with attention.... The resplendent sun which is within the soul does not lose its brilliance and beauty. That resplendence belongs to the soul and nothing can take the beauty away."[13]

Light and Sound as a Current of Divine Love

The terms "light" and "sound" denote to many an aspect of physics, where waves are radiating from a source. However, the Light and Sound referred to by mystics and saints from ancient times are not just waves that follow the law of physics of this physical universe; the current of Light and Sound is spiritual, made of the same essence as the Creator from where it emanates. The current of Light and Sound flowing out from its Source, God, is divine love. The nature of this love is all-conscious, blissful, happiness, compassion, peace, and ecstasy. Coming in contact with the Light and Sound within oneself is connecting with the power of divine love.

St. John of the Cross (1542-1591), refers to the spiritual Light within us and its power to connect us to divine love within us, as he writes:

O guiding night, O night more lovely than the dawn,
O night that has united the lover with his Beloved and changed
    her into love.

—St. John of the Cross[14]

Sant Darshan Singh has explained this as: "The inner Light is brighter than the light of the outer sun. It is a beacon to wayfarers leading them to higher and higher regions. Like St. Teresa of Avila and many other mystics, St. John depicts the relationship of the soul and God as that of lover and Beloved....As the relationship develops, the seeker or lover awakens to his or her true Beloved and is changed into love itself. This is the transformative Power through which the human becomes Divine."[15]

The transformative power of love by contacting the world of Light and Being of Light during a near-death experience has been well documented by doctors and scientists who have been recording such accounts. The Light transforms people by making them more loving, caring, and compassionate. Many even changed their career paths to professions in which they can be of more service to others.

For this same reason much of the writings of the Masters have focused on the transformation of the disciple's character. Those who connect people with the Light and Sound within them have maintained that before this connection it may have been difficult to become a fully human(e) being—one who has developed love and compassion for all creation. Yet, once one comes in contact with the Light and Sound current within, it brings about a change in one's character by developing qualities that make God-realization not difficult. The time spent immersed in the spiritual love of God within helps develop qualities such as love and respect for all, compassion, a desire to serve others selflessly, humility, truthfulness, purity, and nonviolence. The real work of every sincere spiritual aspirant is therefore to develop this divine love, which is who we already are.

The Light and Sound current is the attractive and binding power of the universe and is therefore also the essence of love itself. Love moves the universe, and is the universe itself in its thousand and one myriad forms. The current of Light and Sound as it flows through all realms of creation is the source of all light, whether of the earth or the higher regions. It is the life behind all forms of existence and indeed even of seemingly nonliving and inanimate forms. Even stones and minerals are expressions of this eternal living verity, for these too are parts of creation. Thus, Light, Sound, love, and life are expressions of the primordial essence of God. They are inextricably connected, forming an inseparable unity both in the soul and in God's creation. Just as an ordinary beam of sunlight derives its existence from the sun, so too love cannot be separated from its source, which is this preexistent Light. Thus, life cannot be separated from the attribute of love.

Each being has within the seed of the other's essence. Hence, all forms of life owe their "existence" to this supernal light. Nothing can exist on its own or by itself without being connected to this primal creative essence. Similarly, at the human level, both the body and mind are sustained by this life principle every moment.

For this reason, the single most essential ingredient in all spiritual practice is the cultivation of this unifying force we know as love. It is and remains the *sine qua non* of all spiritual advancement. All authentic inner illumination results in both an increased vitality and greater capacity to love. Love, as seen in some of the testimonies of near-death survivors, is the prerequisite and passport for entry into higher levels of spiritual beatitude. As the soul becomes enveloped and embraced by ever-greater levels of luminosity, it experiences the ever more exhilarating and enchanting fragrance of love. The following words of a practitioner from Latin America who was taught meditation on the Light and Sound by one of the spiritual Masters, Sant Darshan Singh, expressed the unity consciousness increasing in proportion to the ascendancy of Light:

> While in meditation the Master escorted me to a spiritual region where there was very intense Light. There were millions upon millions

of stars each of great piercing brilliance. As I gazed at the vastness of the universe, I understood my own smallness. I was flooded with tears of joy and ecstasy. I realized that every living thing, be it a stone, insect, bird, plant, animal or human, is connected to this great universal beam of Light. I could feel a spiritual unity and oneness with everything and I felt no separation from anyone or anything. I understood that we are not islands unto ourselves and that everything is felt and understood by the Master.[16]

The Passport of Love

Like other great poet-mystics Sant Darshan Singh's mystical verse conveyed the multifaceted nuances and secrets of the spiritual journey in an enchanting way. Sant Darshan Singh Ji Maharaj (1921–1989) brought to the world a renewed understanding of the redemptive power of the Light and Sound as a manifestation of divine love. His outstanding poetry conveyed a new clarity to the often hidden world of mysticism. With pearl-like brilliance and pristine simplicity, he illumined the secrets of the mystical path as they pertained to the stages of inner revelation. As one of India's foremost poet-saints, he is most recognized by his peers for his exquisite verses in the *ghazal* form.

Like all the great teachers of humanity, Sant Darshan Singh professed that all human beings, regardless of backgrounds, are endowed with the same spark of divine Light, and therefore belonged to one humanity.

Saints and mystics since ancient times who have connected people to the inner Light have attested that anyone who has absorbed the secrets of divine love can accelerate their progress on the spiritual path. Indeed, the journey back to God can be summarized in one word—love. For it is love that forms the binding principle of all life, both human and divine. This universal love is the same love as expressed in countless traditions.

> The spiritual path is one of love. God is love. Our soul, being of the same essence as God, is love, and the way back to God is also through love. On this path, the passport we need to gain admittance to the divine kingdom is that of love. The one who can arrange for our passage and can guide us there in the quickest possible time is the living Master. He is, in fact, a resident of that kingdom and is sent to serve as the guide and traveling compassion for all those who wish to enter the eternal land of love.[17]

In this world and the next, it is love alone which keeps all things in existence. Without it, even for a fraction of a second, this entire universe would dissolve. Love is a gift of God and without it life becomes unbearable and sterile. Love beautifies everything and transforms everything it sees into a garden of love and devotion. It is for this reason alone that we have come into this world. Sant Darshan Singh was well known for saying, "Love has only a beginning; it has no end." It is the primary and, for saints and mystics, the most revealing, and yet ineffable, of all God's attributes. In Sant Darshan Singh's words, he reveals the sublime nature of this cosmic force:

> Love is the golden key that opens the door to the kingdom of heaven. Without it, nothing has ever been achieved nor can be achieved on the spiritual path. But, it is difficult to understand the meaning of love, its purpose, and scope. In reality, it is as boundless as God, and to know its full meaning is beyond our limited intellect. Love is innate in our soul, for we are, in reality, drops of the ocean of all love that have been separated from our Source since the beginning of creation. Having originally come from the eternal kingdom, we cannot know lasting peace and happiness until we are reunited with our Source....In fact, love is the essential theme of all the saints and mystics, for it is indeed the passport to the kingdom of heaven.[18]

The theme of Light in mystical poetry dates back to the beginnings of mystical literature. In the following verse, Sant Darshan Singh expresses the perennial conflict between love and intellect on the spiritual path characteristic of many great Masters:

> O tell the darkness of intellect
> to seek the madness of love,
> For this madness is a beam of light,
> and nothing but light.[19]

In this verse he beckons the would-be lover to forsake intellectual wrangling, which in the end only clouds the path, and embrace the inexplicable "madness" of spiritual love. This madness (poetically speaking) is in itself the yearning for Godly Light.

On the path of Divine Love, it is God that provides the food and nourishment for the soul. Left on its own, the intellect remains in a condition of bewilderment. Using language reminiscent of mystic poetry, Sant Darshan Singh likens the spiritual Master to the "Cupbearer of the Tavern (the assembly of lovers of God)," who dispenses this divine Wine (love of God) in the form of inner Light and Sound. For the true lover, the remembrance of the Beloved produces brilliance in the soul, filling it with an everlasting bliss.

> In this night of sorrow, I need neither the candle nor the chandelier,
> For when I remember you, O Beloved, there is nothing else but light.[20]

When the soul crosses from the causal realm into the supracausal region it moves beyond the limitations of mind and intellect. Here, it enters a state of unity consciousness in which "though all things differ all things agree." Sant Darshan Singh gives an eloquent rendering of this vision of universal oneness at the root of all authentic mystical attainment. Here all differences between lover, Beloved, and love vanish into undifferentiated oneness.

> We are but drops of the same fountain of divine beauty,
> We are but waves on the great river of love.
> We are diverse blossom in the garden of the Lord,
> We have gathered in this same valley of Light.
> We who dwell on this earth belong to one humanity;
> There is but one God and we are all His Children.[21]

The road to unity consciousness is a journey in which we are immersed in blissful love. As meditation opens our spiritual vision we then recognizes that same love shining in us also glows within all other human beings and all forms of life. Recognizing that oneness leads to an outpouring of divine love flowing from us to embrace all whom we meet. Through love, we are transformed.

The Significance of Positive Mysticism in Daily Life

One of the most prominent messages and a common theme among saints and mystics is that the pursuit of spiritual realization through meditation is accompanied by leading a life of spiritual love in all aspects of daily life. Finding the Light within through meditation does not lead to a life in which we renounce the world to live alone in a jungle or mountaintop; rather it is a life in which we embrace the world with love. The manifestations of having love for all is inclusive of being nonviolent, caring, selfless, and giving. Sant Darshan Singh coined the term "positive mysticism" to encourage the pursuit of spirituality while fulfilling the innate obligations of a responsible human life—earning a livelihood and responsibly caring for one's family, community, country, and the world. It is said the life of a true mystic is one in which the needs of others comes first. Sant Darshan Singh captures a profound paradox and the essence of humanity's spiritual predicament in the following verse:

> We are communing with the moon and
>   the stars,
> But alas, we have not reached the
>   heart of our neighbor.[22]

The life of a true mystic is one of reaching out in service to one's fellow human beings. Authentic mysticism is always rooted in the service of God's creation, for to serve God we must serve God's creation. Sant Kirpal Singh was often fond of saying "One alone is a true human being, who lives for others not just one's own self."[23] In the excerpt below Sant Darshan Singh's selfless love for others highlights the ideal of engaged spirituality or positive mysticism.

> He opened his door to all and treated them as family. People came with their spiritual and mundane difficulties and he found solutions to them. Anyone who came to him with a heavy burden left feeling light-hearted and free of their problems. He welcomed people at all hours of the day and night. It was not unusual to see him pass days on end without a wink of sleep. His heart was so sensitive that he could not bear to see anyone in pain.[24]

Masters encourage seekers to live a balanced life. This means while spending time in meditation and other spiritual practices, they also engaged in meeting their obligations to their families, career and jobs, community, society, and helping to make a difference in the world. One did one's best in all these endeavors, developing one's physical, mental, and spiritual aspects of life.

Masters and saints have taught that spiritual enlightenment was available to every person as his or her birthright from God. One need not be a saint to practice meditation and attain union with God; it was available to all. As Sant Tulsi Sahib (1763–1843) wrote:

> By practicing the science of inversion, one becomes
>   world famous,
> Even Valmik, a well-known highwayman, acquired
>   the status of a Brahm. [God][25]

> One who is above the sense of mine and thine;
> One who prays to God in total humility;
> The Adept who even bows to his own disciples,
> Tulsi says that such a one is truly a Sadh,
>   a realized soul.[26]

Tulsi Sahib points out by referring to a highwayman as reaching the status of realization with God shows that anyone can attain God-realization. It only takes praying to God in humility to become a realized soul.

Anyone can learn meditation and find the inner Light. Along with meditation one develops positive qualities such as nonviolence, truthfulness, humility, selfless service, and universal love. These qualities become a part of one's nature as one goes about their daily life.

When we look at the life of Baba Jaimal Singh, an early Master, who taught meditation on the inner Light and Sound, we see a number of these attributes beautifully expressed. Sant Kirpal Singh in the book, *Baba Jaimal Singh: A Brief Biography*, recounts the remarkable tale of the spiritual quest of Baba Jaimal

Singh (1838–1903). His story bears the hallmark of past spiritual pioneers, embodying an intense struggle for spiritual liberation coupled with the highest ethical conduct and righteous living. His life bears witness to the specific qualities and training needed for success on the spiritual path.

Born in a village family of devout farmers, the young Jaimal showed remarkable spiritual precocity. Before reaching the age of maturity, he had completed a careful reading of the scriptures, and had memorized the key passages of these spiritual treasures.[27]

His intense yearning manifested into his highly disciplined and regular practice of meditation. On occasion, after attending to his flock of sheep all day, he would pass the entire night in meditation. Such a profound spiritual sadhana is remarkable even in a grown man, but at the age of nine, it presaged true spiritual greatness. These efforts brought him even closer to his goal, and soon he reported to his spiritual teacher that he could glimpse the inner Light, and had seen the stars and moon within. He continued his spiritual practices with renewed zeal, but his quest for an understanding of the meaning of the *Pancha Shabd,* or *Five Melodied Word,* which he had read about in the scriptures, remained unanswered.

Jaimal Singh took initiation with many different teachers during his earlier years of spiritual searching. He learned these teachers' practices, but intuitively understood the limitations of their techniques as well. Before his 15th birthday, he had mastered *japa* (mantra yoga) and *pranayama* (breathing exercises), and studied the mystery of the *Ghor Anhad* (internal Sound).[28]

Through a series of adventures that would test both his faith and his fortitude, he was guided to a little known yogi living deep in a remote jungle. This remarkable ascetic, who spent night after night in silent meditation, was renowned for his disregard of all visitors. However, the young Jaimal Singh was no ordinary seeker, and after three nights of patient and watchful vigil by the yogi's side, the adept finally broke his silence. Confiding affectionately, he said, "My son, I cannot tell you much, but in my meditation I saw that the Guru you seek dwells with his wife in Agra. He is indeed a great soul....He shall unlock to you the treasures of the Pancha Shabd. Proceed there, and I will follow as soon as I can to partake of his bounty."[29] The great sage he was soon to meet was Swami Ji, who lived in the city of Agra and not only knew the meaning of the Panch Shabd, but also was its leading living exponent.

Not long after this vision, Jaimal Singh came face to face with Swami Ji, the Master who would initiate him into the Light and Sound and finally answer the mystery of the Panch Shabd or five-worded Word. After a cordial welcome and a brief but illuminating discourse, the great sage of Agra offered to initiate Jaimal and resolve for the last time his lingering doubts. "As soon as Jaimal Singh sat down for meditation, he got lost in samadhi. The night came and passed away, the day broke, but he continued motionless, lost in the inner bliss he had discovered. Another day saw itself swallowed by the night, and the night saw itself replaced by another day, and yet the youth sat lost to the world around him."[30]

Jaimal's seemingly rapid enlightenment was a product of the maturation of many of the qualities needed for spiritual advancement. His intense yearning for enlightenment and profound discernment all came into fruition as a result of countless lifetimes of spiritual effort. It is these qualities which form the basis of the disciple's inner development and pave the way for inner spiritual progress.

Baba Jaimal Singh illuminated the spiritual discipline necessary and conduct required for following the inner path. He illuminated the path's practical aspects. In the following excerpt, Baba Jaimal Singh reiterates the necessity of daily spiritual practice as the cornerstone of true devotion. He maintained that what stays with us beyond this physical world is the Shabd-dhun or the current of Light and Sound and the help of a spiritual Master who helps us connect with it within us. In this remarkable passage we see how connecting with the inner Light through a meditation practice called simran, and connecting with the inner Sound through a meditation practice called bhajan, can help us reunite our soul with the Divine:

> When doing our bhajan and simran,[31] do not have any world cares in your mind nor let yourself be distracted by any worldly thoughts....You will then experience great bliss, and Supreme Grace will descend on you from the highest region.[32]

The spiritual connection between the inner Light and Sound and God is a constantly reiterated theme in the training of the disciple. Once the soul recognizes its connection to this unspoken and unknowable essence, its work is propelled forward. Spiritual liberation arises through merging the soul back into the inner Light and Sound as quickly as possible. But it requires that during meditation that the mind is still and focused within.

> You ask me how to hold your mind. It is held only through Shabd. Hear its music daily and meditate on the form of the Satguru. Then the mind shall cease to wander and one day, borne on the Shabd-Dhun, shall reach Dasam Dwar (the third inner realm and home of the universal mind). Thus leaving the mental apparatus behind, the soul shall unite with the pure Shabd and through the grace of the Satguru reach Sach Khand. Have no doubt it shall reach there.[33]

The saints have reiterated the necessity of developing intense longing for God. This results in being put in contact with this inner stream of Light and Sound which emanates from Absolute God, and on which the soul can return to its spiritual home. The Light and Sound is embedded deep within our being and, as the soul begins to enjoy this bliss, it is transported home by this innate longing to spend more and more time in this state of bliss and happiness. Thus, the contact with the blissful current of divine love draws the soul to want to immerse itself more and more, propelling the soul along the divine stream until it merges back into the Ocean of God from where it came.

As the aspirant spends time in meditation, his or her attraction and love for God increases exponentially. However, besides going within through meditation, our journey is accelerated through the development of godly virtues including selfless love for others—one of the greatest purifying agents in propelling the soul forward. In fact, to love selflessly helps us return to our Source. Such love is a reflection of the soul's innermost cry for God.

Spiritual Discipline: Meditation on Light and Sound

Through the ages, spiritual Masters have offered an inner path in which spirituality could be practiced as an inner science free from blind faith. Each soul can experiment to find the great "effulgence" in the laboratory of his or her own body, which is the true temple of God. Sant Kirpal Singh often remarked, "Seeing is believing and seeing is above all." By this he meant the mystical journey is beyond conjecture, intellectual inferences, or philosophical discussion. It is when we experience directly this great Light within the temple of our innermost soul that we can know the truth. Spiritual revelation and gnosis begins when the inner spiritual eye of perception and inner ear of audition is opened at a point referred to as the third eye or *tisra til*.

This important critical first step of opening the spiritual eye was the gift of a competent spiritual teacher who himself was an embodiment of this Light. Such a Master at the time of initiation could open one's spiritual eye so a soul can witness the Light and Sound within. After this inner door is opened through their overflowing mercy and grace, the soul truly commences its mystical journey. In the following passage, Hazur Baba Sawan Singh (1858–1948) describes the first glimmerings of illumination after initiation which fulfills the soul's deepest longings and aspirations:

> Hearing Music in the region
> of sukhmana,

Concentrate on the rapturous
  strains;
There, learn the untold story
Which satisfies all longings
  of the heart.[34]

And again:

Within us are universes of Light,
The subtle worlds and
  wondrous regions,
Where the sweet resounding
  Music
Leads us to the everlasting
  throne of the Lord....[35]

As the seeker's inner eye opens, he or she is ushered into realms of unending Light and Sound. Here the soul tastes the first flickering of self-conscious awareness rising upward within his or her soul. In this passage, Hazur Baba Sawan Singh reveals how the illuminating resonance of the Light and Sound begins to accompany the sincere seeker as he or she enters the inner spiritual regions. The mystic adepts and Masters of light consistently taught that such inner mystical experience was the pathway that leads to the throne of God and one's ultimate spiritual attainment.

Hazur Baba Sawan Singh wrote extensively on the practice of meditation on the Light and Sound. Having trained as an engineer for his career coupled with his role as a spiritual Master he explained the practical aspects of the meditation practice in clear and transparent language accessible to all aspirants.

Spiritual discipline consisted of two main practices, a) simran or meditation on the inner Light; and b) bhajan or listening to the Sound. In the following passage, Hazur Baba Sawan Singh outlined these two basic phases of the meditation practice, as the soul ascends up to the point where it sees the thousand-petaled lotus pulsating with inner radiance:

The spiritual uplift consists of:

a) Repetition [or simran practice], bringing into concentration in the third eye the scattered attention and the vital Current from the part of the body below the eyes.

b) Holding the attention in the third eye by making contact with the astral form of the Master.

c) Lifting the soul up by attaching it to the bell [sound].[36]

The description of the process of withdrawal occurs when the soul is fully concentrated at the third eye and not diffused in the lower chakras. Since the attention naturally resides at the "eye center" or seat of the soul there is no need to descend to the lower centers or chakras and then proceed up. By beginning at the third eye, aspirants can contact the Light and Sound immediately, thereby saving valuable time on the spiritual journey. From this point, souls can more efficiently reach the inner regions. In the following excerpt, Hazur Baba Sawan Singh explains the more subtle aspects of the withdrawal of the sensory currents from the body and its gradual reunion with the current of Light and Sound.

> The body is alive on account of the presence of the Soul Current in
> it. The soul is a drop, and the Shabd is the ocean. The soul is sustained
> in the body by Shabd, and the body in its turn by the soul. But so long as
> soul is not lifted up to the higher stages, it remains associated with the
> mind in the lower stages. In the process of concentration both the mind
> and the soul (they are closely associated) are lifted.[37]

The Light and Sound current has its source in the abode of Sach Khand (true Region) and is not associated with any form of matter or subtle matter. It is pure consciousness, love, and Light. People are not aware of this inner experience of this innate bliss and Light because they are focused on the world outside, their physical body, and mind. Unless taught how to invert their attention within they remain unaware of these inner realms of love, Light, and bliss.

This explains why saints try to connect the soul to the Light and Sound because through this inner listening to the Divine current it can experience greater and greater illumination. This inner contact provides love and bliss greater than any in the outer world, thus, drawing the soul to higher spiritual connection. Thus, on their own, outer material desires effortlessly drop away like autumn leaves in the wind. Through continued contact within, the soul comes to understand that material desires are not lasting but can lead to suffering when we lose them. As the soul ascends it discovers a bliss and peace within that are lasting.

Baba Jaimal Singh reveals the essence of spiritual practice which is the meditation upon the Light and Sound principle. The Light and Sound current is in fact the real identity of the soul. Once the disciple has fully merged his/her soul in this Light and Sound its work is done. Remaining fully absorbed in the heavenly Light is the essence of spiritual liberation.

> When you sit for bhajan, [listening to Inner Sound] forget yourself
> and the world around you. Nothing is greater than the Word. Always
> keep in touch with it and let it grow from strength to strength. You

should aspire for the spiritual realms: Sach Khand...[the highest pure-ly spiritual realm]. This alone is worth striving for and noting else is. Practice all this from day to day and your endeavors will one day bear fruit. Remember the advice of the Satguru, forgetting the "self."[38]

Masters and saints through the ages have placed a great emphasis on the value of spiritual guidance at every turn and twist of the journey, maintaining that it is through the help of a skillful spiritual guide that one could connect with the Light and Sound leading back to God.

The Role of the Spiritual Mentor

Since ancient times, the help of a spiritual guide has been recognized for put-ting people in touch with the inner Light and Sound. Having ridden that current themselves back to its source, they are in tune with it and radiate this spiritual energy. Whosoever comes into contact with them can receive a connection to this Light and Sound already within them.

One of the renowned women saints from India, Mira Bai, described the role that her spiritual teacher, whom she referred to as Satguru, played in her quest for the Light of God. In these two verses she says:

I seek a physician who knows the secret of this world and the next,
That I may tell him of my condition and be cured of the malady of
transmigration.

Now I have met Sant Ravi Das, my Satguru,
And he has bestowed on me self-knowledge.[39]

—Mira Bai

Mira Bai intensely searched for God, and it was only when she met her Satguru, Sant Ravi Das, that she was put in touch with the divine Light within her. She describes how all the practices she had followed, the form of meditation she had pursued, brought her no peace, no rest. She had been only in pursuit of shad-ows, of reflections, which were visibly elusive. If she finally found truth, it was by coming to a perfect Master. Through him she was given a firsthand experience of God in absolute state, and having received that experience, all her questing, all her doubts were at rest....Mira's quest did find a resolution. She did discover a Satguru who could resolve the mystery and take her back to her eternal Home.... It was Sant Ravi Das's grace which came to Mira's rescue. He gave her that price-less gift which the perfect adept gives to the seeker. He enabled her to rise above consciousness of the body and transcend the inner realms until she could see for herself what she was. It was only when the soul has risen above the physical, the astral, and the causal, that it at last realizes its true identity. Beholding itself stripped of its various coverings the soul beholds itself and cries out in ecstasy, "I am That...." When the soul has finally realized its identity, it is ready for the final union..., and then commences a process of merger with God.[40]

Speaking of the role of a master, Sant Kirpal Singh has said:

> The work of imparting actual spiritual instructions and guidance is, however, done by a living Master. Highly charged as he is with higher consciousness, he injects the jivas [souls] with his life impulse. Spirituality can neither be bought nor taught, but it may be *caught*, like an infection from one highly infected himself. As Light comes from Light and Life from Life, and a spirit that is bodily ridden can only be moved by a Spirit that is untrammeled by body and mind.[41]

Sant Kirpal Singh in his autobiographical account of how he found his Master illustrates this profound principle at work. It is the Light of the Master who ignites the inner flame within the disciple. The great paradox of the spiritual search is that although it may appear the disciple is searching, it is the teacher who finds the seeker. It is as difficult for the disciple to find the spiritual Master any more than a lost sheep can find the shepherd. For how can one who is spiritually blind and deaf find one who is spiritually awakened? In this sense, the saying, "The Master appears when the disciple is ready" has special meaning.

The fundamental principle that Love and Light emanate from the Master is graphically illustrated in the life of Sant Kirpal Singh. Very early on, he recognized the necessity of a spiritual guide in order to reach the highest pinnacle of spiritual attainment. Kirpal Singh began an arduous search for a spiritual teacher from whom he could receive inner experiences of the Divine. However, the plethora of spiritual Gurus in India was vast. How was he to recognize one who could fulfill his goal of union with God? One day, he received a letter from one of his brothers who was engaged in the same search.

His brother zealously informed him, "A very great Master is here. Will you come?" Kirpal Singh immediately went to the saint and confronted him with an unusual request. "I have intoxication that continues day and night; but sometimes, after three, four or five months, it stops for a day or two. I am very puzzled. Can you help me?"

The man replied, "You will have to lay down everything—your body, mind, and soul—to me. Only then will I help you." Kirpal wrote, "I thought the man is after my body and possessions; he wants my intellect to be blindfolded....I paid him homage and returned home."[42]

Unwilling to submit blindly to someone with no more than a few verbal assurances, he respectfully parted his company. In a matter of such vital importance, only firsthand inner experience, he concluded, could be trusted. It was this reliance on the authority of one's inner experience, which became a touchstone for him....He encompassed this significant teaching in a pithy expression to sincere seekers, "Seeing is above all; seeing is believing."

Not long afterward, fearful of being led astray, Kirpal Singh directed his prayers to God Almighty. "Oh God," he would fervently pray, "I am yearning for You. I want to meet You. The world is full of Gurus and Masters. To whom should I go? Unless I find someone who has reached You, my life's aim will be spoiled. It is said that in olden days You appeared to those who loved You, then why can't You manifest now? If God could give revelations to God's lovers in the past, why could God not give direct revelation to me?"[43]

With this prayer, a great Master began appearing to him in May 1917, during his meditation. Kirpal Singh spent the next seven years communing with this inner spiritual guide without awareness of his identity. He finally met his spiritual Master in a seemingly chance encounter near the River Beas in the Punjab. He was wonderstruck when he saw, in the flesh, Hazur Baba Sawan Singh—the radiant being who had been guiding him on the inner realms for so many years. When Kirpal Singh questioned the Master about why the delay in meeting him physically, Hazur replied with enigmatic simplicity, "This is the most opportune time."

What Sant Kirpal Singh had been seeing was the ethereal or radiant form of the spiritual Master within during meditation. This term has been referred to as *Guru Dev*, signifying the self-luminous form of the Master, which is free from and far above his physical body, and which the spirit actually perceives with its inner subtle Light. When the spirit comes face to face with the radiant form of the Master, its inner journey begins or one can travel in the company of the guide through the spiritual realms back to God. The radiant form which appeared to Kirpal Singh is capable of guiding innumerable souls and works simultaneously in the inner "regions" beyond the physical.

Swami Shiv Dayal Singh [Swami Ji]'s poetic description of the radiant form of his Master gives a brief glimpse into the inner state of one who witnesses it. The spiritual Master is not only the vehicle through which inner ascension is made, that form itself is radiant with Light, love, and bliss. As those who had a near-death experience are enraptured by the love they experience from the being of Light, so do those who encounter the radiant form of a spiritual Master become intoxicated with ecstasy from the divine love with which it embraces those who experience it. This radiant form is so captivating and enchanting as to dwarf all other interests or desires. When the soul meets this form it becomes immersed in a love so pure, and a light so incandescent, as to glorify every atom of its being. Mystical poetry resounds with praise for this inner form, often poetically called by saints and mystics as the "Beloved," and in the following *ghazal* (lyric poem), Sant Darshan Singh gives a tiny taste of the rarified joy the soul experiences in meeting this manifestation of the radiant form of the Master:

> Your form is brilliant Light.
> Your glimpse of love
>   unparalleled.
> Your position among the Saints
>   is that of the moon among the
>   stars.
> There is a unique lotus mark
>   engraved on your holy feet.
> Nature has expended all its
>   perfection by creating your
>   wondrous form.
> Your silvery-white flowing
>   beard and turban of honor,
>   full of glory and grandeur,
>   radiate light in all directions.[44]

In the writings of saints through the ages, they have described how being in the presence of a spiritual Master can produce a profound experience of exaltation and transformation. Sometimes in meditation, aspirants will see the Master who initiated them embedded in and radiating this living Light. If a disciple's attention remains focused, the most amazing spiritual experiences can begin to unfold.

In the following instance, a person while meditating saw the physical form of Sant Rajinder Singh transform into the appearance of previous spiritual Masters. While gazing steadily, the disciple witnessed powerful beams of light emanating from the Master's eyes. These manifestations of Light experienced within the third or inner eye have the capacity to release unimaginable currents of love and bliss, and begin to reshape the disciple in the image of love itself.

> An intense light surrounded him when he sat on the dais. The light
> increased with time and seemed almost blinding yet it was never too

much. At first I thought something was wrong with my eyes, so I turned them in another direction to see if there was light somewhere else, but there wasn't. He was the source of the radiation. His face kept changing into many other unfamiliar faces. At times, his physical body would practically disappear, features would blur, and it would be only light. Sitting there, I felt I was watching a light show. At one point during the program, his darshan came toward me as a concentrated beam of light. It looked like a searchlight coming in my direction. As the light entered my eyes, I was filled with a longing for a completely spiritual existence, unadulterated by the physical body. I wanted to connect with my higher self. The intensity of that longing overshadowed any other desires I may have had; I wanted only God.[45]

These inner visions of Light have the power to transform the soul while strengthening the soul's connection to its Source. It was for this reason Baba Jaimal Singh pointed out that since a living Master has merged his essence in the living Light and Sound, the spiritual radiation emanating from him elevates the soul to the point within, the third or single eye, from where one connects with the Light and Sound current, leading to reunion with God.

The Living Light of Unity

Over many centuries saints in various traditions describe the methods of inverting within through meditation practices so others can experience the same divine union with the Creator. One who currently is teaching people from many regions of the world to meditate on the inner Light and Sound is Sant Rajinder Singh Ji. A common question people ask him is: if people in ancient times could experience the inner Light and transcend to inner spiritual realms leading back to God, is it possible to do so today? In response to this question, Sant Rajinder Singh explains how a person can test the hypothesis for themselves. In doing so, he refers to an "inner science of spirituality" where one can perform the experiment of meditation to find out for one's self if there is Light and Sound within. And, if one immerses oneself: Are there Light/Sound currents within that will lead to higher realms?

He has thus put into the hands of people of various ages, cultures, and backgrounds a method to discover for themselves the mystical experience of inner sight described since ancient times and traditions. Direct inner communion with Divine Presence through the practice of meditation continues to be affirmed by numerous testimonies by practitioners from many lands as they journey inward. Such stories bear witness to the transcultural nature of the experiences of mystical Light and Sound. In many instances, meditators had little or no prior conceptual or experiential grounding in either the theory or practice of meditation on the inner Light and Sound. Here is one practitioner's recounting of his experiences in meditation shortly after formal initiation into the meditation on the Light and Sound:

> On numerous occasions I have been taken up to a gorgeous sky. I don't know how to explain the difference between this and the physical sky except to say that it is like another dimension. There are changing hues of deep blues and purples that are breathtakingly wondrous. The stars are more brilliant than what one would see even on a clear night in an isolated area on earth. Sometimes there are colored lights and shooting stars in the sky. The moon there is very bright; it is a huge, cool sphere of golden, yellow, and white light. What is most remarkable is the calming and soothing vibration there. It's so absolutely peaceful that one wants to stay there, motionless, and not go back. On my return, I always feel uplifted.[46]

Even in this preliminary experience at the threshold of the inner regions, the practitioner experiences a deeply calming and joyful delight. As an aspirant progresses, these experiences may intensify, revealing ecstasy and light well beyond what human language may describe.

> During meditation...I saw the light of a thousand suns, like the midday sun, but so bright that the naked physical eye could not have gazed upon it. I felt my attention going deep into the light—yet there was no heat. I don't know how long the vision lasted, but I continue to enjoy that bliss and ecstasy. It left me with no words to express my gratitude....[47]

The spiritual realizations of universal love and compassion, which accompany the inner revelations of Light and Sound, represent the culmination of the deepest teachings of these saints. In these spiritual journeys, the Masters escort meditators to various inner regions where they can more perfectly understand the true meaning of divine love and its importance in daily living. The following passage recounts how one glimpses the real nature of compassion and how the saints teach about spiritual love by themselves exemplifying that love. The significance of the entire journey can be capsulated and expressed in two words: unity consciousness. This Light is the Light of Unity and the Light of Love itself.

The realization of unity consciousness through meditation can be understood as the essence of spirituality. In the end, one's cultural background, whether humanist, theist, or agnostic becomes immaterial. Meditation and a life of universal love, compassion, and loving service to all of creation ensure spiritual progress. Ultimately, through the alchemy of love and compassion, the soul is purified of material dross into the essence of Light itself.

From its beginnings Masters of meditation on the inner Light and Sound have envisioned a renewed spirituality, born from Eternal Light and open to all. They have envisioned a Light which when enshrined in human hearts, would kindle a flame of divine unity encompassing all humankind in its embrace. From this new emanation would be born fresh perspectives that respected the Living Light within every man, woman, and child, indeed in all sentient beings. It would be a humanity that honored diversity and transcended differences of backgrounds and cultures. This great confluence of spiritual love would bring in a new golden age of spirituality that would unite people everywhere in the loving bonds of true fellowship.

As Sant Rajinder Singh Ji has prayerfully written:

May we bury our weapons of war
So they may be transformed into flowers of tranquility and bliss,
May we lay down our arms
To lift up our arms to the Creator.
May our prayers and meditation transform this world
Into a garden of everlasting joy;
And may each of us spread Light and Love
Bringing peace to the whole world.[48]

Guidelines at the Heart of the Teachings

1. The current of Light and Sound is the primal eternal vibration arising from the Creator that is the causeless cause of all creation. *From One Light all creation was born.*

2. Our souls, being expressions of this effulgent radiance, are also Light. *We are beings of love, Light, and life.*

3. Recognize that all truth, peace, joy, and wisdom lie within you. *If we don't go within, we go without. ~ Sant Rajinder Singh*

4. Understand that the inner goal of self-realization is the birthright of all humans.

5. The human body is made in the image of the cosmic order. *Everything that is found below is found above.*

6. The mystical journey begins with the opening of the "spiritual eye" during meditation and entering into the first spiritual region. *The spiritual journey starts in time and space but ends beyond time and space.*

7. This mystical spiritual eye can be opened by a spiritual master who then appears in his radiant or Gurudev form to guide the aspirant through the inner spiritual regions. *Receive the gift of Light from one who is overflowing with Light.*

8. To prove the hypothesis that there is inner Light and Sound and realms beyond leading to God involves seeing for one's self the inner Light and listening to the inner ringing radiance. *Seeing is above all. Seeing is believing. ~ Sant Kirpal Singh*

9. A competent Master radiates Light, love, and life to all creation. *Spirituality cannot be bought or taught, but caught from one who is a living manifestation of Light. ~ Sant Kirpal Singh*

10. An ethical life is the necessary portal to the life of spirit. *We first must become good people before we can become godly people.*

11. Service to others is like wings by which aspirants can fly directly into the divine Light. *Service before self is the high road to Truth.*

12. Regular meditation on Light and Sound, coupled with ethical virtues including selfless service and loving-kindness, can accelerate our journey back to God. *Love is the* sunum bonum *of life's existence.*

A Contemplative Practice

Below is an introductory technique taught by Sant Rajinder Singh that anyone can try to get an idea of how simple meditation is and how easily it can be practiced. While the full meditation technique of meditation on the inner Light and Sound are taught to those who want to explore inner spiritual realms leading to God-realization, this Jyoti Meditation technique can be practiced by anyone to give one an experience of peace and happiness:

"To meditate, sit in any pose most comfortable. You can sit on a chair, a sofa, or on the floor. Close your eyes gently, just as you do when you go to sleep. Then, look into the middle of what you see in front of you. While gazing sweetly within, slowly repeat a Name of God, divine presence or higher Power with which you feel comfortable. Repeat it mentally, not aloud. This repetition keeps your attention focused on looking within. You may see flashes of Light or circles of Light. This Light could be golden, yellow, orange, pink, red, blue, green, purple, violet, or white. When you are finished meditating, open your eyes. Jyoti Meditation fills us with inner calm, happiness and joy, and helps us radiate that peace to others."

—Sant Rajinder Singh

EPILOGUE

A Caravan of Light and Love

See now again, gently pulsing beneath all being, a river of light. Permit it to rise to the surface. Realize that the one gazing at the river and the river are one. We are the light.

—Rabbi Lawrence Kushner, *The River of Light*

From primordial beginnings to the present moment, our forefathers and foremothers have navigated down the river of life, with its many depths and shallows, and crosscurrents of joys and sorrows. Today, humankind is faced with a host of tremendous challenges, with each problem to be resolved having its own spiritual dimensions as well. The possibilities for positive transformational changes are also plentiful. Increasing numbers of people of all ages around the planet, especially among the younger generation, are exploring ways, individually and collectively, to tap into available resources that will enhance self-understanding and realization of Divine Presence within themselves and in the world. In doing so, more persons are discovering for themselves the proverbial wisdom that "Life is not a problem to be solved but a mystery to be lived."

The ancient Chinese ideograph for "crisis" was formed by combining two characters: one signifying "danger," the other "opportunity." This linking together of danger with opportunity seems profoundly relevant as a symbol for our times. Given current circumstances globally, a number of questions emerge. Can enough common ground be found among persons of good will from diverse cultures and countries to bring together and act upon a unifying ethos for all of humanity? Will our positive actions become more consistent with our species being known as *homo sapiens* (wise people)? What will it take to build nonviolent, sustainable bridges of lovingkindness, social justice, and compassion, beginning within ourselves, our families, and communities, and expanding throughout the planet? And, of vital importance, once we understand more fully the nature of these challenging responsibilities, what will be our ability to respond appropriately with due diligence? "

It is becoming increasingly understood that there can be no real and lasting peace in the world until there is peace between peoples of all backgrounds. Vietnamese Buddhist sage Thich Nhat Hanh counsels in his *Love Letter to the Earth*: "For us to survive, both as individuals and as a species, we need a revolution in consciousness. It can start with our collective awakening." South African Archbishop Desmond Tutu in his heartfelt counsel reminds us that "My humanity is bound up in you, for we can only be human together." And as Pope Francis II, speaking in January 2015 has emphasized: "We must be clear and unequivocal in challenging our communities to live fully the tenets of peace and coexistence found in each religion, and to denounce acts of violence when they are committed."

It is encouraging to witness increased participation in interfaith dialogue[1] and active involvement by groups promoting people-oriented socio-economic changes. Also, a growing movement, the interspiritual, is attracting persons from a wide range of perpectives—theists and non-theists, humanists, and evolutionary transformationists, among others. A recent book, *The Coming Interspiritual Age,* points to this broad movement as a growing recognition that the basic core of deepest spiritual experience draws upon the same wellspring(s).[2]

As the ongoing journey of humankind continues to unfold, there exists opportunities to conceive and participate in what could be poetically described as a gathering caravan of Light and Love. As an early harbinger of this welcoming message, the poet-saint Sant Darshan Singh once proclaimed:

> I started alone on the journey of love,
>   filled with faith and zeal,
> At every step travelers joined me,
>   and soon we were a caravan.[3]

It is significant that there is a place for everyone in such a caravan. Each participant has something unique and of value to offer to the others, and reciprocally to learn from his/her fellow travelers on their shared journey as well.

Also, it is vital in every community to have teachers and mentors that have the interest and capacity to share what they have learned from their own life experiences with others.

Human beings have an innate potential to experience contact with divine Light and Sound. There are references in esoteric traditions that say the way back home to the creative Source takes place most directly under the guidance of a competent spiritual Teacher. Such a Master, saint, mentor, or by whatever other name they are known, is one who can facilitate a practical demonstration of the experience of Inner Light and Sound within the "laboratory of the soul" of a sincere aspirant. This precious gift is offered with deep humility by the teacher, be it to an individual student or to all of humanity.

Human beings have innate potential to develop contact with Divine Light and Sound, and ultimately to merge with it. An authentic Teacher can provide access to this mystical reality at the time of a disciple's or student's initiation onto the spiritual path. Such Teachers who in their own lifetime personally have received ongoing access to this Light, joyfully offer this priceless gift to those who earnestly seek to explore its true value.

The word enlightenment has been seen historically primarily in a secular sense—as in describing the movement in the latter part of 18th century Europe known as the Enlightenment. Yet as the word itself can be broken down into its separate syllabic components, *en-lighten-ment*, its root meaning becomes "in-the-light." This in turn can be envisaged, not only as a metaphor, but as an alternative way of significantly pointing to a "hidden treasure" to be unearthed and recovered.

Enlightenment thus reframed may be seen as a vital source for spiritual unification within the luminous core of a human being's authentic Self, and a vital component inspiring the quality of life's ongoing journey. When recently asked to distill the essence of the ultimate relationship between enlightenment and inner Light and Sound, Sant Rajinder Singh Ji responded:

> When we sit in {meditative} silence, stilling our thoughts, and gazing within, we find inner Light and divine Music reverberating within. This inner Light and Sound is a current or stream that connects our soul back to God. By concentrating on this inner Light and Sound, our soul can soar on this divine current back to its source, the Divine. By doing so, we fulfill the purpose for which saints and Masters came to this world, reuniting our soul with God. We also are gifted with spiritual experiences of the vistas within and the divine beauty, joy, bliss, and lasting happiness that come with spiritual enlightenment.[4]

The English term "mystic" comes from the Greek *mystikos*, "secret, hidden," which in turn is derived from *mystes*, "one who has been initiated." A mystic is thus literally one initiated into that which is normally secret or hidden. How can the "mystical" be demystified, becoming common knowledge shared by all? We can begin today to become more aware of the many veils impeding our inner vision. Perhaps it can begin with the recognition that life itself is the greatest gift of all, and that the "miraculous" can occur whenever or wherever we learn to see the extraordinary within the ordinary.

As the poet William Blake beautifully observed centuries ago in his "Auguries of Innocence":

To see a World in a Grain of Sand
And a Heaven in a Wild Flower,
Hold Infinity in the palm of your hand
And Eternity in an hour.

What we traditionally recognize as wisdom can be experienced and nurtured in many places—such as within the insightful verses of a joyful song that has inspired persons of all ages: "This Little Light of Mine. I'm going to let it shine." May these "little lights" of ours shine forth, so that each person might realize their birthright and share in the "inheritance of the saints in the light" (Colossians 1:12 NRSV). Join with myriad voices singing in unison and inviting passers-by to join in: "All around the world, I'm going to let it shine...." And as all those "little lights" come together in beloved community, may they become a prayerful emancipating torch for all of humankind. May they bring the spirit of Peace, Light, and Lovingkindness—shared by and for people everywhere, that could illuminate the entire earth.

Bibliography
Books and Other Cited Materials in Chapter Text

1. Judaism and the Soul's Quest for Eternal Light

Armstrong, K. (2007). *The great transformation: The beginning of our religious traditions.* New York, NY: Anchor Books.

Ashlag, Y. (2002). *In the shadow of the ladder: Introductions to Kabbalah.* Safed, Israel: Nehora Press.

Besserman, P. (1978). *Kabbalah: The way of the Jewish mystic.* Garden City, NY: Doubleday.

Chittister, J. (2007). *Welcome to the wisdom of the world.* Grand Rapids, MI: Wm. Eerdmans.

Cooper, D. (1997). *God is a verb: Kabbalah and the practice of mystical Judaism.* New York, NY: Riverhead Books.

Coopersmith, A. (2011). *A journey from Haight Street to Jerusalem.* Granada, CA: One World Lights.

Dan, J., & Kiener, R. (1986). *The early Kabbalah.* NJ: Paulist Press.

Faierstein, M. M. (Trans.). (1999). *Jewish mystical autobiographies: Book of visions and book of secrets.* New York, NY: Paulist Press.

Fine, L. (1984). *Safed spirituality: Rules of mystical piety, the beginning of wisdom.* New York, NY: Paulist Press.

Firestone, T. (2003). *The receiving: Reclaiming Jewish women's wisdom.* San Francisco, CA: HarperSanFrancisco.

Goldstein, R. (2006). *Betraying Spinoza: The renegade Jew who gave us modernity.* New York, NY: Nextbook: Schocken.

Heschel, A. J. (1951). *The Sabbath: Its meaning for modern man.* New York, NY: Farrar.

Idel, M. (1988). *The mystical experience in Abraham Abulafia.* Albany, NY: State University of New York Press.

Jacobs, L. (1977). *Jewish mystical testimonies.* New York, NY: Schocken Books.

Jacobson, S. (2002). *Toward a meaningful life: The wisdom of Rebbe Menachem Mendel Schneerson.* New York, NY: Harper Collins.

Kaplan, A. (1982). *Meditation and Kabbalah.* York Beach, ME: S. Weiser.

Kaplan, A. (1985). *Jewish meditation: A practical guide.* New York, NY: Schocken Books.

Kapstein, M. T. (2004). *The presence of light: Divine radiance and religious experience.* Chicago, IL: University of Chicago Press.

Krassen, M. (1998). *Uniter of heaven and earth.* New York, NY: SUNY Press.

Kushner, L. (2000). *The River of Light: Jewish Mystical Awareness.* Woodstock, VT: Jewish Lights.

Kushner, L., & Polen, N. (2004). *Filling words with light: Hasidic and mystical reflections on Jewish prayer.* Woodstock, VT: Jewish Lights.

Matt, D. C. (Trans.) (1983). *Zohar: The book of enlightenment.* New York, NY: Paulist Press.

Raphael, S. P. (1994). *Jewish views of the afterlife.* London, UK: Jason Aronson.

Sacks, J. (2015). *Not in God's name.* New York, N.Y., Schocken Books.

Sacks, J. (2005). *To heal a fractured world: The ethics of responsibility.* New York, NY: Random House.

Samuel, G. (2007). *The Kabbalah handbook: A concise encyclopedia of terms and concepts in Jewish mysticism.* New York, NY: Jeremy Tarcher.

Schachter-Shalomi, Z. (2003). *Wrapped in a holy flame: Teachings and tales of the Hasidic masters.* San Francisco, CA: Jossey-Bass.

Schneersohn, J. I., & Schneerson, C. M. (1996). *The making of Chassidim: A letter written by the previous Lubavitcher Rebbe.* Brooklyn, NY: Sichos in English.

Schneerson, M. M. (1986). *On the essence of Chassidus.* Brooklyn, NY: Kehot Publication Society.

Schochet, J. I. (1988). *Mystical concepts in Chassidism: An introduction to Kabbalistic concepts and doctrines.* Brooklyn, NY: Kehot.

Scholem, G. G. (1961). *Major trends in Jewish mysticism.* New York, NY: Schocken Books.

Shapiro, Rami (2004). *Open Secrets: The letters of Reb Yerachmiel ben Yisrael.* Rhinebeck, New York: Monkfish Book Publishing.

Smith, H. (2006). *Let there be light: Modern cosmology and Kabbalah: A new conversation between science and religion.* Novato, CA: New World Library.

Spitz, E. K. (2000). *Does the soul survive?: A Jewish journey to belief in afterlife, past lives, and living with purpose.* Woodstock, VT: Jewish Lights.

Steinsaltz, A. (2003). *Opening the Tanya: Discovering the moral and mystical teachings of a classic work of Kabbalah.* San Francisco, CA: Jossey-Bass.

Steinsaltz, A. (2006). *The thirteen petalled rose: A discourse on the essence of Jewish existence and belief.* New York, NY: Basic Books.

2. The Transfigured Presence: Christianity and the Gospel of Light

Angela, of Foligno (1993). *Complete works* (P. Lachance, Trans.). New York, NY: Paulist Press.

Augustine, of Hippo (1984). *Augustine of Hippo, selected writings* (M. T. Clark, Trans.). New York, NY: Paulist Press.

Beer, F. (1992). *Women and mystical experience in the Middle Ages.* Rochester, NY: Boydell Press.

Böhme, J. (1981). *The "key" of Jacob Boehme* (W. Law, Trans). Edinburgh, UK: Magnum Opus Hermetic Sourceworks.

Catherine, of Siena (1980). *The dialogue* (S. Noffke, Trans.). New York, NY: Paulist Press.

Climacus, John (1980). *The Ladder of Divine Ascent,* (Colm and Russell Trans.) New York, NY: Paulist Press.

Dupre and James Wiseman, OSB (2001). *Light from Light; An anthology of Christian mysticism.* Paulist Press, Second edition, New York:/Mahwah N.J.

Eckhart, & Davies, O. (1994). Selected writings. London ; New York: Penguin Books. Fox, G. (1963).

Eckhart, M. (1969). *Meister Eckhart: A modern translation* (R. B. Blakney, Trans.). New York, NY: Harper & Row.

Eckhart, M. (1981). *Meister Eckhart, the essential sermons, commentaries, treatises, and defense* (E. Colledge & B. McGinn, Trans.). New York, NY: Paulist Press.

Eckhart, M. (1994). *Selected writings* (O. Davies, Trans.). New York, NY: Penguin Books.

Fox, G. (1963). *The journal of George Fox* (R. M. Jones, Ed.). New York, NY: Capricorn Books.

Fox, M. (1982). *Meditations with Meister Eckhart.* Santa Fe, NM: Bear & Co.

Gould, S. J. (1998). *Leonardo's mountain of clams and the Diet of Worms: essays on natural history* (1st ed.). New York, NY: Harmony Books.

Head, N. (1861). *Daily walk with wise men; or, religious exercises for every day in the year.* (n. p.).

Hildegard, of Bingen (1994). *The letters of Hildegard of Bingen* (J. L. Baird & R. K. Ehrman, Trans.). New York, NY: Oxford University Press.

Hughes, R. D. (2008). *Beloved dust: Tides of the spirit in the Christian life.* New York, NY: Continuum.

Kavanaugh, K. & Rodriguez, O. (1987).*The collected works of St John of the Cross,*Washington, ICS Publications.

Markides, K. C. (1987). *Homage to the sun: The wisdom of the Magus of Strovolus.* New York, NY: Arkana.

Mechthild, of Magdeburg (1998). *The flowing light of the Godhead* (F. J. Tobin, Trans.). New York, NY: Paulist Press.

Merton, T. (1966). *Conjectures of a guilty bystander.* Garden City, NY: Doubleday.

Philokalia (1979). *The Philokalia: The complete text* (compiled by St. Nikodimos of the Holy Mountain and St. Makarios of Corinth; translated by G. E. H. Palmer, P. Sherrard, & K. Ware). London, UK: Faber and Faber.

Plested, M. (2004). *The Macarian legacy: The place of Macarius-Symeon in the Eastern Christian tradition.* New York, NY: Oxford University Press.

Porete, M., & Babinsky, E. L. (1993). *The mirror of simple souls.* New York, NY: Paulist Press.

Pseudo-Dionysius, the Areopagite (1987). *Pseudo-Dionysius: The complete works* (C. Luibhéid & P. Rorem, Trans.). New York, NY: Paulist Press.

Seuse, H., & Tobin, F. J. (1989). *Henry Suso: The exemplar, with two German sermons.* New York, NY: Paulist Press.

Smith, Huston (2009). *Worlds Religons,* New York, NY: Harper One.

Steere, D. V. (1984). *Quaker spirituality: Selected writings.* New York, NY: Paulist Press.

Steegmann, Mary G. (Translator), Algar Thorold (2007).*The Book of divine consolation of the blessed Angela of Foligno* Kessinger Publishing.

Steuart, R. H. J. (2006). *The mystical doctrine of St John of the Cross.* Bloombury Publishing.

Teresa, of Avila (1957). *The life of Saint Teresa of Avila by herself.* New York, NY: Viking Penguin.

Teresa, of Avila (1979). *The interior castle.* New York, NY: Paulist Press.

Teresa, of Avila (1987). *The collected works of St. Teresa of Avila* (2nd ed.). Washington, DC: ICS Publications.

Teasdale, Wayne (2001).*The Mystic Heart, discovering a Univesal Spiritualtiy in the Worlds Relgions.* New York; New Library.

Thompson, R. V. (2007). *A voluptuous God: A Christian heretic speaks,* Kelowna, BC: Wood Publishing House.

Ward, B. (2003). *The desert fathers: Sayings of the early Christian monks.* New York, NY: Penguin Books.

Wilber, K. (1997). *The eye of spirit: An integral vision for a world gone slightly mad.* Boston, MA: Shambhala.

3. Hinduism: The Light That Illumines the Self

Armstrong, K. (2007). *The great transformation: The beginning of our religious traditions.* Canada: Vintage Press.

Aurobindo, Sri. (2006). *The life divine* (4th ed.). Twin Lakes, WI: Lotus Press.

Callewaert, W. M. (1988). *The Hindu biography of Dadu Dayal.* Delhi, India: Motilal Banarsidass.

Coomaraswamy, A. K. (1977). *Coomaraswamy: Selected papers, metaphysics.* Princeton, NJ: Princeton University Press.

Das, J. N. *Vedic conception of sound in four features.* Retrieved from: veda.harekrishna.cz/encyclopedia/vedicsound.htm

Easwaran, E., & Nagler, M. N. (2009). *The Upanishads.* Tomales, CA: Nilgiri Press.

Eliade, M. (1965). *Mephistopheles and the androgyne: Studies in religious myth and symbol.* Chicago, IL: Sheed and Ward.

Feuerstein, G. (1988). *The Tantra path of ecstasy.* Boston, MA: Shambala.

Feuerstein, G. (2001). *The Yoga tradition: Its history, literature, philosophy, and practice.* Prescott, AZ: Hohm Press.

Fisher, M. P. (2011). *Living religions* (8th ed.). New York, NY: Prentice Hall.

Hawley, J. S. (2005). *Three Bhakti voices: Mirabai, Surdas, and Kabir in their time and ours.* New Delhi, India: Oxford University Press, 2005.

Metzner, R. (1986). *Opening to inner light: The transformation of human nature and consciousness.* New York, NY: J. P. Tarcher.

Miller, B. S. (1986). *The Bhagavad-Gita, Krishna's counsel in time of war.* New York, NY: Bantam Classics.

Muller-Ortega, P. E. (1989). *The triadic heart of Śiva, Kaula Tantricism of Abhinavagupta in the non-dual Shaivism of Kashmir.* Albany, NY: State University of New York Press.

Namdev (1970). *Shri Namdev Gatha* (Trans. Visoba Khechar). Bombay, India: Maharashtra Government Press.

Novak, P. (1994). *The world's wisdom.* New York, NY: Harper One.

Reps, P., & Senzaki, N. (1999). *Zen flesh, Zen bones: A collection of Zen and pre-Zen writings.* Boston, MA: Tuttle Publishing.

Saraswati, S. C. (2012) *By God's grace: The life and teachings of Pujya Swami Chidanand Saraswati.* San Rafael, California. Mandala Publishing.

Shankara (1975). *Crest jewel of discrimination: Timeless teachings of non duality* (Trans. Swami Prabhavanada and C. Isherwood). Hollywood, CA: Vedanta Press.

Singh, K. (1978). *Naam or Word.* Bowling Green, VA: SK Publications.

Singh, K. (1980). *The crown of life: A study in yoga* (4th ed.). Bowling Green, VA: SK Publications.

Siva Samhita: A Critical Edition, English Version (Trans. Swami Maheshanda, B. R. Sharma, Shir G .S. Sahay, Shri R. K. Bodhe, B. K. Jha, & R. C. Bhardwaj). (2009). Pune, India: O.P. Tiwari Secretary Kaivalydhama S.M.Y.M. Samiti's.

Smart, Ninian (1998). *The Worlds Religons,* Oxford: Cambrigde Press 2nd Edition

Yogananda, P. (1946). *Autobiography of a yogi.* Los Angeles, CA: Self-Realization Fellowship.

4. Luminous Mind: Buddhism and the Heart of Clear Light

Ajahn, B. (2006). *Mindfulness, bliss, and beyond: A meditator's handbook.* Boston, MA: Wisdom Publications.

Bodhidharma (1987). *The Zen Teaching of Bodhidharma* (Red Pine, Trans.). San Francisco, CA: North Point Press.

Broughton, J. L. (1999). *The Bodhidharma anthology: The earliest records of Zen.* Berkeley, CA: University of California Press.

Bstan, 'dzin Rgya Mtsho, Dalai Lama XIV, & Berzin A. (1997). *The Gelug-Kagyü tradition of Mahamudra.* Ithaca, NY: Snow Lion Publications.

Bucknell, R. S., & Stuart-Fox, M. (1986). *The twilight language: Explorations in Buddhist meditation and symbolism.* New York, NY: St. Martin Press.

Chandrakirti (2004). *Introduction to the middle way: Chandrakirti's Madhyamakāvatāra* (J. Mipham, Trans.). New Delhi, India: Shechen Publications.

Ching, J. (2000). *The religious thought of Chu Hsi.* New York, NY: Oxford University Press.

Cleary, T. (Trans.). (1987). *Flower ornament scripture/Entry into the realm of reality.* Boston, MA: Shambhala.

Cleary, T. F. (Trans.). (1988). *The Taoist classics: The collected translations of Thomas Cleary.* Boston, MA: Shambhala.

Coleman, Graham, Jinpa Thupen & Dorje, Gyurme, Trans. by (2007) *The Tibetan Book of the dead; the first Complete translation.* New York, NY; Penguin Books.

Conze, E. (1954). *Buddhist texts through the ages.* Oxford, UK: B. Cassirer.

Desmond, T. (2016). *Self-compassion in psychotherapy: Mindfulness-based practices for healing and transformation.* New York, N. Y., W. W. Norton and Company, Inc.

Dumoulin, H. (1994). *Zen Buddhism: A history* (Vol. 1, India and China: With a New Supplement on the Northern School of Chinese Zen). New York, NY: Macmillan4.

Gyatso, Tenzin; Alexander Berzin (1997). *The Gelug/Kagyu tradition of Mahamudra.* New York: Snow Lion Publications.

Hanh, T. N. (2012). *Awakening of the heart: Essential Buddhist sutras and commentaries.* Berkeley, California. Parallax Press.

Kapstein, M. T. (2004). *The presence of light: Divine radiance and religious experience.* Chicago, IL: University of Chicago Press.

Karma-Lingpa, T., & Padmasambhava (2006). *The Tibetan book of the dead: The great liberation by hearing in the intermediate states* (Translated by G. Dorje and edited by G. Coleman with T. Jinpa). New York: Viking.

Kim, H. J., & Leighton, T. D. (2004). *Eihei Dōgen: Mystical realist.* Boston, MA: Wisdom Publications.

Kornfield, J. (1977). *Living Buddhist masters.* Santa Cruz, CA: Unity.

Kornfield, J. (2008). *The wise heart: A guide to the universal teachings of Buddhist psychology.* New York, NY: Bantam.

Low, A. (2006). *Hakuin on Kensho: The four ways of knowing.* Boston, MA: Shambhala.

Porter, B. (1993). *Road to heaven: Encounters with Chinese hermits.* San Francisco, CA: Mercury House.

Rinpoche, G. (2002). *Meditation, transformation, and dream yoga* (S. Khandro & B. A. Wallace, Trans.). Ithaca, NY: Snow Lion Publications.

Simmer-Brown, J. (2002). *Dakini's warm breath: The feminine principle in Tibetan Buddhism.* Boston, MA: Shambhala.

Singh, H. (1980). *Taming the mind.* Bowling Green, VA: Sat Sandesh.

Tenzin, W., & Dahlby, M. (1998). *The Tibetan yogas of dream and sleep.* Ithaca, NY, Snow Lion Publications.

Watson, B. (1993). *The lotus sutra.* New York, NY: Columbia University Press.

Wick, G. S. (2005). *The book of equanimity: Illuminating classic Zen koans.* Boston, MA: Wisdom Publications.

Wilber, K. (1999). *Integral psychology.* Boston, MA: Shambhala.

Wong, E. (Trans.). (1992). *Cultivating stillness: A Taoist manual for transforming body and mind* (E. Wong, Trans.). Boston, MA: Shambala.

Zhengjue, Hongzhi (2000). *Cultivating the empty field: The silent illumination of Zen Master Hongzhi* (T. D. Leighton, Trans.). Boston, MA: Tuttle.

6. Ineffable Light: Visions of Light in Life, Death, and in the Afterlife

Atwater, P. M. H. (1999). *Children of the millennium: children's near-death experiences and the evolution of humankind.* NYC, NY: Three Rivers Press.

Atwater, P. M. H. (2003). *The new children and near-death experience.* Rochester, VT: Bear & Co.

Bailey, L. W., & Yates, J. (1996). *The near-death experience: A reader.* New York, NY: Routledge.

Basford, T. K. (1990). *The near-death experience.* New York, NY: Garland.

Cohen, J. M., & Phipps, J. F. (1979). *The common experience.* Los Angeles, CA: J. P. Tarcher.

Dante Alighieri. *The divine comedy.* Trans. A. S. Kline. http//www.poetryintranslation.com/klineasdante.htm

Davies, P. (1983). *God and the new physics.* New York, NY: Simon and Schuster.

Edgerton, F. (Trans.). (1944). *Bhagavad Gita.* New York, NY: Harper TorchBooks.

Eliade, M. (1970). *Death, afterlife, and eschatology.* New York, NY: Harper Row.

Enright, D. J. (1983). *The Oxford dictionary of death.* New York, NY: Oxford University Press.

Goswami, Amit (2004). *The quantum doctor.* Charlottesville, VA: Hampton Books.

Goldman, D. (1988). *The meditative mind.* Los Angeles, CA: Jeremy Tarcher.

Grey, M. (1985). *Return from death.* London, UK: Arkana.

Harris, B., & Bascom, L. (1990). *Full circle: The near death experience and beyond.* New York, NY: Pocket Books.

Insinger, M. (1991). The impact of a near-death experience on family relationships. *Journal of Near-Death Studies, 9,* 141–181.

James, W. (1901). *The varieties of religious experience.* New York, NY: Signet.

Kapleau, P. (1971). *The wheel of death.* New York, NY: Harper TorchBooks.

Kramer, K. (1988). *The sacred art of dying.* New York, NY: Mahwah/Paulist Press.

Kubler-Ross, E. (1989). *On death and dying.* New York, NY: Macmillan.

Levine, S. (1982). *Who dies.* Garden City, NY: Anchor Press/Doubleday.

Levine, S. (1987). *Healing into life and death.* Garden City, NY: Anchor Press/Doubleday.

Lommel, P. V. (2010). *Consciousness beyond life: The science of near-death experience.* New York, NY: Harper Collins.

Lorimer, D. (1990). *Whole in one: The near-death experience and the experience of interconnectedness.* London, UK: Arkana.

Lundahl, C. R. (1982). *A collection of near-death readings.* Chicago, IL: Nelson-Hall.

Lusseyran, J. (2006). *And there was light: Autobiography of Jacques Lusseyran, blind hero of the French Resistance* (2nd ed.). Sandpoint, ID: Morning Light Press.

McColman, C. (2000). *The aspiring mystic: Practical steps for spiritual seekers.* Holbrook, MA: Adams Media.

Meltzer, D. (Ed.) (1984). *Death: An anthology of ancient texts, prayers, and stories.* San Francisco, CA: North Point Press.

Moody, R. A. (1975). *Life after life.* Covington, GA: Mockingbird Books.

Moody, R. A. (1988). *The light beyond.* New York, NY: Bantam.

Nugent, C. (1994). *Mysticism and death.* New York, NY: SUNY Press.

Oris, K., & Haraldsson, E. (1977). *At the hour of death.* New York, NY: Avon.

Radin, D. (1997). *The conscious universe.* New York, NY: Harper Edge.

Rawlings, M. (1978). *Beyond death's door.* Nashville, TN: Thomas Nelson.

Ring, K. (1985). *Heading toward omega: In search of the meaning of the near-death experience.* New York, NY: Quill Press.

Rinpoche, Sogyal (1994). *The Tibetan book of living and dying.* San Francisco, CA: Harper.

Russell, P. (2002). *From science to God: A physicist's journey into the mystery of consciences.* Novato, CA: New World Library.

Sabom, M. B. (1982). *Recollections of death.* New York, NY: Harper & Row.

Schroeder, G. L. (1997). *The science Of God.* New York, NY: Broadway Books.

Singh, Kirpal (1981). *The mystery of death* (4th ed.). Bowling Green, VA: SK Publications.

Singh, Rajinder (2006). *Inner and outer peace through meditation* (3rd ed.). Naperville, IL: Radiance Publishers.

Talbot, M. (1981). *Mysticism and the new physics.* New York, NY: Bantam.

Vincent, K. R. (1994). *Visions of God.* New York, NY: Larson Publications.

Wentz, E. (Trans.) (1960). *The Tibetan book of the dead.* New York, NY: Oxford University Press.

7. Meditation and the Splendor of Inner Light

McLeod, W. H, & Schomer, K. (1987). *The Sants: Studies of devotional tradition in India.* Berkeley CA: Berkeley Religious Studies Series, and Motilal Banarsidass.

Rumi, Jalalu'ddin. *Mathnawi,* Book I, Opening lines, verse 1–30. All translations of Rumi unless otherwise noted are taken from *The Mathnawi of Jalalu'ddin Rumi,* Books 1–6 (Edited and translated by R. A. Nicholson). (1926/2006). Published and distributed by the Trustees of the E. J. W. Gibb Memorial.

Russell, P. (2002). *From science to God: A physicist's journey into the mystery of consciences.* Novato, CA: New World Library.

Shahib, Tulsi (1966). *Ghat Ramayana,* Pt. II. Allahabad, India: Bellevedere Press.

Shahib, Tulsi (1972). *Shabdavali,* Pt. II, Holi Deepchandi 8. Allahabad, India: Bellevedere Press.

Singh, Darshan (1979). *Secret of secrets.* Bowling Green, VA: SK Publications.

Singh, Darshan (1986). A *tear and a star.* Bowling Green, VA: SK Publications.

Singh, Darshan (1988). *The wonders of inner space.* Bowling Green, VA: SK Publications.

Singh, Darshan, (1989). *Love at every step: my concept of poetry.* Vijay Nagar, Delhi, India: SK Publications.

Singh, Darshan (1993). *Streams of nectar.* Naperville, IL: SK Publications.

Singh, Darshan (1982). *Spiritual Awakening.* Bowling Green, VA: SK Publicstions.

Singh, Darshan (1989). *Love at every step: my concept of poetry.* Vijay Nagar, Delhi, India: SK Publications.

Singh, Darshan (1996). *Love has only a beginning: Stories of family and relatives,* Vol. II. Bowling Green, VA: SK Publications.

Singh, Kirpal (1971). *Man know thyself* (8th printing). Bowling Green, VA: SK Publications.

Singh, Kirpal (1978). *Naam or Word.* Delhi, India: SK Publications.

Singh, Kirpal (1981). *Portrait of perfection.* Bowling Green, VA: SK Publications.

Singh, Kirpal (1995). *The spiritual path: An anthology of the teachings of Kirpal Singh.* Bowling Green, VA: SK Publications.

Singh, Kirpal (1998). *A Great Saint: Baba Jaimal Singh—Life and teachings,* 6th ed. Delhi, India: SK Publications.

Singh, Rajinder (2013). *Empowering your soul through meditation.* Lisle, IL: Radiance Publishers.

Singh, Rajinder (2000). *Flowering of grace: Stories of living master Sant Rajinder Singh Ji.* Bowling Green, VA: SK Publications.

Singh, Rajinder, (2011). *Spark of the divine.* Lisle, IL: Radiance Publishers.

Singh, Rajinder (2012). *Meditation as medication for the soul.* Lisle, IL: Radiance Publishers.

Singh, Rajinder (2007). *Inner and outer peace through meditation.* Lisle, IL: Radiance Publishers.

Singh, Rajinder (2006). *Spiritual pearls for enlightened living.* Lisle, IL: Radiance Publishers.

Endnotes

Introduction

[1] For a profound interpretation of the nature of Inner Light and Sound, see the pionering work by Kirpal Singh, *Naam or Word*, 4th ed. (Bowling Green, VA: SK Publications, 1972).

[2] Darshan Singh, *Streams of Nectar* (1993), p. 191.

[3] Jalal ad-din Rumi, "Four Poems on the Night," trans. by John Moyne and Coleman Barks, in *World Poetry*, ed., by Katherine Washburn, John S. Major, and Clifton Fadiman (New York: W. W. Norton, 1998), p. 478.

[4] Editor David Appelbaum's introductory Focus to a stimulating issue on "Light," in *Parabola: Myth Tradition and the Search for Meaning, 26*:2, May 2001, p. 5.

[5] Huston Smith, *Why Religion Matters: The Fate of the Human Spirit in an Age of Disbelief* (New York, NY: Harper Collins, 2001). See especially the chapters on Light, pp. 137–144, and Spirit, pp. 255–271.

[6] Daniel Siegel, *Mindsight: The New Science of Personal Transformation* (New York, NY: Bantam Books, 2010).

Chapter 1: Judaism and the Soul's Quest for Eternal Light

[1] See Kushner & Polen, 2004, pp. 153–154.

[2] For all Jewish biblical citations in this chapter, unless otherwise noted, we are using the translations and annotations of the Stone Edition of the *Tanach* (the Torah, Prophets, and Writings), 2nd edition printed in 2012.

[3] In the introduction to his insightful study *Uniters of Heaven and Earth*, Miles Krassen (1998, p. 6) writes that "it is especially important to understand the nature of the spiritual experience idealized and cultivated by the Hasidic masters...In addition to mystical experiences, Rabbi Meshullam Feibush Heller's approach to Hasidism places perhaps equally great weight on a commitment to ethical value, namely humility."

[4] Ashlag, 2002, p. 106.

[5] Translation of quoted psalms are from A. J. Rosenberg (Ed.), *The Complete Tanach Library.*

[6] Jewish tradition maintains that 73 of the Psalms were composed works by King David based on the writings of 10 ancient psalmists (including Adam and Moses). By contrast, many modern scholars see these psalms as the product of several authors or groups of authors, a good many unknown.

[7] In the introduction to her study *The Great Transformation,* Karen Armstrong (2007, pp. xv–xxiii) holds that, given the current predicaments of contemporary humankind, "we can find inspiration in the period that the German philosopher Karl Jaspers called the Axial Age, because it was pivotal to the spiritual development of humanity....During this period of intense creativity, spiritual and philosophical geniuses pioneered an entirely new kind of human experience, [showing us] what a human being can be."

[8] Armstrong, 2007, p. 452–456. She notes that, "the Jewish Axial Age had been cut short, stifled perhaps prematurely, by the difficulties of dispersion and resettlement, but it was brought to fulfillment by marvelous secondary and tertiary flowerings."

[9] Ibid., p. 456.

[10] References to the throne, for example, are found in 1 Kings 22:19, Isaiah 6:1–8, and Daniel 7:9–10.

[11] Kaplan, 1982, p. 41.

[12] Samuel, 2007, pp. 188–189.

[13] See, for example, "Aaron Roth's essay 'Agitation of the Soul' " in Jacobs, 1977, pp. 245–259.

[14] Scholem, 1961, pp. 49–50.

[15] Jacobs, 1977, pp. 3–4.

[16] Besserman, 2001, pp. 2–3.

[17] This biographic account is drawn from Idel (1988, pp. 2–6), which provides a summation of Abulafia's inner experiences and influential teachings.

[18] Idel, 1988, p. 79.

[19] This passage, from a book written in 1295 that set forth the basic ideas of prophetic Kabbalism, was translated by G. Scholem in Qiryat Sefer 1 (1924, p. 134), and appears in *Major Trends in Jewish Mysticism* (1961, p. 150).

[20] The practice of gematria "existed in Greek, Babylonian and Syrian culture before finding its way into Kabbalah." Jewish mysticism held that the Torah, understood at different levels, contained all the wisdom of Creation. Gematria served as a popular means to seek access to higher meanings and mystical secrets hidden within the texts, "much the way a detective searches for the secret of a code. Breaking the code opens the door to higher levels of reality, bringing the hidden into the known" (Samuel, 2007, pp. 110–111).

[21] Ibid., p. 56.

[22] Samuel, 2007, p. 288.

[23] Ashlag, 2002, pp. 63–65.

[24] Ibid., pp. 67–70.

[25] See chart of 32 Mystical Paths according to the Ari (Cooper, 1997, p. 87).

[26] Much of the material on the three highest sephirot discussed in the previous paragraphs is drawn from Kaplan (1985, pp. 179–186).

[27] Cooper, 1997, pp. 211–215.

[28] "The Zohar on the High Priest's Ecstasy," in Jacobs (1977, pp. 80–87).

[29] Quoted in Jacobs (1977, p. 93).

[30] See "The Religious World of Safed" in the introduction by Lawrence Fine (1984, pp. 7–10) to *Safed Spirituality.*

[31] For a creative interpretation of the concept of tikkun ha-olam, see Rebecca Goldstein (2006, pp. 111–112).

[32] Jonathan Sacks, *To Heal a Fractured World* (New York, NY: Random House, 2005), p. 72.

[33] Fine, 1984, p. 63. For the broader context for these teachings by Luria, see "Rules for Mystic Piety," pp. 61–80.

[34] Firestone, 2003, p. 245.

[35] Ibid., pp. 215–216.

[36] Ibid., p. 228.

[37] Jacobs, 1977, pp. 149–153. The translation here follows the version printed in the Ben Porat Yoself (pp. 100a–b), as this was the version known to the Hasidim.

[38] Kaplan, 1982, p. 284.

[39] Magid Deverav LeYaakov (Jerusalem, 1971, p. 52).

[40] Kaplan, 1985, p. 41.

[41] In this expanded discourse, "the Rebbe precisely defines the unique relationship Chassidus has with the other parts of the Torah and the traditional forms of interpretation; with Kabbalah; with the various dimensions of the soul; with the concept of Moshiach; and with the Divine attributes" (Schneerson, 2003, p. 14).

[42] Jacobson, 2002, p. 282.

[43] Schneerson, 1986, pp. 91–92.

[44] Quoted in Schneerson, 1986, pp. 8–9. "There are four 'worlds' or basic levels, each of which is a general category of Divine manifestation, ranging from the highest level, where there is total unity with G-d, down to this lowest physical world which we inhabit where the infinite is all but concealed....Kether is the level which transcends all worlds, and which is the 'Crown' to the Sefirot. It is identified with the Supernal Will, and it is that which links G-d, the infinite Ein Sof, with all His finite created worlds....When new light emanates from Kether, all the Sephirot are rejuvenated, as it were, transformed into something higher than before."

[45] "As the expression of Divine Emanation, Shekhinah expresses and manifests fully as the final sephirah, Malkhut (kingdom) which receives and expresses the energy of all the proceeding in the Kabbalistic Tree of Life...Maimonides believed that Shekhinah was the aspect of the Divine that was revealed to the Biblical Prophets in their visions" (Samuel, 2007, pp. 308–309).

[46] Heschel, 1951. See especially the chapters "A Palace in Time," pp. 12–25, and "Intuitions of Eternity," pp. 72–77, among others.

[47] Menachem M. Schneerson, *Victory of light: A Chasidic discourse*, originally published in Hebrew in 5747 (1986), p. 7.

[48] Samuel, 2007, pp. 246–247.

[49] See, for example, Raphael, 1994.

[50] Spitz, 2002, p. 23.

[51] Ibid., p. 24.

[52] Ibid., p. 26.

[53] Ibid., p. 174.

[54] Shapiro, 2004, p. 114.

[55] In the realm of the Sephirot, *Yesh* literally means "to exist," and refers to the world of seemingly separate forms. *Ayn*, meaning emptiness, is ultimately a reference to the Ayn Sof, that which has no ending.

[56] Steinsaltz, 2006, p. 33.

[57] Kaplan, 1985, p. 54.

[58] See the chapter "Mantra Meditation" in Kaplan, 1985, pp. 54–63.

[59] Other influential teachers participating in the Jewish Renewal movement include Rabbis Tirzah Firestone, David Cooper, Elliot Ginsberg, Leah Novick, Shefa Gold, Lynn Gottlieb, Miles Krassen, Goldie Milgram, Marcia Prager, Daniel Siegel, Shohama Wiener, David Wolfe-Blank, Stan Levy, Art Green, Arthur Waskow and David Ingbar.

[60] From Rabbi Arthur Waskow's letter of July 4, 2014, published in Rabbi Michael Lerner (ed.), *Tikkun:* to heal, repair and transform the world. Website of remembrances, following the death of Reb Zalman: http://www.tikkun. org/nextgen/remembering-reb-zalman-membersof-our-tikkun-community-share-their-memories.

[61] http://www.tirzahfirestone.com/biography. Accessed January 26, 2014.

[62] Firestone, 2003, p. 247.

[63] Samuel, 173–74. Hebrew letters also double as numbers: *lamed* (l) is 30 and *vav* (v) is 6. Together *lamed* and *vav* (lv) mean thirty-six: hence the phrase Lamed Vav Tzaddikim.

[64] Avram Davis (ed.), *Meditation from the Heart of Judaism*, p. 36.

[65] Firestone, 2003, p. 228.

Chapter 2: The Transfigured Presence:
Christianity and the Gospel of light

[1] Smith, Huston, *World religions,* p. 206.

[2] See, e.g., the September 30, 1963, interview with Kirpal Singh on www.ruhani satsangusa.org/wcau.htm

[3] "The Acts of the Apostles, the fifth book of the New Testament, recounts the history of the earliest church in Jerusalem and in Palestine...It is almost the only source for Christian history in the period 30–64 CE, though in using it the reader must reckon with the author's idealized picture of the earliest church as a unified body under the Apostles and guided by the Holy Spirit, and with his liberty in composing speeches." John Bowker (Ed.), *The Oxford Dictionary of World Religions* (New York, NY: Oxford University Press, 1997), p. 15.

[4] See, e.g., the Sept. 30, 1963, interview with Kirpal Singh on www.ruhanisatsang usa.org/wcau.htm

[5] Augustine, 1984, pp. 70–71.

[6] Climacus, 1982, pp. 54–56.

[7] Ibid., p. 54.

[8] Ibid., p. 55.

[9] Homily 1.2, trans. Jennings, italics ours.

[10] Wilber, 1997.

[11] Daskolos refers to the method of leaving the body as *examatosis* and refers to his disciples as "researchers after truth." See Markides, 1987.

[12] Pseudo-Dionysius, 1987, p. 53.

[13] Ibid., p. 54.

[14] Ibid., p. 151.

[15] Ibid., p. 76.

[16] Hildegard, 1994, p. 23.

[17] Mechthild, 1998, p. 77.

[18] Ibid., p. 83.

[19] Ibid., p. 83.

[20] Ibid., p. 83.

[21] Ibid., p.179.

[22] Porete,1993, p. 149.

[23] Ibid., p. 153.

[24] Ibid., p. 191.

[25] Davies, 1994, p. 216.

[26] Paradiso, XXX, 61–66.

[27] Angela, 1993, p. 190.

[28] Angela, 1980 p. 190.

[29] Steegmann and Thorold, 1995, p. 364.

[30] Ibid.

[31] Kavanaugh, K. and Rodriguez, O., 1979, p. 67.

[32] *The life of St. Teresa,* translated by J. M. Cohen, London, 1957, pp. 197–198.

[33] Kavanaugh, K. and Rodriguez, O., 1987, p. 65.

[34] Ibid., p. 91.

[35] Kavanaugh, K. & Rodriguez, O. 1987. p. 104.

[36] Smart, 1998, p. 276.

[37] A noted scholar on Christian mysticism, Bernard McGinn, makes the point that a doctrine of deification can also be found among Roman Catholics, such as Augustine, the Cistercians, Porete, and Eckhart. (Personal correspondence with Prof. McGinn.)

[38] Philokalia, Vol. 1, p. 18.

[39] Philokalia, Vol. 4, p. 13.

[40] Philokalia, Vol. 4, p. 18.

[41] Philokalia, Vol. 4, p. 20.

[42] Philokalia, Vol. 4, p. 59.

[43] Philokalia, Vol. 4, p. 39.

[44] Philokalia, Vol. 4, p. 75.

[45] Philokalia, Vol. 4, p. 62.

[46] Philokalia, Vol. 4, p. 29.

[47] Philokalia, Vol. 4, p. 47.

[48] St. Symeon the New Theologian, Hymn 27, 125–132.

[49] Philokalia, Vol. 4, p. 376.

[50] Philokalia, Vol. 4, p. 414.

[51] Philokalia, Vol. 4, p. 419.

[52] Philokalia, Vol. 4, p. 420.

[53] Philokalia, Vol. 4, p. 378.

[54] Philokalia, Vol. 4, p. 292.

[55] Philokalia, Vol. 4, p. 382.

[56] Philokalia, Vol. 4, p. 362.

[57] Philokalia, Vol. 4, p. 288.

[58] Böhme, 1981.

[59] See *The supersensual life*, at gnosis.org/library/super.htm

[60] From the journals of George Fox. ccel.org/ccel/fox_g/autobio.txt

[61] Ibid.

[62] R. M. Jones, *Social law in the spiritual world: Studies in human and divine inter-relationship* (Philadelphia, PA: John C. Winston, 1904), pp. 167–168.

[63] See Arthur Stein and Brian Toomey, "Contemplative practice and social commitment: The Quakers and engaged Buddhism,"*Integral Explorations: Journal of Culture and Consciousness*, January 2003, Vols. 7–8, pp. 130–151.

[64] natcath.org/NCR_Online/archives 2/2007d/121407/ss121407e.htm

[65] Merton, 1966, p. 450.

[66] Ibid., p. 449.

[67] Ibid., pp. 140–142.

[68] One of the key issues explored by the Parliament was the necessity to search for common ground, a shared "global ethic" to which all of the world's religions basically adhered.

[69] Thompson, Robert V., 2007, p. 213.

[70] Teasdale, 2001, pp. 75–76.

[71] Markides, 1987, pp. 169–170.

[72] Ibid., pp. 169–170.

[73] Ibid., p. 120.

[74] See Feldman and Jack Kornfield, 1991, pp. 291–292.

Chapter 3: Hinduism: The Light That Illumines the Self

[1] Feldman & Kornfield, 1991, p. 235.

[2] *Upanishads, Katha, Isa, Kena, and Mundaka*, 1949, p. 288.

[3] Armstrong, 2007, pp. 19–29.

[4] Eliade, 1962, p. 30.

[5] Coomaraswamy, 1977, p. 100.

[6] Eliade, 1962, p. 26.

[7] Hume, 1931, p. 373.

[8] *Thirty Minor Upanishads*, 1914, p. 256, at sacred-texts.com

[9] Eliade, 1962, p. 28.

[10] Ibid.

[11] Ibid., p. 15.

[12] *Upanishads,* 2009, pp. 107–109.

[13] Ibid.

[14] Kirpal Singh, 1978, Preface to introduction.

[15] http://veda.krishna.com/encyclopedia/vedicsound.htm

[16] Jahnava Nitai Das. http://www.bvashram.org/articles/104/1/The-Vedic-Conception-of-Sound-in-Four-Features/Page1.html

[17] *Upanishads,* 2009, pp. 107–109.

[18] Reference here to the sound of the drum appears not only in the Hindu traditions but is found as well within many additional religious/spiritual paths within the South Asian subcontinent.

[19] In his *Autobiography of a Yogi,* Paramahansa recounts his own master's remark on this translation, "'the path of the yogi is singular enough as it is,' he remarked. 'Why counsel him that he must also make himself cross-eyed? The true meaning of *nasikagram* is 'origin of the nose,' not 'end of the nose.' The nose originates at the point between the eyebrows, the seat of spiritual vision.'" (Yogananda, 1946, Chap. 16).

[20] Miller, 1986. Gita: 6, 11–14.

[21] Miller, 1986. Gita: 6, 19–21.

[22] Miller, 1986. Gita: 11, 4.

[23] Miller, 1986. Gita: 11, 10–14.

[24] Miller, 1986. Gita: 11, 17–19.

[25] For many, including Gandhi who read the text daily, the text was seen as an allegorical account of the battle against the lower self for spiritual growth, and thus was not read as condoning war or violence against others in the physical world.

[26] http://www.yogajournal.com/advertise/press_releases/10

[27] Feuerstein, 2001, p. 507.

[28] *Siva Samhita,* 2009, p. 16.

[29] Ibid., p. 211.

[30] *Gheranda Samhita,* ii, v, p. 77.

[31] Metzner, 1986, p. 89.

[32] Yoga Vasishtha, p. 475.

[33] Yoga Vasistha, p. 407.

[34] Yoga Vasishtha, p. 321.

[35] Yoga Vasishtha, pp. 21.

[36] Kirpal Singh, 1980, p. 122.

[37] Shankara, 1975, pp. 3–4.

[38] Ibid., pp. 4–5.

[39] Ibid., Preface.

[40] Ibid., p. 7.

[41] Ibid., p. 53.

[42] Ibid., p. 54.

[43] Muller-Ortega, 1986, p. 3.

[44] Reps & Senzaki, 1999, p. 196.

[45] Feuerstein, 2001, p. 177.

[46] Muller-Ortega, 1986, p. 188.

[47] Ibid., pp. 98–99.

[48] Ibid., p. 188.

[49] Darshan Singh, 1989, pp. 36–37.

[50] Ibid.

[51] *Shri Namdev Gatha,* 1970, p. 563, poem 1359.

[52] Ibid., p. 875:2.

[53] Callewaert, 1988, p. 23 (in Dada Janama Lila, 15:18:13).

[54] Callewaert, 1988, p. 22.

[55] Ibid., p. 36.

[56] Ibid., p. 36.

[57] Ibid., pp. 36–37.

[58] Ibid., p. 37.

[59] Ibid., p. 49.

[60] Gupta, 2004, p. 17.

[61] Mohan Singh, *An Introduction to Punjabi Literature,* p. 152.

[62] *Garib Das Granth*, 1924, p. 481.

[63] Ibid., p. 26.

[64] Ibid., p. 14.

[65] Ibid., p. 2.

[66] Gupta, 2004, p. 218.

[67] Ibid., p. 333.

[68] Ibid., p. 464.

[69] Novak, 1995, p. 46.

[70] Fisher, 2011, p. 201.

[71] Sri Aurobindo, 2006, p. 507.

[72] Ibid., p. 907.

[73] Ibid., p. 1084.

[74] Ninian Smart, 1998, p. 422.

[75] Yogananda, 1998, pp. 166–167.

[76] Ibid., pp. 166–168.

[77] Paramahansa Yogananda, 1990, p. 31.

Chapter 4: Luminous Mind: Buddhism and the Heart of Clear Light

[1] Brahm, 2006, p. 22.

[2] Bhram, 2006, p. 22.

[3] Bhram, 2006, p. 23.

[4] Kornfield 1977, p. 315–316.

[5] Kornfield, 1977, pp. 249–250.

[6] Kornfield, 1977, p. 252.

[7] Zhengjue, 2000, pp. 31, 33.

[8] Bodhidharma, 2000, p. 33.

[9] Dumoulin, 2005, pp. 8–9.

[10] Some scholars consider Master Tang Hoi to be the first monk to bring Zen Buddhism to China.

[11] Bodhidharma, 2000, p. 77.

[12] Broughton, 1999, p. 67.

[13] Bodhidharma, 2000, p. 33.

[14] Wick, 2005, p. 118.

[15] Zhengjue, 2000, pp. 33, 40.

[16] Kim & Leighton, 2004, p. 39.

[17] Hazur Baba Sawan Singh, "Taming the Mind," *Sat Sandesh* (1980, April): 34. Print.

[18] Cleary, 1987, p. 330.

[19] Wong, 1992, p. 32.

[20] Kohn, Taoist http://www.amazon.com/Daoist-Body-Cultivation-Traditional-Contemporary/dp/1931483051

[21] Cleary, 1987, p. 280.

[22] Ibid., p. 280.

[23] Ibid., p. 317.

[24] Ibid., p. 298.

[25] Ibid., p. 290.

[26] Ibid., p. 294.

[27] Cleary, p. 298.

[28] Cleary, p. 298.

[29] Ching, 1988, p. 122.

[30] Low, 2006, p. 53.

[31] More precisely, the Bodhisattva plays varying roles in different Mahayana schools. In some it is an enlightened being, in others a being who advances spiritually to a point just preceding enlightenment and vows to withhold their enlightenment until all beings have been freed. Additionally, archetypal Bodhisattvas such as Mañjuśrī and Avalokiteśvara serve as objects of devotional piety, lay worship, and iconography.

[32] Chandrakirti, 2004, p. 156.

[33] Watson, *Lotus Sutra*, Chapter 1, p. 13.

[34] Watson, *Lotus Sutra*, Chapter 26.

[35] Larger Sukhavativyuha Sutra: http://www12.canvas.ne.jp/horai/larger-sutra-1.htm

[36] A mudra is a "seal of the Buddha."

[37] Unno, 2004, p. 33.

[38] According to the Tibetan tradition, the Bardol Thodol was dictated to Yeshe Tsogal, the semi-mythical great bliss queen, by Padmasambhava, who brought

Buddhism and tantra to Tibet from India. The root text however was buried in the hills of central Tibet, to be rediscovered by Karma Lingpa in the 12th century. It is likely, however, that other texts and oral traditions of similar content were common in the intervening four centuries.

39 Coleman, Graham, Jinpa Thupen & Dorje, Gyurme, 2007, p. 228.

40 Ibid.

41 Ibid., p. 276.

42 Ibid., p. 247.

43 Ibid., p. 239.

44 Ibid., p. 280.

45 Personal interview with Tibetan Geshe Thupten Tendhar, South Kingston, RI, 2010, 12–16.

46 Conze, 1973, p. 99.

47 Gyatso & Berzin, 1997, p. 219.

48 Ibid., p. 243.

49 Rinpoche, 2002, p. 78.

50 Ibid., 2002, p. 75.

51 Interested readers are invited to consult the Bön Master Tenzin Wangyal Rinpoche's *The Tibetan Yogas of Dream and Sleep, the Dzogchen Master Namkhai Norbu's Dream Yoga,* and *The Practice of Natural Light* and Gyatrul Rinpoche's *Meditation, Transformation, and Dream Yoga.*

Chapter 5: Shamanic Light: From the Archaic Past to Present Time

1 Quoted (p. 53) in "Indigenous Sacred Ways," in Mary Pat Fisher's *Living Religions,* eighth edition, pp. 33–72.

2 Eliade, Mircea. *Shamanism: Archaic Techniques of Ecstasy* (Princeton, Princeton Univ., 2004), p. 4.

3 Ibid., p. 243.

4 Ibid., p. 248.

5 Ibid., p. 87.

6 Ibid., p. 101.

7 Conner, Nancy & Keeney, Bradford (Eds.), *Shamans of the World: Extraordinary First-Person Accounts of Healings, Mysteries, and Miracles* (Boulder, CO: Sounds True, 2008), p. 161.

8 Ibid., p. 207.

9 Eliade, p. 60.

10 Ibid., p. 61.

11 Eliade, 1962, p. 25.

[12] Ken Wilber, *One Taste: The Journals of Ken Wilber* (Boulder, CO: Shambala, 2000), p. 184.

[13] Conner & Keeney, p. 241.

Chapter 6: Ineffable Light:
Visions of Light in Life, During Death, and in the Afterlife

[1] Kirpal Singh, 1981, p. 26. From Jalalu'ddin Rumi, *Mathnawi*, Book III, verse 3900–3907.

[2] Kramer, 1988, p. 62.

[3] Ibid., p. 70.

[4] Edgerton, 1944, 8:12–14.

[5] Vincent, 1994, pp. 3–5.

[6] www.NDERF.org. Near Death Experience Research Foundation, August 22, 2013

[7] Light and Music here referring to the various experiences known in different scriptures as Word, Naam, Jyoti, and Sruti, Shabda, and Music of the spheres.

[8] Lommel, 2010, pp. 71–80.

[9] Ibid., p. xviii.

[10] Dante Alighieri, *The Divine Comedy,* trans. A. S. Kline, http://www.poetryin translation.com/klineasdante.htm

[11] Atwater, P. M. H., 1999.

[12] Lommel, 2010, p. 150.

[13] Sogyal Rinpoche, 1994, p. 323.

[14] Ibid., p. 330.

[15] Ibid., p. 331.

[16] Rev. Howard Storm, *My Descent into Hell,* www.near-death.com. See Notable NDEs on home page. All accounts reprinted here are with the permission of the authors as noted on the website quoted above.

[17] Ibid., www.near-death.com. See Notable NDEs on home page.

[18] The work of Dr. Peter Russell who pioneered much of the early research into meditation makes numerous connections to the work of quantum theorists and the mystical experiences of inner light in his book *From Science to God: A Physicist's Journey into the Mystery of Consciences* (Novato, CA: New World Library, 2002), pp. 67–69. In essence, all matter is solidified Light.

[19] www.near-death.com See Notable NDEs on home page on Christian Andréason.

[20] Ibid.

[21] See Sant Rajinder Singh, 2004.

[22] www.near-death.com See Notable NDEs on home page, on Christian Andréason.

[23] Many points of corroboration or tacit agreement can be found in publications which discuss NDEs and their relationship to science, mysticism and the "new

Physics," including Paul Davies, *God and the New Physics* (New York, NY: Simon and Schuster, 1983); Michael Talbot, *Mysticism and the New Physics* (New York, NY: Bantam, 1981); Dean Radin, *The Conscious Universe* (New York, NY: Harper Edge, 1997); Amit Goswami, *The Quantum Doctor* (Charlottesville, VA: Hampton Roads, 2004).

24 www.near-death.com. See notable Near Death on Home page; pp. on Christian Andréason.

25 Ibid.

26 Excerpt is taken from her website www.TiffanySnow.com. Her books include *Psychic Gifts in the Christian Life; and Distant Healing, Bilocation, Medical Intuition, and Prayer in a Quantum World.*

27 www.TiffanySnow.com

28 The light body is referred to in the mystical literature of most traditions.

29 www.TiffanySnow.com

30 http://www.near-death.com/krebs.html

31 www.near-death.com. Reading the detailed account of her story is highly recomended.

32 Ibid.

33 www.near-death.com. See Notable NDE Home page Mellon-Thomas Benedict.

34 Ibid. Reprinted by permission of his friends Dr. Lee Worth Bailey and Jenny Yates. See their excellent book entitled *The Near-Death Experience: A Reader* (New York, NY: Routledge, 1996).

35 Ibid., p. 3.

36 Ibid., p. 4.

37 Ibid., p. 5.

38 http://www.neardeathsite.com/benedict4.php

39 http://www.neardeathsite.com/benedict4.php

40 www.near-death.com. See Notable NDEs Laurelynn account. Reprinted from her book *Searching for Home.*

41 Ibid.

42 Ibid., www.near-death.com, pp. 3–4.

43 Ibid., p. 4.

44 Ibid., p. 5.

45 Ibid., pp. 6–7.

46 Lusseyran, 2006, pp. 16–17.

47 Cohen & Phipps, 1979, p. 11.

48 Ibid., pp. 142–143.

49 Cohen & Phipps, 1979, pp. 152–153.

50 Cohen & Phipps, 1979, p. 8.

[51] Grey, 1985.

[52] Moody & Perry, 1988, pp. 55–67.

[53] Insinger, 1991, pp. 141–181.

Chapter 7: Meditation and the Experience of Inner Light and Sound

[1] Darshan Singh, *Love at Every Step: My Concept of Poetry* (SK Publications, Delhi, India, First Edition, 1989) p. 30.

[2] Rajinder Singh, 2014, p. 1–2.

[3] Kirpal Singh (SK Publications, 1987), p. 27.

[4] Rajinder Singh, *Empowering Your Soul Through Meditation,* 2007. pp. 4–7.

[5] Rajinder Singh, *Spark of the Divine,* 2011, p. 16.

[6] Ibid., 2011 p. 17–18.

[7] Ibid., 2011, p. 18.

[8] Ibid., 2011, p. 19.

[9] Ibid., 2011, p. 19.

[10] Ibid., 2011, p. 20.

[11] Jalalu'ddin Rumi, *Mathnawi* (translator unknown), Book I, Opening lines, verse 1–30. [All other translations of Rumi cited in this book, unless otherwise noted, are taken from *The Mathnawi of Jalalu'ddin Rumi,* Books 1–6 (edited and translated by R. A. Nicholson), published and distributed by the Trustees of the E. J. W. Gibb Memorial, 1926/2006.]

[12] Rajinder Singh, 2011, p. 22–23.

[13] Darshan Singh, *Streams of Nectar,* pp. 165–167.

[14] Ibid., p. 183.

[15] Ibid., p. 182-184.

[16] Interview by author, May 1987.

[17] Darshan Singh, 1988, p. 147.

[18] Ibid., 1988, p. 148.

[19] Darshan Singh, 1986, p. 15.

[20] Ibid., 1986, p. 29.

[21] Darshan Singh, 1989, p. 78.

[22] Darshan Singh, *A Tear and a Star,* 1986, p. 58.

[23] Kirpal Singh, *Morning Talks,* 1970.

[24] Darshan Singh, 1996, p. xii.

[25] Kirpal Singh, *Naam or Word,* 1978, p. 17.

[26] Darshan Singh, *Streams of Nectar,* 1993, p. 391.

[27] Kirpal Singh, 1998, pp. 16–17.

[28] Ibid., 1998, pp. 17–18.

[29] Ibid., p. 30.

[30] Ibid., p. 35

[31] The terms simran and bhajan are the Sant Mat terms for meditation on the inner Light and Sound current. The first is the spiritual practice of meditation on the inner light, and the second is the practice of absorption into the Divine Music or Dhun. The terms surat and nirat refer to the seeing and hearing faculties of the soul or, more precisely, the inner cognitive and perceptual consciousness of the soul. Within each is the essence of both God and the spiritual master.

[32] Kirpal Singh, 1998, pp. 94–95.

[33] Ibid., 1998., pp. 96–97.

[34] Sat Sandesh, Dec., 1986, p. 33

[35] Sat Sandesh, Dec., 1986, p. 32.

[36] Sat Sandesh, August, 1978, p. 24.

[37] Sat Sandesh, August, 1978, p. 23.

[38] Sat Sandesh, Dec., 1977, p. 23.

[39] Darshan Singh, *Streams of Nectar: Lives, Poetry and Teachings of Saints and Mystics* (SK Publications), 1993, pp. 156–158.

[40] Ibid., p. 156–160.

[41] Kirpal Singh, 1974, *Godman* (SK Publications), p. 26, 3rd printing.

[42] Kirpal Singh, *Portrait of Perfection*, 1981, p. 9.

[43] Ibid., p. 9.

[44] Sat Sandesh, July, 1978, p.9.

[45] Rajinder Singh, 2000, p. 108–109.

[46] Rajinder Singh, 2000, p. 117–118.

[47] Ibid., p. 113–114.

[48] Rajinder Singh, "Peace in the New Millennium," *Sat Sandesh* (SK Publications, Bowling Green, VA), Dec., 2000, p. 13.

Epilogue: A Caravan of Light and Love

[1] Pastor Don Mackenzie, Rabbi Ted Falcon and Iman Jamal Rahman. (2009). *Getting to the Heart of Interfaith: The Eye-opening, Hope-filled Friendship of a Pastor, a Rabbi and an Iman* (Woodstock, Vermont, SkyLight Paths Publishing).

[2] Kurt Johnson and Robert Ord, *The Coming Interspiritual Age* (2013).

[3] Singh, Darshan, *A Tear and a Star* (SK Publications, Bowling Green, VA, 1986), p. 50.

[4] Singh, Rajinder, *Sat Sandesh* (SK Publications, Naperville, IL, Dec., 2013), p.15.

Glossary and Index of Key Words

Judaism

Ayin: Hebrew, lit. "no-thingness." In Chassidic terminology describes a person who transcends self-centeredness and commits oneself to service of God.

Adam Kadmon: Hebrew. Mystically, a level within the Godhead, the first emanation from which provided the archetype for human beings. The "crown of creation."

Atzilut: Hebrew. The World of Emanation. In Kabbalistic terms it is the highest of the four spiritual worlds, the realm of spiritual existence which is at one with the Infinite Divine Light.

Aur Ein Sof: Infinite light of God, emanating from Ein Sof, permeating all of creation with supernal light and love.

Chabad: Hebrew. An acronym for Chochmoh, Binah, Da'at (wisdom, understanding and knowledge). The name of a Chassidic movement—predicated on the concept of studying and understanding God and His relationship with the world. Founded by Rabbi Schneur Zalman of Liadi in 18th century Russia, is also known today as Chabad-Lubavitch.

Devekut: Hebrew. Refers in Kabbalah to the spiritual attitude of "clinging to God." The ultimate goal of the soul's journey, achieving union with Creator.

Ein Sof: Hebrew, "The Endless Oneness." Ein Sof in Kabbalah is understood as the Eternal God prior to creation of the world.

Halacha: Hebrew, "the Way." Elaboration of Jewish religious practices to be assiduously followed in daily living, especially within Orthodox or Hasidic traditions.

Ha-Shem: Means "the Name": Leviticus 24:11. Jewish tradition discourages using sacred names of God, except in prayer. Hashem is otherwise substituted when mentioning the divine presence.

Hasidism: Hebrew. A movement of ecstatic piety initiated by Rabbi Baal Shem Tov in 17th century Poland. Emphasizes service of God through the mystical in addition to the legalistic dimension of Judaism, and the power of prayer, joy, love of God and one's fellows.

Kabbalah: Hebrew. (Qubbalah, Arabic). Literally, that which is received. Broadly speaking, encompasses all of esoteric teachings of Jewish mysticism, from Mt. Sinai Oral Law onwards. Explores how God's "hidden life" may best be perceived within Creation, through revelation and speculation.

Merkavah: Hebrew, meaning "chariot." Major early school of Jewish Kabbalistic mysticism (ca. 1–200 CE). Began with Prophet Ezekiel's vision of ascending to the heavenly throne; became a meditation practice for many later "Riders of the Chariot" over the centuries.

Mishnah: Basic core of Talmud and first great text of rabbinic Judaism, compiled around 200 CE.

mitzva: Hebrew (pl. *mitzvot*). One of the Torah's 613 commandments; a good deed or religious precept. According to Chassidut, the word mitzvah stems from the root *tzavta,* attachment, the mitzvah creating a bond between God and one doing the deed.

Pardes: Probably of Persian origin, meaning "orchard." Refers biblically to the Garden of Eden. In medieval times it became an acrostic, signifying four approaches to study of the Torah: Pshat (simple, literal meaning), Ramas (allegorical), Debash (midrashic), and Sod (mystical).

Prophet: Hebrew. *Navi, navi'im* plural. The prophets spoke on "behalf of YHWH," often emphasizing ethical monotheism and challenging the populace with their call for social justice (e.g., Isaiah, Amos, Micah).

Rebbe: Hebrew. A respectful form of addressing an exceptional, and often beloved, Jewish teacher of Torah, and a spiritual guide of the community. Tradition begun in Eastern Europe among Hasidim.

Sephirot: Hebrew (singular *sephira*). Divine attributes or emanations, which are manifested in each of the Four Worlds and are the source of the corresponding ten faculties *(kochot)* of the soul. Ranges "downward" at each level from the Keter (crown) to Malchut (sovereignty).

seven-branched candelabrum: A basic symbol of Light within Judaism, which embodies cosmic images of all Time and Space. Also, symbolic of Redemption, and the eternal light (Nar Tamid) and the Sabbath.

Shekhinah: Hebrew. The feminine aspect of the Divine Presence of God in the world, symbolized in many ways in Jewish mysticism and traditions. She is welcomed in song and prayer each Friday at sunset as the beloved Sabbath Queen or bride.

Shema: Hebrew. A central Jewish prayer recited twice daily beginning, "Hear, O Israel: the Lord Our God, the Lord is One." At a deep mystical level, it is taught that, prayed with full awareness, the Shema brings one's whole being into the experience of the Aur (Light) of God's Unity.

Talmud: Hebrew. Instruction, learning. Monumental collections of rabbinic discussion on Jewish law, ethics, philosophy. Jerusalem Talmud 220 BCE, Babylonian Talmud ca. 600 CE.

Tanach: Hebrew. The written Torah, an acronym formed by the words Torah, Nevi'im (prophets), and Ketuvim (writings). Compiled in 5th century BCE.

Tikkun: Hebrew. Literally means "repair," whether it be compassionately healing the human soul (Tikkun Hanefesh), or binding up the wounds of the world (Tikkun Olam).

Torah: The central scripture in Judaism received by Moses on Mt. Sinai; in general, refers to the five books of the written and the oral Torah.

Tree of Life: Hebrew, Etz Chayim. The Tree of Life and Tree of Knowledge of good and evil are central to the Garden of Eden story. Trees are symbolic of energetic balance, rooted in the material world with branches in supernal realms.

Tsimtsum: Hebrew (lit. "contraction"). A means of conceptualizing the process of Divine self-contraction and self-limitation, thus making possible the concept of limited, worldly existence. Explicated by Rebbe Luria of Safed.

Yahweh: Hebrew. The word Yahweh is a modern scholarly convention for name of God, transcribed into Roman letters as YHWH and known as the Tetragrammaton. Traditionally rendered as "I am who I am" after Moses' "burning bush" experience.

Yom Kippur (Day of Atonement): A day-long period of spiritual repentance, prayer, fasting, and moral resolve, ten days after Rosh Hashanah.

zaddik *(tsaddik)*: A Jewish mystic who displays outstanding qualities of faith, piety, and generosity of spirit. In Hasidism it often refers to a Master. Legend holds that goodness in the world is upheld at all times by virtue of the righteousness of thirty-six *zaddikim.*

Zohar: Hebrew, *Sefer-ha Zohar, the Book of Splendor.* A major Kabbalistic 13th century work, which speaks of emanation of Godhead into the world, transcendence of self, and maintaining covenant with the Creator.

Christianity

Abgeschiedenheit: German for "disinterestedness." This was a concept articulated first by the German mystic Jacob Boehme, which meant the stripping away of all identification with finite and limited qualities in order to enter the unlimited being of Godhead.

Apophatic theology: The Christian theology born from the idea that God is beyond all possible positive assertions, beyond the good and the bad, the existent and non-existent, serving as the ground beyond all pairs.

Assensus: Latin for "assent." This aspect was taken for granted in early Christian doctrine, but its deeper meaning was closer to belief as fidelity, confident trust, and connection.

Aÿlon: Literally, the "light which shines beyond all fire." It was purity of heart which led to the experience of inner light or "illumination." This light was indescribable, and its activity beyond rational apprehension.

Centering Prayer: A method of contemplation practiced at St. Joseph Abbey in Spencer, Massachusetts. Based on ancient Christian documents, such as the fourteenth-century anonymous treatise *The Cloud of Unknowing*. This practice of centering prayer focused one's attention inwardly, while repeating a "Prayer Word"—a sacred word or phrase internally with the tongue of thought.

Empyrean: In Christian cosmology a supra-physical sphere of existence where evolved souls partake of varying levels of connection with God. Dante in his *Paradiso* recounts his experiences in this region.

Energeia: (Gk., *energeiai*) According to St. Gregory this is the "divine energy," which is unknowingly perceived and visibly seen within the soul. It is experienced by the pure at heart during contemplative practice or deep prayer. This "divine energy" was thought to be the deifying illumination or "light" as distinct from God's essence or *ousia*.

Hesychast prayer: (*hesychasm*, literally stillness). In practice, the Hesychastic prayer bears clear resemblance to mystical prayer or meditation in Eastern religions, although there are differences in techniques. Like other forms of contemplative practice it involves acquiring an inner mental stillness, withdrawing from the physical senses, and focusing on the names of God or divinity.

Philokalia: (Greek, literally "love of spiritual beauty"). *The Philokalia* is an anthology of spiritual texts penned between the fourth and fifteenth centuries by various masters of the Jesus Prayer and *hesychasm* ("stillness"). In the eighteenth century these texts were compiled and edited into the present-day work by St. Nicodemus of the Holy Mountain and St. Macarius of Corinth.

Pistis: Greek. A Greek term connoting faith, which often relates more closely to the idea of persuasion and assurance than to faith as blind belief. This particular concept of faith in Christianity is a central notion taught by Jesus Christ himself in reference to the Good News (cf. Mk 1:15).

Pseudo-Dionysius: (the Areopagite). The enigmatic fifth-century Syrian theologian lived at the time of transition between Christian antiquity and the Medieval era.

Scivias: Written by twelfth-century Rhineland mystic Hildegard von Bingen. It is a series of twenty-six visions providing spiritual interpretations on the sacraments, the origin, nature, and end of creation, and the process of sanctification. In this record she recounts her encounter with divinity, producing a magnificent fusion of divine inspiration and human intellect.

Hinduism

Aham Brahma Asmi *or* **Aham Bahu Syam:** In Hindu mystical terminology this refers to the state of mystical oneness achieved through intense meditative discipline leading to oneness. Literally, it means "the soul and God are of the same essence." In other words, the individual soul, or Atman, is no different than Brahman or absolute consciousness.

Anahad sabad: Literally, the "unstruck sound," or "that which is heard without the agency of matter." It was this term which Kabir, the great mystic of the fifteenth-century, used to describe the Light and Sound principle.

Antar Jyoti: In the Brihadaranyaka Upanishad 4.3.7 a Sanskrit term which refers to the "Light within the heart" or "inner light."

Apara vidya: In Sanskrit this refers to the knowledge of this world gained through the agency of the five senses and intellect. More commonly known as ordinary knowledge of sense objects gained by the use of the intellect.

Atman: The Sanskrit word for "soul/Self" in Hindu non-dualist philosophy.

Chakras: Sanskrit. According to Hindu yogic texts these are the subtle energy centers responsible for sustaining the physical body. In Hindu metaphysical and tantric/yogic traditions and other belief systems *chakras* are wheels in the subtle human body. *Chakras* are part of the subtle body, not the physical body, and as such, are the meeting points of the subtle (non-physical) energy channels, called *nadiis*.

Dhunamuk: This denotes the inner subtle vibration caused by the *Shabda* or *Udgit* and is heard only through the subtle sense of perception. This is the sound of the eternal, as opposed to the temporal.

Dhyana: The practice of meditation or contemplation predicated upon one-pointed attention and leading to *samadhi* or union. It is the penultimate limb of Patangali's eight-fold path to enlightenment.

Jagrat: Refers to the state of deep sleep or unconsciousness. One of the four states of consciousness found in classical yogic philosophy.

Jyoti: Literally, "light." This refers to the inner light experienced through the *Shiv netra*, or eye of spiritual perception.

Jyoti prajanaman: This is the Sanskrit term for the procreative Eternal Light responsible for the creation, maintenance, and dissolution of creation.

Karma: In Hindu philosophy the concept of karma can denote action or the consequences of one's actions. Our future experiences are shaped by thoughts, words, and actions in the present: "As we sow, so shall we reap," in this lifetime and/or in the hereafter.

Madhyama: In early yogic texts represents the mental consciousness or awareness of self through the agency of the five senses.

Naad/Nada: In Hindu mystical terminology this is the "inner Sound current" known also as the *Shabda, anahad Shabd,* and *Naam.*

Nadiis: Literally, "tube" or "pipes" in Sanskrit. According to the Patangali's yogic texts these are energy veins located within the subtle body responsible for distributing the inner finer energies known as "pranas" to the physical body.

Para vidya: In Sanskrit this refers to the knowledge attained only through direct revelation within the mystical inner being. It is by necessity beyond both the intellect and five senses.

Pashyanti: According to Nitin Das, *pashyanti* represents the intellectual consciousness often referred to as the discriminating faculty—the power to determine right from wrong.

Prakriti: According to Patanjali, this refers to the sum total of all mental and physical activity. The goal of all yoga is to still or stop the oscillations of *prakriti* in order that the light of consciousness shines forth.

Shaktipat: In Siddha Yoga terminology this refers to the giving of initiation. The Siddha master imparts his own consciousness into the disciple, thereby initiating a powerful inner transformation.

Shaivas (*Shaivism* or *Saivism*): Sanskrit, *śaiva paṁtha,* literally "associated with Shiva"), is one of the four most widely followed sects of Hinduism, which reveres the god Shiva as the Supreme Being. Followers of Shaivam believe that Shiva is All and in all, the creator, preserver, destroyer, revealer, and concealer of all that is.

Shruti: Literally, in Sanskrit "that which is heard." More broadly it refers to the inner sound or "Nada" reverberating throughout creation. This sound or music emanates from the source of consciousness or the absolute.

Sushupti: This refers to the state of normal waking consciousness experienced between deep sleep and dreaming during waking hours.

Svapna: Refers to the state of "dreaming" when the soul is in the throat chakra. The third of four states of consciousness in yogic philosophy.

Udgit: In Sanskrit another name for the "inner sound principle" resonating throughout all creation. The name first appears in the Upanishads and later is referred to again in yogic texts.

Vaikhari: In classical yogic texts it represents the physical consciousness.

Varnamuk: This refers to the outer sounds of creation perceived through the agency of hearing and created through the interplay of the five elements upon one another. Sounds are produced through vibrations of matter upon matter.

Vrittis: Literally, "whirls" in Patangali's Yoga-sutras. This refers to the oscillations of the mind or thought forms, which appear on the lake of consciousness.

Yoga shcitta virtti nirodha: A direct quote from Patanjali Yoga-sutras describing the goal of all yogic discipline, namely "to stop the oscillation and disturbance of the mind stuff."

Buddhism

Anapana-sati: Sanskrit, literally, "mindfulness of the incoming and outgoing breath." This has traditionally been used as a preliminary practice in Tibetan, Zen, and Theravadan Buddhism. According to tradition, *Anapanasati* was originally taught by the Buddha in several sutras, including the Ānāpānasati Sutta. .

Bardo Thodol: The Tibetan Book of the Dead. This funerary text is the best-known Tibetan religious document which, according to tradition, was dictated by Padmasambhava, who brought Buddhism and tantra to Tibet.

Bhavanga: Pali, literally, the "ground of becoming." *Bhavanga* is the most fundamental aspect of mind in Theravada Buddhism. It has been compared to the Mahayana concept of store-consciousness. The Theravada tradition identifies it with the phenomenon described as "luminous mind."

Eko hensho: The meditative injunction, which translates as "learn to withdraw, turning the light inwards, illuminating the self." This was the essential form of meditative practice in esoteric Taoism.

Dharmakaya: Sanskrit. Literally, "truth body." This is the body of light or imperishable body—in other traditions known as the light body, radiant body, or spiritual body.

Dzochen: A Tibetan Buddhist term referring to a more advanced form of meditation often practiced among the *geluk-pa,* or followers of the *virtuous way,* and other branches of Tibetan Buddhism. In this form the practitioner begins to connect with the Clear Light.

Hekigan-roku: Chinese for, literally, the"Blue Cliff Record." This was a collection of one hundred Chán Buddhist koans compiled in China during the twelfth century Song dynasty.

Jhāna (Pali): Literally, meaning "absorption." The equivalent of *dhyāna* in Sanskrit, which is related to *dhyan* or contemplation. Here the yogi begins to merge with the object of contemplation, and the concentration becomes steady and continuous.

Komyo shingon: Japanese for the "Mantra of Light," which in English translates roughly as Clear Light Mantra. It is one of the most common contemporary practices, being promoted for lay practitioners and found, not only among Shingon adherents, but also among adherents of other Japanese Buddhist traditions as well.

Madhyamaka: System of thought associated with Nargarjuna's path of the middle way. It was seen as a middle way between what he saw as the twin pitfalls of essentialism and nihilism, or in more common terms, over-indulgence versus extreme asceticism.

Mòzhào chán: Chinese for the "silent illumination." Designates an approach to practice and enlightenment that strongly emphasizes the inherently enlightened buddha-nature in all sentient beings.

Neidan: Meaning the inner, esoteric, or subtle alchemy, which circulates the breath and whereby one enters into the light. One expert has said, "If the breath is not circulated, it is not *neidan*. If the breath is circulated, but no light is seen within, it is not *neidan* meditation. If the breath and the light circulate together, but then the practitioner feels kundalini arising, that is not *neidan*."

Nyingmapa: The oldest of the four major schools of Tibetan Buddhism (the other three being the *Kagyu, Sakya* and *Gelug*). "Nyingma" literally means "ancient" and is often referred to as the Nga'gyur *school of the ancient translations* because it is founded in the first translations of Buddhist scriptures from Sanskrit into Tibetan, in the eighth-century.

Pi kuan: Chinese, for the "wall-examining examining practice" now associated with Zen Buddhist meditation practice.

Pāli Canon: The standard collection of Theravada Buddhist scriptures. Used primarily by the Mahayana and Theravadan traditions.

Phowa: Tibetan. That which causes transference of consciousness to one of the intermediate god realms, or in the case of Dzogchen, to the Dharmakaya itself (Sanskrit, literally, "truth body").

Shingon: Japanese form of Buddhism literally meaning "True Words." Shingon Buddhism is one of the major mainstream schools of Japanese Buddhism and one of the few surviving esoteric Buddhist lineages that started in the third- to fourth-century AD.

T'ai chi ch'uan (and Qigong): forms of martial arts which employ subtle energy to enhance concentration, intention, and purity of the practitioner.

Zen: Chinese term for the Chán tradition. Etymologically linked to the Sanskrit *dhyna* and Pāli *jhanna*, literally "meditation." Zen is a school of Mahayana Buddhism that developed in China during the sixth-century. Zen emphasizes the attainment of enlightenment and the personal expression of direct insight into the Buddhist teachings.

Zhēnyán: Literally, "True Words," which, in turn, is the Chinese translation of the Sanskrit word Mantra.

About the Authors

Arthur Stein

Arthur Stein (Art) is currently Professor Emeritus of Political Science and a co-founder of the Center for Nonviolence and Peace Studies at the University of Rhode Island (URI). Art received an interdisciplinary Ph.D. in International Relations from the University of Pennsylvania, and subsequently has done studies identifying the root causes and potential resolution of several transnational, ethnic, and cultural conflicts. He is an educator, author, interfaith participant, and scholar-practitioner in various aspects of nonviolent social change.

His books include *Seeds of the Seventies: Values, Work and Commitment in Post-Vietnam America*. For his teaching and community service, within and well beyond the classroom, Art has been recognized for his "commitments to human rights and ecological concerns that have inspired thousands of students over the years." He has been a speaker, "scholar in residence," and workshop facilitator at numerous universities, colleges, and civic programs worldwide

Dr. Stein has had long-term interests and involvement in the fields of comparative religion and spirituality, ethics, wisdom traditions, mysticism, meditation and other contemplative practices. He has innovated and offers such courses as "Wisdom Traditions of the World's Cultures and Religions," and "Meditation, Mindfulness and Peacebuilding: Within Ourselves and Globally." For over 40 years he has practiced meditation. He has participated as a presenter and/or facilitator in each of the five global Parliaments of the World's Religions held between 1993–2015.

Art and his wife Clare live in Wakefield, Rhode Island.

He can be reached at artstein36@gmail.com.

Andrew Vidich

Andrew Vidich Ph.D. is an award winning author, educator, and transformational speaker in the fields of spirituality, mysticism, and death and dying. He is the author and/or editor of five books. Dr. Vidich has been an adjunct assistant professor of religion at Manhattan College and at Iona College in New Rochelle where he has taught courses in the nature and experience of religion, meditation, and death and dying. He lectures and presents seminars and trainings at educational and religious institutions, conferences, radio and TV shows, throughout the world on a variety of leadership topics.

He is a founding member of The Interfaith Council of New York, a not-for-profit interfaith organization, as well as a member of the council of trustees of The Temple of Understanding, a global interfaith organization, which promotes understanding and cooperation across all religions and faiths. He has been meditating for over 45 years. He has participated as a presenter and/or facilitator in each of the five global Parliaments of the World's Religions held between 1993–2015.

Andrew and his wife TAMIR live in upper-state New York.

Index